Hiking
Wisconsin

Help Us Keep This Guide Up to Date

Every effort has been made by the authors and editors to make this guide as accurate and useful as possible. However, many things can change after a guide is published—trails are rerouted, regulations change, techniques evolve, facilities come under new management, etc.

We would love to hear from you concerning your experiences with this guide and how you feel it could be improved and kept up to date. While we may not be able to respond to all comments and suggestions, we'll take them to heart and we'll also make certain to share them with the authors. Please send your comments and suggestions to the following address:

The Globe Pequot Press
Reader Response/Editorial Department
P.O. Box 480
Guilford, CT 06437

Or you may e-mail us at:

editorial@GlobePequot.com

Thanks for your input, and happy travels!

AFALCON GUIDE®

Hiking
Wisconsin

Eric Hansen

FALCON GUIDES ®

GUILFORD, CONNECTICUT
HELENA, MONTANA

AN IMPRINT OF THE GLOBE PEQUOT PRESS

Cover photo: Tom Algire
Maps and interior photos: Eric Hansen

ISSN 1537-3479
ISBN 978-0-7627-1172-7

Manufactured in the United States of America
First Edition/Fourth Printing

♻ Text pages printed on recycled paper.

To the thousands of men and women
who give so generously of their time
so that Wisconsin remains
a place well worth hiking.
They build and maintain trails,
attend conservation hearings,
and campaign against those
who would turn our rivers
into discharge channels for mines
and our forests into industrial tree farms.

Contents

Acknowledgments ix
Legend x
Overview Map xi
Introduction 1
   Hiking Wisconsin 1
   Ice Age National Scenic Trail 2
   North Country National Scenic Trail 2
   Land Acquisition to Protect Hiking Trails 3
   Saving This Place We Call Wisconsin 3
   Weather 4
   Seasons 4
   Clothing 5
   Ticks and Lyme Disease 6
   Being Prepared 6
   Treading Lightly on the Land 7
Using This Guide 8
Hike Finder 10

THE HIKES

Lake Superior Lowland 17
   1 Amnicon Falls 17
   2 Superior Shoreline 19
   3 Lost Creek Falls 22
   4 Sea Caves 25
   5 Oak Island 28
   6 Trout Point 31
   7 Tombolo 34

Northern Highlands 37
   8 Manitou Falls 37
   9 Brule–St. Croix Portage 40
  10 Anderson Lake 43
  11 Marengo River/Porcupine Lake 46
  12 Marengo River/Swedish Settlement 52
  13 Morgan Falls/St. Peter's Dome 55
  14 Copper Falls 58
  15 Potato River Falls 61
  16 Penokee Range 64
  17 Sandrock Cliffs 66
  18 St. Croix 70
  19 Blue Hills/Devils Creek 74
  20 Escanaba Lake 76
  21 Star Lake 80
  22 Clark Lake 83
  23 Deer Island Lake 86
  24 Hidden Lakes 90

25 LaSalle Falls 93
26 Glacial Potholes 96
27 Chippewa Moraine Loop.................................100
28 Chippewa Moraine/Plummer Lake 104
29 Jerry Lake 107
30 Chippewa Lobe 110
31 Timm's Hill 113
32 Wood Lake 116
33 Ed's Lake 119
34 Jones Spring 122
35 Long Slide Falls 125
36 Mead State Wildlife Area 128

Western Upland 131
37 Chippewa River 131
38 Trempealeau River 134
39 Perrot Ridge 137
40 McGilvray Bottoms 141
41 Rush Creek Bluff 144
42 Wyalusing State Park 147
43 Berghum Bottoms 150
44 Kickapoo River 153
45 Pine Cliff 156
46 Ferry Bluff 160
47 Blackhawk Ridge 163

Central Sandy Plain 166
48 Wildcat Mound 166
49 North Bluff 170
50 Lone Rock 173

Eastern Moraines and Lake Michigan Plain 177
51 Eagle Bluff 177
52 Deathdoor Bluff...180
53 Rock Island 182
54 Newport State Park 186
55 Ridges 190
56 Moonlight Bay 194
57 Point Beach 198
58 Emmons Creek 201
59 Devil's Lake East Bluff 205
60 Devil's Lake to Parfrey's Glen 208
61 Parfrey's Glen 211
62 North Kettle Moraine 214
63 Lake La Grange 217
64 Beulah Bog...219

Appendix A: Glossary 222
Appendix B: Useful Addresses for More Information 223
Appendix C: Good Reading 226

About the Author...227

Acknowledgments

This book would not have been possible without the help of many people. I would like to thank the nearly fifty avid hikers who found time to return my questionnaires and inform me of their favorite routes. Many of those folks are active in the Wisconsin Let's Go Hiking Club, Sierra Club, Milwaukee Nordic Ski Club, North Country Trail Association, or the Ice Age Park and Trail Foundation.

Steve Sorensen, of Ashland, shared his knowledge of many hikes in that area. Drew Hanson, Geographer of the Ice Age Park and Trail Foundation, supplied savvy trail data, a steady stream of encouragement, and text review.

Thanks also to the countless land agency personnel who patiently answered my questions.

I am grateful to copy editor Sharon DeJohn, Joshua Rosenberg, and the rest of the staff at The Globe Pequot Press for their knowledgeable assistance.

Special thanks to my spouse, Anne Steinberg, for frontline editing that kept me on track and a faith in this project that smoothed the rough spots.

Any errors are mine, not theirs.

Legend

Interstate	5		Natural Area/ Wildlife Refuge	
U.S. Highway	134		Bridge	
State Highway	190 47		State Border	GEORGIA
Forest Road	4165 49		Gate	
Trailhead	◯		Cave	
Interstate Highway	⟹		Ranger Station/ Visitor Center	
Paved Road	⟹		Buildings/Shelters	■
Dirt Road	⟹		Campground	Λ
Railroad			Cemetery	†
Featured Trail(s)			Observation Tower/ Viewpoint	
Secondary Trail(s)			Harbor Light/ Lighthouse	⊙
Cross Country/ Ski Trail			Mountain	
Snowmobile Trail			Dome	
Cruise Line			Hill	
River/Creek			Map Orientation	N
Intermittent Stream				
Falls			Scale	0 .5 1 Miles
Lakes/Rivers				
Marsh/Wetland				
Sea Caves				
Bluff				

Overview Map

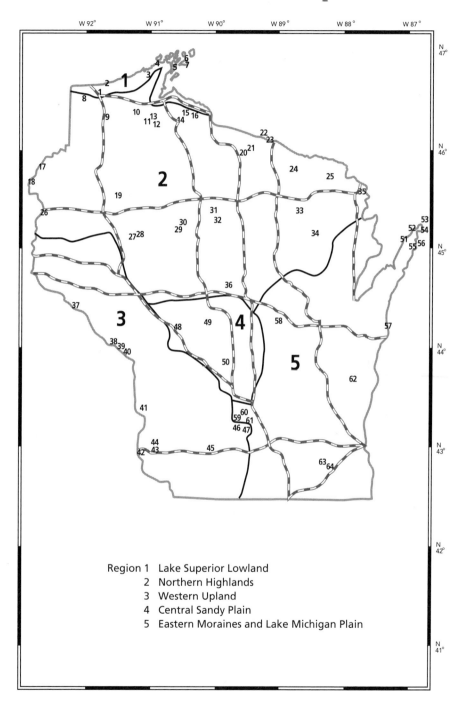

Region 1 Lake Superior Lowland
         2 Northern Highlands
         3 Western Upland
         4 Central Sandy Plain
         5 Eastern Moraines and Lake Michigan Plain

Introduction

HIKING WISCONSIN

If a foreign visitor were to ask me about hiking in Wisconsin, I would sum it up in three words: water, woods, and wolves. Bordered by two of the Great Lakes and the Mississippi River, filled with thousands of inland lakes and sparkling streams, the state's abundance of pristine water attracts natives and neighbors alike. A vast second-growth forest of hardwoods and evergreens, concentrated in the Northern Highlands and Central Plain, covers 46 percent of the state. An impeccable authority indicates the quality of that forest's quiet corners: Wild timber wolves, returning of their own free will, have reoccupied much of Wisconsin's forest land, raising pups as far south as the center of the state.

I would tell the visitor that I can leave my Milwaukee home, drive three hours, and walk past the tracks of one of the eight breeding packs of wolves in the central forest. Or I could travel west, to a quiet bluff-top prairie offering broad views of the Mississippi River and the hardwood forests clinging to steep slopes along its shores. Upstream, an hour's drive north of the Twin Cities, I would walk beside one of the cleanest large rivers in the country, the St. Croix, while eagles scan for dinner. There huge glacial potholes, scoured 60 feet deep and 12 feet wide into bedrock, illustrate the epic glacial forces that shaped the St. Croix valley and much of the state.

A little north of there the choices become difficult. Should I walk to the fourth-highest waterfall east of the Rocky Mountains, a stunning 165-foot drop, or opt for solitude at a charming backcountry cascade? Or should I follow part of the North Country Trail's 60-mile passage through a remote forest, passing lakes where the haunting cries of loons echo?

I couldn't leave this part of the state without communing with Lake Superior, possessor of a full eighth, and some of the purest, of the planet's fresh water. Two outings along its shores are classics: a walk along one of the pristine beaches and a hike to one source of that sand, the spectacular wave-carved sandstone sea caves and cliffs east of Cornucopia.

Sometime I would have to head south, but not before making a walking sojourn with another timeless natural wonder, the 17,000 acres of virgin forest, sprinkled with twenty stunningly clear lakes, at Sylvania. A small jog downstate would bring me to another favorite woodland walk, the Ice Age National Scenic Trail near the Yellow River, where fishers and wolf pups romp and the otherworldly Goblin Fern haunts the forest duff. Then memories of the primeval bark of sandhill cranes, nesting osprey, and herons would pull me to a marsh walk along dike roads in the Central Plain.

A detour to Wisconsin's east coast would be in order. I would journey to Door County and roam the rockbound peninsula south of Moonlight Bay, where rare orchids compete with wave-washed shores for my attention. Rolling down the coast, Point Beach's 6-mile-long strand would have no trouble getting me out of the car.

Almost home, I would stop in the Kettle Moraine country, grateful that such a treat was near Milwaukee. Miles of Ice Age Trail to follow, shady woods, a tumbled, playful topography, and otter tracks along the streams would persuade me to linger.

I know these places and their rejuvenating powers, and I would gladly return to them. However, this book, and the hiking choices within it, is for you. Whatever your tastes, whichever corner of the state you find yourself in, there is a path waiting for you, a way to reconnect with the natural world. The directions are here.

ICE AGE NATIONAL SCENIC TRAIL

Not that long ago, 15,000 years back, massive glaciers covered most of the land we know today as Wisconsin. Vast sheets of ice, led by six lobes, scoured rock debris across much of the state, bulldozing everything in their path. It was an era when ice covered wide areas of the northern part of North America, but nowhere else on the continent is the glaciers' path as clear as it is here. Wisconsin's glacial landscape is a renowned showcase for that era.

Terminal moraines, rock rubble from the glaciers' front, are one of their most prominent relics. In the early 1950s an idea surfaced to create a linear ice age park and trail along the moraine's 1,000-mile-long line across the state, the mark of the glaciers' last advance. Today, major parts of that dream are a reality. Six hundred miles of trail are now open along the proposed path.

Four long segments of the Ice Age Trail are noteworthy: the Chippewa Moraine in Chippewa County, the Jerry Lake Segment in Taylor County, and the trail sections in the Northern and Southern Units of the Kettle Moraine State Forest.

Hikers can access trail maps and local chapter contacts as well as a history of Wisconsin's glacial landscape by contacting the foundation's office or Web site.

Ice Age Park and Trail Foundation
207 East Buffalo Street, Suite 515
Milwaukee, WI 53202-5712
(800) 227–0046 or (414) 278–8518
www.iceagetrail.org

NORTH COUNTRY NATIONAL SCENIC TRAIL

In the 1960s the Chequamegon National Forest built a 60-mile-long footpath in northwest Wisconsin and named it the North Country Trail. At the time, there were no great ambitions for it to be more than a trail through Wisconsin's Northwoods.

However, the name caused a stir. In the years that followed, the idea of a North Country Trail stretching across a wide tier of northern states spread, and a movement to build that trail was born.

Today the North Country National Scenic Trail has 1,600 miles of trail in place on a route that stretches 4,000 miles, from northern New York to North Dakota.

Here in Wisconsin, that first, 60-mile-long trail segment continues to attract hikers looking for long, quiet walks. Its hold on that niche may last, but its claim to fame in the scenery category faces a strong challenge from a new stretch of trail in the Penokee Range. Other newer trail segments are in the Brule River State Forest, Pattison State Park, and Copper Falls State Park.

Trail maps and up-to-date reports on new trail additions are on the North Country Trail Association's Web site at www.northcountry.org. Hikers may also find information on the trail's proposed Wisconsin route, a 150-mile-long swath running from Hurley west to the Minnesota border.

North Country Trail Association
c/o Cable Natural History Museum
P.O. Box 416
Cable, WI 54821-0416
(715) 798–3890
nctrail@cablemuseum.org

LAND ACQUISITION TO PROTECT HIKING TRAILS

Few would argue the point that corridors of natural habitat are essential to a healthy wildlife population. It is time to apply that logic to the spiritual health of our species. When it comes to the habitat of hiking trails, all too often fragmentation takes hold. For a hiker, coming around a corner to find one hundred acres of four-year-old aspen, an obvious remnant of a clear cut, is a disheartening experience. A fair number of linear hiking trails in the state cross land that is subject to commercial pressures to show a profit by logging. Hikers lobbying land managers is one solution. Conservation easements would be another. Land acquisition to protect trail corridors solves the problem.

The state of Wisconsin has a plan, the Knowles-Nelson Stewardship Program, to acquire and preserve green acres. It is important that land acquisition for hiking trails be a priority for that program. To find out how you and other hikers can effectively advocate for trail corridors, contact the Ice Age Park and Trail Foundation or the North Country Trail Association.

SAVING THIS PLACE WE CALL WISCONSIN

"For the strength of the pack is the wolf and the strength of the wolf is the pack."

You, and others like you, can make the critical difference in whether the places we enjoy today are worth visiting in the years to come. Your knowledge of savvy methods to respond to the threats to Wisconsin's wild lands is a key part of the strategy to protect them. Citizen watchdogs are the eyes and ears that blow the whistle on polluters and other illegal activity.

You are not alone. You can plug into a broad union of like-minded folks at the Wisconsin Stewardship Network (WSN), a group working to restore our state's rich conservation tradition. A glance at their steering committee list reveals the variety of the network's backers. That diverse support—anglers and environmentalists, duck hunters, hikers, and bird watchers—builds a strong voice for the land that heals us all.

Several threats to our natural landscape loom large. First, there is a sustained effort to locate a mine on the headwaters of the Wolf River. Second, there is a scheme afoot to construct a huge electrical transmission line from Duluth to Wausau, cutting a broad swath through our northern forest. A spur of that line would service the mine. Factory farms, with their ominous "waste lagoons," pose a third threat.

As drastic as those three menaces are, another is even more serious: persistent attempts to weaken the state's environmental protections. You can do a great service for yourself, other hikers, and the community at large by keeping abreast of these issues. Information is power.

In addition, while you are out hiking watch for questionable activities, like a bulldozer working on the edge of a wetland. Your willingness to make a phone call could save that wetland from illegal filling. "I can list a hundred times that we got non-permitted activities stopped on the weekend because a warden responded quickly to a citizen call," says John Holmes, a retired conservation warden, quoted on the WSN's Web page. "If you see something suspicious, act fast before environmental damage happens."

The Wisconsin Stewardship Network
122 State Street
Madison, WI 53703
(608) 268–1218
www.wsn.org

WEATHER

Weather, in Wisconsin, is a source of local pride, often seen as a test of character. At its fiercest, it will challenge you with near hundred-degree heat and below-zero wind chills. Fortunately, there is a lot of fine hiking weather between those extremes. In addition to the obvious seasonal variations, there is often a wide difference between the weather in the north and south of the state. Another, more regional distinction is worth noting: The Great Lakes moderate temperatures along their shores, resisting heat and cold that may be dominant only a few miles inland.

For hikers more than a casual distance from their vehicle, it pays to know the forecast and be prepared for worst-case scenarios, such as cold rain showers accompanied by strong winds. Several hikes in this book follow Great Lakes shorelines. Be aware that coastline routes are glorious in good conditions but merciless in their exposure to high winds when the weather gets rowdy.

SEASONS

Spring hiking, with its woodland wildflowers, colorful birds, and open sight lines through the leafless forest, can be the best of the year. It is a time when marsh walks along dike routes can lead to extravagant bird migration scenes.

Bug presence is minimal and weather is often temperate and ideal for walking. The weather can be volatile, though; keep track of forecasts and bring appropriate clothing. Right after the snow melts, trails are frequently wet or muddy. A trip to the central sand counties, or a beach walk along Lakes

Michigan or Superior, is a good option then. Trails that keep to the top of a moraine, such as the Ice Age Trail in the Northern Kettle Moraine area, drain well and tend to dry before others.

Summer, with its long hours of daylight, lends itself to lengthy hikes, with time to linger at distant destinations. Hot temperatures are a comfort factor directly related to how much of a hike is in the deep shade of the forest canopy. Shady forest trails of the north tend to be reasonably comfortable throughout the summer. Many southern trails weave in and out of the shade and can be warm in the midday heat. Beach walks and open dike routes in marshes can be downright hot during the middle of the day. One way to escape the heat is to walk near the Great Lakes shorelines and enjoy cooler lake effect temperatures.

Bugs are numerous in early summer and slowly decline as the season progresses. Thunderstorms can soak hikers and expose them to dangerous lightning.

Fall is the favorite season of many hikers. It is hard to disagree with the merits of a forest ablaze with color. Shorter daylight hours dictate an earlier return from hikes. Full rain gear is a good idea for the cooler temperatures and lingering rain showers of fall. Bug season ends, and hikes that would be miserable in June are prime in late September. Hunters are out and about, so wearing some blaze orange is prudent.

Winter snow cover on hiking trails is a sure thing in the central and northern portions of the state. That deep snow may bring an end to the hiking season, but for snowshoe and ski enthusiasts it is a pleasant opportunity to travel the trails in another manner. In the southern part of the state snow cover is less dominant and hiking is possible at times. Cold weather and the arrival of safe ice offer a unique opportunity there: walking into wetlands and bogs.

CLOTHING

Two truths are the basis of a savvy clothing strategy. First, layer your clothing and you will have options. Temperature, wind, shade, and precipitation can change during a hike. If you have clothing choices you will be able to add or subtract a layer and be more comfortable when those changes occur. You will be able to walk without becoming overheated, cold, or wet. Second, synthetic thread does not absorb water as cotton thread does. Essentially, this means that any moisture in the fabric dries quicker because it is between the threads, not within them. This fundamental advantage of synthetic clothes keeps the hiker drier, with less chance of becoming chilled. In cool temperatures or high winds, that advantage can become a critical safety factor.

The season and length of your hike determine what is essential. A cap and sunblock could be the bottom line for a short warm weather hike, but consider a long-sleeved shirt and pants for protection from the sun, bugs and briars.

Rain gear quality should reflect the relative threat of becoming chilled and hypothermic. On a short, warm weather hike that threat may be low, but in cooler temperatures, and on longer outings, take along full rain gear as well as a sweater and warm hat.

Hiking boots are a basic part of your clothing system. Boots that feature a waterproof/breathable liner will keep your feet toasty in a chilly autumn rain and ease the going when trails are wet.

TICKS AND LYME DISEASE

Wisconsin has its share of insects that can be annoying at times, but one is capable of damage worse than a minor sting: the tiny deer tick. Adults of that species are no larger than one of the letters in the "one dime" imprint on that coin's surface. They inhabit grass and brush, attaching themselves to passing warm bodies. Some deer ticks carry Lyme disease, an illness that affects the nervous system, heart, skin, and joints. It is important to recognize the disease's signs and symptoms, which include skin rash, chills or fever, fatigue, and arthritis-like joint and muscle pains. If the disease is caught in the early stages, antibiotics are usually successful in treating it.

Be sure to do a complete check of your body and clothes for ticks after hiking in tick habitat. Hikers should educate themselves about the disease as well as methods of prevention and treatment. There is a geographical pattern to the occurrence of Lyme disease in Wisconsin. The northwest part of the state has the higher rates, with reported cases tapering off to the southeast.

For more information, contact your local office of the Wisconsin Department of Natural Resources or the American Lyme Disease Foundation at

Mill Pond Offices
293 Route 100
Somers, NY 10589
www.aldf.com

BEING PREPARED

Being prepared has its equipment aspects but in the end is mental. We set out on hikes, a set of assumptions in place. We are confident that our physical capabilities and gear can deal with the conditions and terrain we expect to find. In a way we are using a mathematical formula that goes like this: confidence + conditioning + gear + conditions that are reasonable and as expected = successful outing. Trouble arises when one of the factors in this formula changes and the formula no longer computes. That change could be a severe heel blister, twisted ankle, sudden lightning storm, or cold rain squall. At that point, conditions may exceed our capacity to deal with them. There is no warning light on a dashboard, but savvy hikers recognize that moment's approach and trim their sails appropriately.

Even a small fanny pack has room for a small amount of gear that can make a big difference when problems arise. At a minimum, take a compass, energy bar, water, knife, aspirin, bandages, antibacterial ointment, matches, and space blanket emergency bag. Tightly folded garbage bags take up less room than your wallet and can pinch-hit as an emergency shelter or rain gear.

TREADING LIGHTLY ON THE LAND

Zero impact is to hiking and camping what catch-and-release is to fishing. It all boils down to one concept: With a little forethought, we will still be able to enjoy the outing we are taking today in five years.

If you pack it in, pack it out. Leave nothing but footprints. Human sanitation is especially important in the backwoods, away from toilets. Dig a six-inch-deep hole, well away from any stream or water, relieve yourself, and cover the hole with dirt. Pack out your used toilet paper in a plastic storage bag.

The Summit Rock Trail overlooks the Dalles of the St. Croix (Glacial Potholes hike).

Using This Guide

One goal framed the research and writing for this book: to find and catalog the best natural ambiance in the state. The questions that guided me were: Which hikes offer a strong connection with the natural world? Where are the routes that offer outstanding samples of what is unique in our ecosystem? I sought out hikes that were quiet and a pleasure to the eye and offered treats such as waterfalls, wildlife, vistas, and old growth woodlands.

Deciding not to just take trails at face value, I looked for new wrinkles. For example, many of the hikes in this book don't begin at the official trailhead. The hikes may also combine sections of different trails to create the best experience for the hiker. At times I recommend unmarked routes, often in state wildlife areas, and for some hikes I have developed off-trail segments.

Field research was done through more than 800 miles of hiking. The author walked every mile of trail described in this guidebook. The purpose of this guidebook is to organize that pool of knowledge in a way that allows readers to locate outings suitable to their abilities and tastes.

Readers can make an initial screening of the hike chapters by checking the hike finder chart that follows this section. A hike locator map offers a quick scan of which hikes are in a given area.

Hike chapters begin with a summary of the facts readers need to evaluate that hike. Hike highlights offers a brief answer to the question, "Why go?" The location heading describes the region the hike is in and the distance from a town. "Type of hike" places each hike in one of four categories:

1. Loop hike. A loop hike begins and ends at the same point without walking the same stretch of trail more than once. At times, finishing the loop may require a small amount of road walking to return to the starting point.

2. Lollipop hike. A lollipop hike is a loop with a stem. If the loop segment of the lollipop is very small in proportion to the stem, it falls into the category of out-and-back hikes.

3. Shuttle hike. A shuttle hike involves walking from one point to another, using a second vehicle or a bicycle for the return trip.

4. Out-and-back hike. An out-and-back hike involves hiking to a location, then retracing your steps to the point of origin.

Mileage for each hike appears after the heading "Total distance." Keep in mind that precise measurement of trail miles is time consuming and rarely done. Most mileage figures, whether from official sources or the author's notes, are usually an estimate.

Each hike has an overall difficulty rating:

1. Easy. These are well-marked trails and have reasonably good footing. There are no obstacles worth mentioning, and the length is less than 6 miles.

2. Moderate. These hikes are on marked or obvious trails, old woods roads, or lanes. They are less than 10 miles long, and footing may be rougher in places than on easy hikes.

3. Difficult. This rating reflects either a hike length of more than 10 miles or conditions or navigation that require considerable skills and/or perseverance. Difficult hikes may be on unmarked trails or old woods roads or involve considerable off-trail travel. The footing may be rough and there may be steep climbs.

"Best months" lists the time period during which the hike is normally snow-free and reasonable to walk. Early or late season snowstorms can change those dates.

Any map listed that is from a land agency or trail organization shows the featured hike or a large portion of it. These maps are often basic but perfectly adequate for easy hikes and some moderate ones. United States Geological Survey (USGS) topographical maps are useful for some moderate and difficult hikes. Unfortunately it is not unusual for these maps to pre-date the existence of the hiking trail in question. Topographical maps that show the area but not all of the trail mentioned have (inc.), for incomplete, after them. Having both the land agency map and the topographical map is a good idea. Wisconsin's landscape has many attributes, but significant elevation change is not one of them. Therefore, elevation profiles are not included in this book.

A "Permits and fees" section lists items such as state park vehicle stickers or backpacking permits that may be needed for the hike.

Each hike summary also includes a brief description of how to find the trailhead from a nearby town. Finally, there are headings listing any nearby camping and whom to contact for more information.

If there are other aspects of a hike that are important for you to know before your outing, they are listed after the "Special considerations" heading.

Hike Finder

Hikes to take if you're looking for (The author's favorites, by category, are indicated with *):

Quiet Inland Lakes	
Quiet Inland Lakes	Anderson Lake *
	Chippewa Moraine Loop
	Chippewa Moraine/Plummer Lake *
	Clark Lake
	Deer Island Lake *
	Escanaba Lake *
	Hidden Lakes *
	Jones Spring
	Lake La Grange
	Marengo River/Porcupine Lake *
	Wood Lake
Great Lakes Shorelines	Deathdoor Bluff
	Eagle Bluff
	Moonlight Bay *
	Newport State Park
	Oak Island
	Point Beach *
	Sea Caves *
	Superior Shoreline *
	Tombolo
	Trout Point *
Rivers and Streams	Amnicon Falls *
	Berghum Bottoms *
	Blue Hills/Devil's Creek *
	Brule–St. Croix Portage
	Chippewa River *
	Copper Falls
	Emmons Creek *
	Ferry Bluff
	Glacial Potholes
	Kickapoo River *
	LaSalle Falls *
	Long Slide Falls
	Lost Creek Falls *
	Manitou Falls *
	Marengo River/Swedish Settlement
	McGilvray Bottoms
	Morgan Falls/St. Peter's Dome
	Parfrey's Glen
	Perrot Ridge
	Potato River Falls
	Sandrock Cliffs
	St. Croix *

Hike Finder

Hikes to take if you're looking for (The author's favorites, by category, are indicated with *):

Rivers and Streams (Continued)	Tombolo Trempealeau River Wyalusing State Park *
Waterfalls	Amnicon Falls * Copper Falls LaSalle Falls * Long Slide Falls Lost Creek Falls * Manitou Falls * Morgan Falls/St. Peter's Dome * Parfrey's Glen Potato River Falls *
Overnight Backpacking Trips	Anderson Lake Chippewa Lobe Chippewa Moraine/Plummer Lake Clark Lake Deer Island Lake * Escanaba Lake Hidden Lakes * Jerry Lake * Jones Spring Lake La Grange Marengo River/Porcupine Lake * Newport State Park North Kettle Moraine Oak Island * Penokee Range Rock Island St. Croix Trout Point * Wildcat Mound *
Walk-in Base Camps	Anderson Lake * Chippewa Moraine/Plummer Lake Clark Lake Deer Island Lake * Escanaba Lake Hidden Lakes * Jones Spring Newport State Park Oak Island * Penokee Range Rock Island Trout Point * Wildcat Mound

Hike Finder

Hikes to take if you're looking for (The author's favorites, by category, are indicated with *):

Long, Hard Day Hikes	Chippewa Lobe
	Chippewa River *
	Deer Island Lake *
	Devil's Lake to Parfrey's Glen
	Hidden Lakes *
	Jerry Lake *
	Marengo River/Porcupine Lake *
	Newport State Park
	North Kettle Moraine
	Oak Island
	Penokee Range
	St. Croix
	Superior Shoreline *
	Trout Point
	Wildcat Mound *
Solitude	Anderson Lake
	Berghum Bottoms
	Blue Hills/Devils Creek
	Brule–St. Croix Portage
	Chippewa Lobe
	Chippewa Moraine/Plummer Lake
	Chippewa River
	Deer Island Lake *
	Hidden Lakes
	Jerry Lake *
	Kickapoo River
	Lone Rock *
	Lost Creek Falls *
	Marengo River/Porcupine Lake *
	Marengo River/Swedish Settlement
	Penokee Range
	Rush Creek Bluff *
	Superior Shoreline *
	Trout Point *
Wildlife Viewing Opportunities	Anderson Lake
	Berghum Bottoms
	Chippewa Lobe
	Chippewa Moraine Loop
	Chippewa Moraine/Plummer Lake
	Chippewa River *
	Clark Lake
	Deer Island Lake *
	Emmons Creek

Hike Finder

Hikes to take if you're looking for (The author's favorites, by category, are indicated with *):

Wildlife Viewing Opportunities (Continued)	Jerry Lake * Kickapoo River Lone Rock Marengo River/Porcupine Lake * Mead State Wildlife Area * North Bluff * Oak Island Sandrock Cliffs St. Croix Superior Shoreline * Tombolo Trempealeau River * Trout Point * Wildcat Mound * Wood Lake Wyalusing State Park *
Views from High Places	Blackhawk Ridge Deathdoor Bluff * Devil's Lake East Bluff Eagle Bluff Ferry Bluff * Glacial Potholes Lone Rock * Marengo River/Porcupine Lake Marengo River/Swedish Settlement Morgan Falls/St. Peter's Dome North Bluff Oak Island * Penokee Range * Perrot Ridge Rush Creek Bluff * Timm's Hill Wyalusing State Park
Loops or Lollipops	Blackhawk Ridge Chippewa Lobe Chippewa Moraine Loop * Clark Lake * Copper Falls Devil's Lake East Bluff Eagle Bluff Ed's Lake Escanaba Lake * Glacial Potholes

Hike Finder

Hikes to take if you're looking for (The author's favorites, by category, are indicated with *):

Loops or Lollipops **(Continued)**	Hidden Lakes * Jones Spring Kickapoo River * Mead State Wildlife Area * Moonlight Bay * Newport State Park * Perrot Ridge * Point Beach Ridges Rock Island Sandrock Cliffs Star Lake * Tombolo Wood Lake Wyalusing State Park *
Hikes through Memorable Woods	Anderson Lake Berghum Bottoms Blue Hills/Devils Creek Chippewa Moraine Loop Chippewa Moraine/Plummer Lake Chippewa River Clark Lake * Deer Island Lake * Devil's Lake East Bluff Ed's Lake Escanaba Lake * Hidden Lakes * Jerry Lake * Lone Rock Marengo River/Porcupine Lake * Marengo River/Swedish Settlement * Moonlight Bay Morgan Falls/St. Peter's Dome Newport State Park * Oak Island * Penokee Range * Pine Cliff Point Beach Ridges St. Croix Wyalusing State Park *
Places of Human Historical Interest	Brule–St. Croix Portage * Ferry Bluff Marengo River/Swedish Settlement

Hike Finder

Hikes to take if you're looking for (The author's favorites, by category, are indicated with *):

Places of Human Historical Interest (Continued)	McGilvray Bottoms Morgan Falls/St. Peter's Dome Perrot Ridge * Rock Island Wood Lake Wyalusing State Park *
Places of Geological or Glacial Interest	Amnicon Falls * Chippewa Moraine Loop Chippewa Moraine/Plummer Lake Copper Falls * Devil's Lake East Bluff * Glacial Potholes * Lone Rock * Manitou Falls * Morgan Falls/St. Peter's Dome Parfrey's Glen Sea Caves

Amnicon Falls

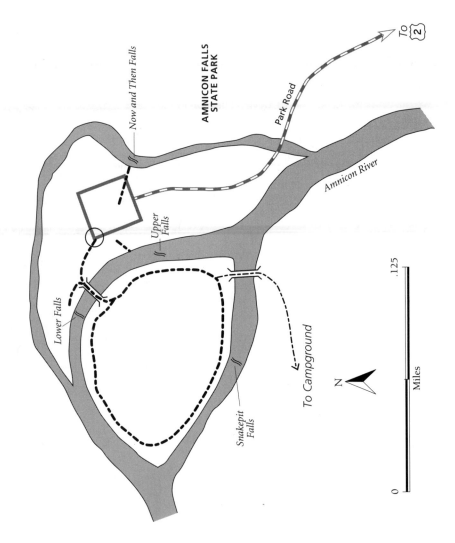

AMNICON FALLS STATE PARK

Now and Then Falls

Park Road

To 2

Amnicon River

Upper Falls

Lower Falls

To Campground

Snakepit Falls

N

Miles

0 .125

Lake Superior Lowland

A flat plain, rich in red clay deposits, runs along Wisconsin's Lake Superior shoreline. This level to mildly rolling landscape, once the lake bed of Glacial Lake Duluth, slopes gently upward to the south and ends 5 to 20 miles inland where higher ground rises.

It is a band of boreal forest habitat, with Canada-like flora and fauna. Clay banks border many of the beaches, reaching almost 200 feet in height on Oak Island's north end. That clay bluff is the highest point on Wisconsin's Superior shore, but sandstone sea caves, chiseled by time and waves, are the area's most well-known landscape art.

Lake Superior, an inland sea that possesses a full eighth of the planet's fresh water, as well as some of its purest, is the focus of most hiking trails here. Hikers can expect cold springs, cool summers, and relatively warm autumns in this region, due to the lake effect climate.

1 Amnicon Falls

Highlights:	A short walk to a fine collection of three waterfalls and numerous cascades on the Amnicon River.
Location:	Northwest Wisconsin, 13 miles southeast of Superior.
Type of hike:	Lollipop day hike.
Total distance:	.5 mile.
Difficulty:	Easy.
Best months:	The park is open from the first weekend in May to the first weekend in October. At other times you are welcome to park at the gate and walk in to the falls, a distance of a little more than .3 mile.
Maps:	Amnicon Falls State Park map or USGS South Range quad (inc.).
Permits and fees:	State park vehicle sticker required.
Finding the trailhead:	From the intersection of U.S. Highways 2 and 53 in Superior, drive 13 miles southeast on U.S. 2 to its intersection with Douglas County Route U. Turn left (north) and drive .3 mile to the entrance road for Amnicon Falls State Park. Turn left (west) and proceed west and north .4 mile to the falls parking lot.
Special considerations:	Wet rocks and whitewater are in abundance here, a dangerous combination for the careless or toddlers running loose.
Camping:	The park has thirty-six drive-in sites just southwest of the falls.
For more information:	Amnicon Falls State Park, see Appendix B.

The hike: When I think of Amnicon Falls, I think of an art gallery, one with a theme of falling water. Visitors wander from display to display, sampling each for its nuance, then moving on to see what the next exhibit offers. With three waterfalls, and sometimes the aptly named Now and Then Falls as a fourth, there is a lot to contemplate here. This is a compact place, and if you want to choose your own route you can easily do so without fear of getting lost.

I recommend following the itinerary of the self-guided tour brochure available at the park office for its educational value. This geology booklet explains the complex history of the park's rock. If you follow the tour's numbered posts, you start out going west from the parking lot, past the covered bridge to a view of the Lower Falls and its sandstone cliffs. Next, cross the bridge to the island and turn left (south) facing the thundering cascade of the Upper Falls.

The route continues around the island in a clockwise manner. At the island's southeast corner turn west, past smaller cascades and a bridge leading to the river's west bank.

This westward turn takes the path downstream along the west branch of the river to Snakepit Falls, a twisting, turning series of three drops. From

Upper Falls, one of a series on the Amnicon River.

there, continue west, then north, until you are back at the covered bridge and the Lower Falls.

Cross the bridge and turn right (south) to a steel ladder that descends into the mist below the Upper Falls. The parking lot is nearby, but one more treat awaits you if the river flow is not low. Walk to the southeast corner of the parking lot and walk 20 feet south on a broad path to Now And Then Falls. This channel of the river, and the waterfall, go dry if the river's flow slackens.

2 Superior Shoreline

Highlights:	A magnificent, wild Lake Superior shoreline.
Location:	Northwest Wisconsin, 15 miles east of Superior.
Type of hike:	Out-and-back day hike or overnight backpack.
Total distance:	6 miles.
Difficulty:	Difficult.
Best months:	June–September.
Maps:	USGS Cloverland quad.
Finding the trailhead:	From Maple, drive north 4 miles on Douglas County Route F and turn left (west) on Wisconsin 13. After .5 mile turn right (north) on Beck's Road (graded gravel). Drive 4.9 miles north and park on the side of the road at the top of the lakeside bluff.
Special considerations:	Moderately difficult, requiring considerable wading in good conditions. Dangerous in poor conditions. An off-trail route along a narrow beach that is underwater during periods of high waves or storm surges. A good weather forecast, including moderate wave height, and good judgment are prerequisites for this hike. See cautions in the text.
Camping:	Backpack camping with free permit from Brule River State Forest.
For more information:	Brule River State Forest, see Appendix B.

Key points:
- 0.0. Pearson Creek mouth (end of Beck's Road and beginning of hike).
- 0.5 Haukkala Creek mouth.
- 1.7 Nelson Creek mouth.
- 2.7 Unnamed Creek mouth.
- 3.0 Second unnamed creek mouth. Turnaround point.

The hike: This hike is along a splendid, untamed shoreline, chock full of solitude and broad lake views. An otter accompanied me when I did this walk, swimming offshore, for half a mile. Ospreys patrolled the coast. A wolf-kill deer, blood not yet congealed, lay just off the beach. Paw prints spoke of a hurried departure. I had seen a blur, and probably had flushed them.

This is a very special place, worthy of thoughtful behavior on your part. In addition to the beauty of the landscape there is another reason for being

Superior Shoreline

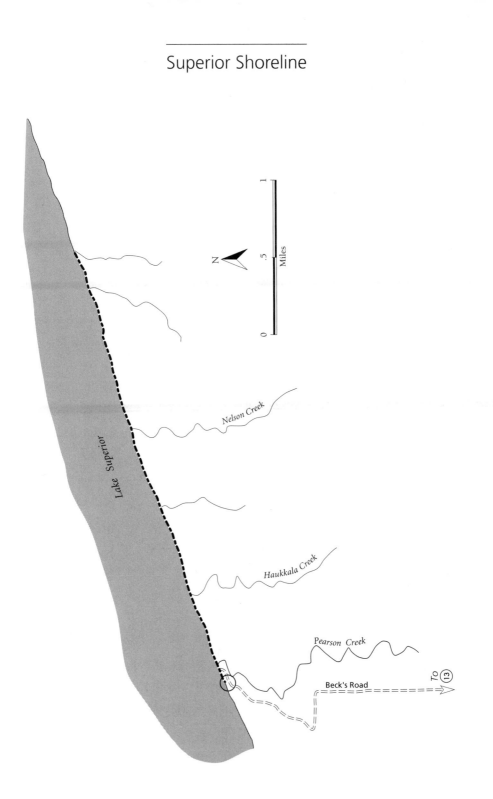

careful. Under poor conditions, high waves or storm surges, the beach will be under water. The hike could become a life-and-death epic.

The route is a narrow beach. In benign conditions, the only obstacles are the creek mouths and deadfall trees whose limbs cross the beach and reach into the lake. Wading the numerous creek mouths is usually a knee-deep affair if you find the sand bar. The sand bar is usually C shaped, with the bulge going out into the lake. Watch for the break of the waves on the bar to locate it. Trekking poles are helpful.

The occasional deadfalls, found once a mile or so, are worse. You can either tunnel through them on the beach or wade around them. On a good day, wading is a mere knee-deep affair. However, when the waves come up, knee deep becomes a waist-high soaking or worse, and hypothermia, becoming seriously chilled, is a concern. The clay banks lining much of the beach tend to discourage any attempt to climb above obstacles.

Before you do this hike you should check the forecast, and be prepared to change your plans if the lake gets rowdy. Exiting from the beach may not be easy.

You should also wear boots that you can wade in. In good conditions you will spend 95 percent of your time strolling down the beach. However, because of the creeks and deadfalls, your feet and shins will be either wet or in the process of drip drying all the time.

Still interested? If you have a good forecast, begin your outing by descending the lakeside bluff on the steep end of Beck's Road. At the bottom of the slope, you will find yourself alongside the lagoon of Pearson Creek, your first crossing. Mark this spot or memorize it. These creek mouths have a habit

The pristine, untamed Lake Superior shore east of Pearson Creek.

of looking similar later in the day and it is possible to walk right by on your return. Don't ask how I came by that wisdom.

Find the sand bar at the mouth and wade to the east side. Walk the beach eastward, taking in the broad lake views. Fifteen miles to the north, the Minnesota shore, dark and high with forested ridges, looms on the horizon. Far to the west, the tall buildings of Duluth are barely visible. At mile 0.5 another creek mouth appears, Haukkala Creek, similar in size to Pearson Creek.

Find the sand bar and wade to the east side. That initial pattern sets the tempo, almost like a rhythmic chant, for this outing. Wade, stroll the beach for awhile, then wade again.

Follow the shoreline east, passing a few minor drainages, and at mile 1.7, you will find Nelson Creek. The exact configuration of the beach at these creek mouths changes with every storm, a study in the dynamics of current, water, waves, and sand.

Cross Nelson Creek and continue walking east. A mile after Nelson Creek, at mile 2.7, a minor, unnamed creek enters from the south. Depending on conditions there may be no water flowing. A little farther east, at mile 3.0, another drainage enters from the southwest. This is a good turnaround point.

3 Lost Creek Falls

Highlights:	A short walk to a beautiful waterfall in a remote, quiet setting.
Location:	Northwest Wisconsin, 2 miles southwest of Cornucopia.
Type of hike:	Out-and-back day hike.
Total distance:	3 miles.
Difficulty:	Difficult.
Best months:	May–October.
Maps:	USGS Bark Bay (inc.) and Cornucopia (inc.) quads.
Finding the trailhead:	From Cornucopia, drive 1.8 miles west on Wisconsin 13. Turn left (south) on Klemik Road (dirt) and go 1.2 miles to an overgrown, weedy snowmobile trail with a yellow gate on the east side of the road. Park on the shoulder of Klemik Road.
Special considerations:	Confidence in your route-finding ability is a requirement for this hike, as reflected by the difficult rating.
Camping:	There are twenty drive-in sites at Herbster Township Park, 7 miles west of trailhead.
For more information:	Bayfield County Forestry Department, see Appendix B.

Lost Creek Falls

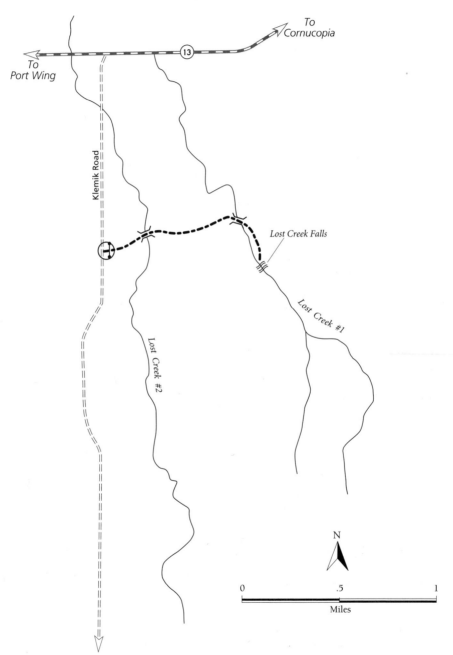

To Cornucopia

To Port Wing

13

Klemik Road

Lost Creek Falls

Lost Creek #1

Lost Creek #2

N

To Siskiwit Lake

0   .5   1

Miles

Key points:

0.3   Bridge over Lost Creek #2
1.2   Bridge over Lost Creek #1
1.5   Lost Creek Falls

The hike: Follow these directions and you will find yourself at an overgrown, unmarked trailhead in an area whose major geographical features bear the names Lost Creek #1, Lost Creek #2, and Lost Creek #3. Persevere. After an inauspicious beginning the route finding is straightforward, the walking pleasant, and the woods gain ambiance. Your reward is a charming water-fall set in a sandstone glen where solitude is a reasonable expectation.

From the yellow gate walk east on a faint road, waist high with weeds in June, marked for snowmobile travel. For the first .25 mile, 30-foot-tall aspen trees line your route. Just before a steel-framed bridge over Lost Creek #2, the surrounding woods change to older aspen, hardwoods, and pines. Ignore two spur roads that lead north, one just before the bridge and one after. Continue east on what is now a well-worn woods road. The road swings north before turning south and descending to the bridge (with wood railings) over Lost Creek #1.

Follow the road southeast some 600 yards and watch for a trail on the west side of the woods road where the road ascends and turns eastward. At this point you should be able to hear the sound of falling water. The water-fall is about 100 yards southwest of this junction, but you will end up walking nearly twice that distance as the rocky path twists and turns through the woods.

Lost Creek Falls, a delicate gem in a quiet setting.

Lost Creek Falls, a small, delicate gem, plunges 15 feet over a sandstone ledge in a mossy glen. On a fine Saturday in June I could not find a single sign of other visitors, not even footprints on the path.

4 Sea Caves

Highlights:	Spectacular mainland sea caves.
Location:	Apostle Islands National Lakeshore, northwest Wisconsin, 15 miles northwest of Bayfield.
Type of hike:	Out-and-back day hike.
Total distance:	4.8 miles.
Difficulty:	Moderate.
Best months:	May–October.
Maps:	National Geographic/Trails Illustrated Apostle Islands National Lakeshore Map, USGS Squaw Bay (inc.) quad.
Finding the trailhead:	From Cornucopia, drive 4.2 miles east on Wisconsin 13. Turn left (north) on Meyers Road and drive north .3 mile to the trailhead. There are picnic tables and a toilet here.
Special considerations:	Use extreme caution near the edge of the cliffs. Undercut and honeycombed sandstone makes a sea cave what it is, and what you are standing on may not be solid rock.
Camping:	There are twenty drive-in sites at township parks at Little Sand Bay (10 miles east) and Herbster (10 miles west).
For more information:	AINL, see Appendix B

Key points:
```
0.0   Meyers Road Trailhead.
0.8   Mawikwe Road.
1.8   Sea caves.
2.4   Turnaround point as trail goes inland.
```

The hike: Sandstone sea caves, carved by waves and ice, are the signature landmark of the Apostles Islands area. A mile of shoreline east of Meyers Road offers the only opportunity to view them on the mainland, and the walk in is a minor price to pay. It is an undulating 2 miles, crossing several ravines.

From the northeast corner of the trailhead parking lot on Meyers Road, take the Lakeshore Trail east. This broad, brushed-out trail starts in young woods sprinkled with orange hawkweed flowers in June and immediately descends into a small drainage. This is the first of several creek crossings along the route. The trail passes the end of Mawikwe Road, a rough dirt road, at mile 0.8.

For nearly 2 miles this trail stays in the woods, with only an occasional glimpse of Lake Superior. Doubts vanish with a bang as you arrive at a spec-

Sea Caves

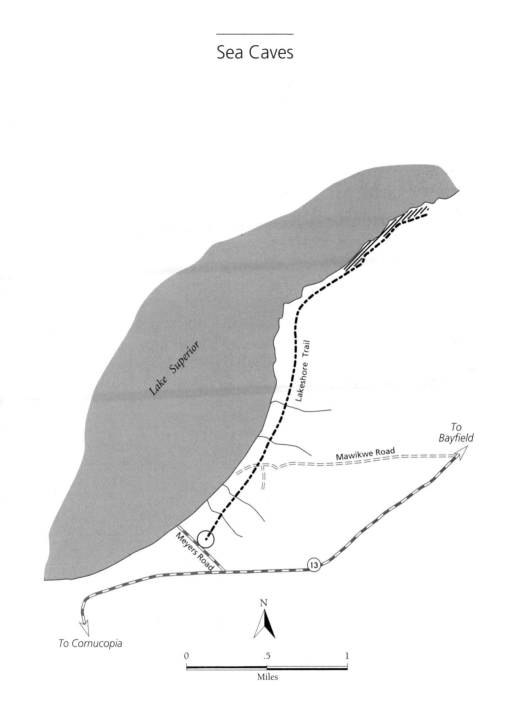

Lake Superior

Lakeshore Trail

To Bayfield

Mawikwe Road

Meyers Road

13

To Cornucopia

N

0   .5   1

Miles

Natural bridge and chasm among sea caves on the Lake Superior shore.

tacular sea chasm at mile 1.8, a deep and intricate cleft knifing into the shoreline. Two separate arches of chockstones, soil, and small birch trees bridge the small canyon.

This spectacular chasm begins a .5-mile-long parade of sea caves, cliffs, and a small dripping waterfall. Several promontories offer vantage points for long views of the shoreline. At mile 2.4 the trail moves inland, a logical place to turn around and retrace your steps to Meyers Road.

5 Oak Island

Highlights:	The highest point on Wisconsin's Lake Superior shore, pristine beaches, and 11 miles of shady hiking trails.
Location:	Apostle Islands National Lakeshore, northwest Wisconsin, 8 miles north of Bayfield.
Type of hike:	Out-and-back base camp backpack or day hike.
Total distance:	7.8 miles.
Difficulty:	Moderate.
Best months:	June–September.
Maps:	National Geographic/Trails Illustrated Apostle Islands National Lakeshore Map, USGS Oak Island (inc.) and York Island (inc.) quads.
Permits and fees:	Camping permit required. Available from Apostle Islands National Lakeshore, see Appendix B.
Finding the trailhead:	If not arriving by private boat, catch the cruise boat (see below) at the Bayfield harbor and get off at the dock on the west side of Oak Island. A vault toilet, water pump, two campsites, and a ranger residence are there.
Special considerations:	From late June to early September Apostle Islands Cruise Service has twice daily service to Oak Island (715–779–3925, www.apostleisland.com). Water taxi service is available at other times. Oak Island, known as the "least buggy" island, is the highest and driest of all the Apostle Islands.
Camping:	Five individual campsites and two group campsites are on the island.
For more information:	AINL, see Appendix B

Key points:
0.0 Oak Island dock.
1.2 Northwest Beach Trail Junction.
1.7 Overlook Trail Junction.
2.8 North Bay Trail Junction.
3.9 North Bay campsite

Recommended itinerary: I recommend a base camp backpack trip with two nights at North Bay. Day one would be a 3.9-mile backpack into North Bay with a 3.8-mile (roundtrip) after dinner walk to the Overlook. The second day would feature a 14.3-mile day hike around the Loop Trail with a side trip to the Northwest Beach. Day three is the 3.9-mile return backpack to the dock.

The hike: When you stand on the clay banks at Oak Island's northern tip, you can't help but wonder who else has stood here or passed by. This spot, known as The Overlook, is a commanding height with a view that takes in ten islands. It is easy to imagine that Voyageurs or Native Americans posted

Oak Island

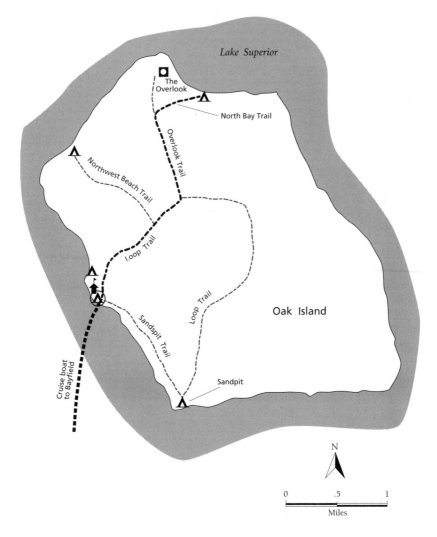

Lake Superior

The Overlook

North Bay Trail

Overlook Trail

Northwest Beach Trail

Loop Trail

Loop Trail

Sandspit Trail

Oak Island

Sandpit

Cruise boat to Bayfield

N

0   .5   1
Miles

lookouts on this strategic location, watching for the canoes of friend or foe. A canoe, traveling Lake Superior's south shore, would have to pass nearby or risk the open waters of the lake.

Walk north one hundred yards from the dock on Oak Island's west side and a trail sign will direct you onto the Loop Trail, a shady path in a pleasant, mature hardwood forest. The trail ascends slowly and gains 400 feet in the next 1.7 miles. After 1.2 miles you pass the junction of the Northwest Beach Trail and at mile 1.7 you top out near the highest point in the Apostles Islands and turn left (north) on the Overlook Trail.

At mile 2.8 the North Bay Trail turns right (east) and drops to the beach. You may want to continue on the .7 mile to The Overlook, but that destination also makes a fine after dinner hike after you have set up camp. From the viewpoint, you can see Hole-in-the-Wall, a sea arch on the island's northeast shore. The North Bay Trail dead ends at mile 3.8, the designated campsite set in trees just off the beach.

Doubts about the wisdom of passing up campsites closer to the dock tend to vanish within moments of arrival as you look around. There's a broad lake view, a .5-mile-long beach perfect for morning or moonlight strolls, and the view through your tent door isn't exactly hard on the eyes, either. Eagles cruise the shoreline and mergansers dot the waves.

You may opt to spend your second day here, looking for a perfect driftwood seat to practice the fine art of Lake Superior gazing. If you would rather roam, I suggest a complete tour of the island's trails in a counterclockwise direction.

Walking in that direction leaves you with a choice 2.6 miles from North Beach when the Northwest Beach Trail heads north. It will cost you 3.2 miles round trip and 300 feet of vertical to take a look, but the pristine beach and enjoyable trail are worth it. If you took the side trip, at mile 7.0 you will be back at the dock and have a chance to load up on water from the pump. Go south on the Sandspit Trail, crossing numerous small drainages and often staying within sight of the lake. The Sandspit itself at mile 8.5, on the island's southwest corner, offers broad lake views and an artesian well for water.

From the Sandspit, head north on the Loop Trail, steadily ascending 400 feet in the first mile before descending a hundred feet as you swing east of the island's summit ridge. In this area, at about mile 10.0, watch for the remains of an old logging camp. An intricately embossed wood stove and other metal artifacts are near the trail. The familiar Overlook Trail Junction is at mile 11.0. Turn north, and another 2.2 downhill miles brings you in to camp. To return to the dock on day three, retrace your steps from the first day.

Options: Day hiking on Oak Island is possible. Backpackers have other choices besides the recommended itinerary. Four locations other than North Beach, one just 50 yards from the dock, have campsites, and all offer easy access to the loop trail system described above.

6 Trout Point

Highlights:	Broad lake views and abundant wildlife at a remote campsite on a pristine shore.
Location:	Apostle Islands National Lakeshore, northwest Wisconsin, 12 miles northeast of Bayfield.
Type of hike:	Out-and-back base camp backpack.
Total distance:	12.6 miles.
Difficulty:	Moderate.
Best months:	June–September.
Maps:	National Geographic/Trails Illustrated Apostle Islands National Lakeshore map, USGS Stockton Island (inc.) quad.
Permits and fees:	Camping permit required, available from Apostle Islands National Lakeshore, see Appendix B.
Finding the trailhead:	If not arriving by private boat, catch the cruise boat (see below) at the Bayfield harbor and get off at the Presque Isle Docks on Stockton Island. Vault toilets, a water pump, nineteen campsites, and a ranger station are there.
Special considerations:	From late June to early September Apostle Islands Cruise Service has daily service to Stockton Island (715–779–3925, www.apostleisland.com). Water taxi service is available at other times.
Camping:	Trout Point is an individual campsite. Three group sites and an individual site are at Quarry Bay, and nineteen sites are at Presque Isle.
For more information:	AINL, see Appendix B

Key points:
- 0.0   Presque Isle Docks
- 0.6   Tombolo Trail Junction.
- 1.6   Trout Point Trail Junction.
- 6.3   Trout Point.

Recommended itinerary: This is a perfect destination for a two-night base camp trip. The first day would be a 6.3-mile backpack to Trout Point. Day two would be dedicated to beachcombing, wildlife watching, and relaxation, with a return to Presque Isle Docks on day three.

The hike: Trout Point, on Stockton Island's quiet north shore, may be the most remote walk-in campsite in the Apostle Islands. When you sit here it is easy to feel as if you have inherited an entire private ecosystem. Somehow, the view seems both intimate and boundless as your eyes wander from the nearby beach to the watery horizon and far-off shores. Morning and evening shows are spectacular as the changing light turns the water a zillion shades of blue. Groups of loons swim by the campsite while others join mergansers in the offshore waters. Ospreys and bald eagles scan from treetop perches or cruise the shoreline on dawn patrol.

Trout Point

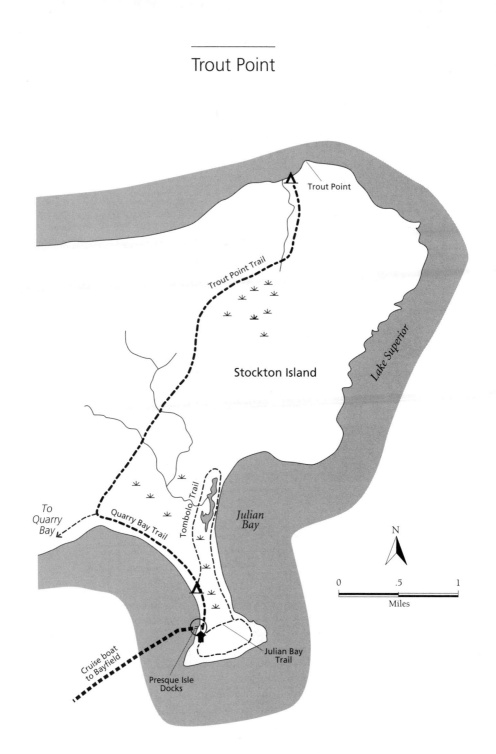

Trout Point

Lake Superior

Trout Point Trail

Stockton Island

Tombolo Trail

Julian Bay

To Quarry Bay

Quarry Bay Trail

Julian Bay Trail

Cruise boat to Bayfield

Presque Isle Docks

N

0   .5   1
Miles

The remote Lake Superior shoreline west of Trout Point.

Comparing Trout Point with Presque Isle, on the opposite side of the island, is a study in contrasts. Presque Isle is the most visited place in the Apostles, and a steady hum of boat traffic is not unusual.

From the Presque Isle Docks walk north on the broad, well-worn Quarry Bay Trail, passing a long string of shoreline campsites. Stay straight (northwest) at mile 0.6 as the Tombolo Trail goes right. At 1.6 miles turn right (north) on the Trout Point Trail; here your transition from frontcountry to backcountry begins in earnest. The Trout Point Trail is a shady, narrow footpath, sparsely used, and a low maintenance priority. It will get you where you want to go, but the next 3.5 miles are notable mostly for the robust insect population.

At mile 5.3 the woods gain ambiance as a northward flowing brook marks the last mile of the walk. You follow the drainage to the lake, finally emerging at the campsite near a 1917 lumber camp. To return to Presque Isle Docks, retrace the steps of your first day.

Options: Staying a third night at Presque Isle would ease the pressure to move quickly on the day you are walking in (or out) to Trout Point. It would also give you a chance to walk the Tombolo Trail. This fascinating trail combines with the Julian Bay Trail to make a 4-mile loop that traverses a wetland on a sturdy boardwalk before traveling Julian Bay's long beach.

7 Tombolo

Highlights:	A boardwalk crossing of a notable dune and bog ecosystem and a splendid beach walk.
Location:	Stockton Island, Apostle Islands National Lakeshore, northwest Wisconsin, 12 miles northeast of Bayfield.
Type of hike:	Loop day hike.
Total distance:	3.8 miles.
Difficulty:	Moderate.
Best months:	June–September.
Maps:	Trails Illustrated Apostle Islands, USGS Stockton Island (inc.) quad.
Finding the trailhead:	If not arriving by private boat, catch the cruise boat (see below) at the Bayfield harbor and get off at the Presque Isle Docks on Stockton Island. Vault toilets, a water pump, nineteen campsites, and a ranger station are there.
Special considerations:	From late June to early September, Apostle Islands Cruise Service has daily service to Stockton Island (715–779–3925, www.apostleisland.com). Water taxi service is available at other times. A lagoon at Julian Bay sometimes requires a brief, shallow wade.
Camping:	Nineteen walk-in campsites are at Presque Isle. Obtain permit from Apostle Islands National Lakeshore (see Appendix B).
For more information:	AINL, see Appendix B.

Key points:
- 0.0   Presque Isle Docks.
- 0.6   Tombolo Trail Junction with Quarry Bay Trail.
- 2.1   Tombolo Trail turns south on Julian Bay's beach.
- 2.7   Creek at lagoon mouth (intermittent, may be either open water or sand).
- 3.4   Julian Bay Trail.
- 3.8   Presque Isle Docks.

The hike: Ask most visitors to the Apostle Islands how the lake shapes the shoreline and they would point to the sea caves. Those sandstone caverns are a clear example of waves, ice, and time nibbling away at rock with grains of sand washing away. Waterborne sand, perhaps even the same grains, is also an element in the landscape of this hike. Here, however, the process adds to the shoreline, forming sand bars that mature into vegetated dunes as the lake recedes.

A tombolo, a spectacular example of these creative powers, is a land bridge (connection) that forms between two previously isolated bodies of land. In this case, rocky Presque Isle, once a mile off shore, became a part of Stockton Island. The story of that transformation unfolds as you walk this short loop hike.

Tombolo

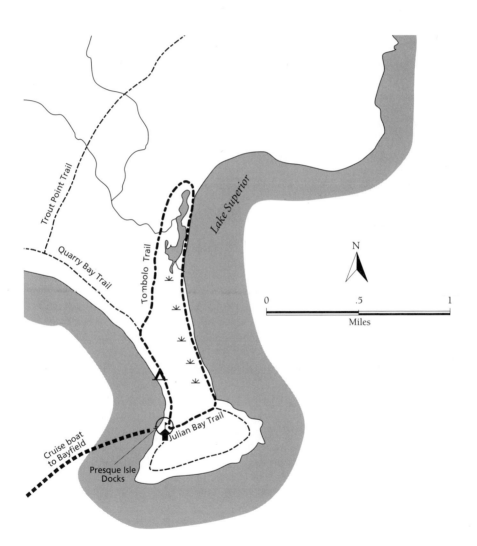

Trout Point Trail

Quarry Bay Trail

Tombolo Trail

Lake Superior

Julian Bay Trail

Cruise boat
to Bayfield

Presque Isle
Docks

N

0   .5   1
Miles

The Tombolo Trail follows Julian Bay's beautiful beach.

From the Presque Isle Docks walk north past tall pines and waterfront campsites on the broad Quarry Bay Trail, .6 mile to the beginning of the Tombolo Trail. Turn right (north) on the smooth, well-defined, but narrow footpath.

After passing through open, piney woods for .5 mile, a lagoon/bog complex appears to your east, dry land ends, and the trail becomes a sturdy boardwalk. A pattern of alternating sand ridges and linear bogs emerges from the wetland. In aerial photos these ridges appear as a series of broad arcs, each the mark of a shoreline of the past. The boardwalk crosses a small stream and a portion of the bog before reentering the woods.

The trail rounds the north end of the lagoon area and at mile 2.1 emerges on the youngest of the sand ridges, Julian Bay's beautiful beach. Follow the waterline south; at mile 2.7 the mouth of the lagoon sometimes requires a brief wade. I found a pleasant, knee-deep channel 50 feet wide.

Continue south on the beach. When the grassy dunes and sand end and shady woods begin at mile 3.4, the route leaves the topography of the tombolo for that of Presque Isle. Turn right (east) on the wide Julian Bay Trail and take that .4 mile to the Presque Isle Docks where the hike began.

Northern Highlands

Wisconsin's largest region, the Northern Highlands, covers the third of the state south of the Lake Superior lowlands. Heavily forested and sprinkled with thousands of lakes, it is a broad upland sitting on a granite base, sloping slightly to the south. That bedrock base shows up often in the region's waterfalls, including the fourth highest east of the Rocky Mountains. The glaciers passed this way, and many Ice Age land forms, from moraines to potholes, are visible today.

Large breeding populations of bald eagles, ospreys, and loons nest on the lake shores, while black bear and fisher roam the woodlands. Some 200 timber wolves call the Northern Highland forest home.

Hiking trails here cross vast forests, border clear streams and lakes, and skirt wildlife-rich marshes. Walkers will find relief from summer heat under the shady forest canopy.

8 Manitou Falls

Highlights:	Two outstanding waterfalls, one 165 feet high and the fourth highest east of the Rocky Mountains, connected by a river side path.
Location:	Northwest Wisconsin, 13 miles south of Superior.
Type of hike:	A lollipop with two stems.
Total distance:	4.4 miles.
Difficulty:	Easy.
Best months:	May–October.
Maps:	Park handout or USGS Sunnyside (inc.) and Borea (inc.) quads.
Permits and fees:	State park vehicle sticker required.
Finding the trailhead:	From the intersection of U.S. Highway 2 and Wisconsin 35 in Superior, drive south 12.9 miles on Wisconsin 35 and turn left (east) into Pattison State Park. Drive 500 feet east, past the park office, and park in the west end of the large parking lot there.
Camping:	Pattison State Park has fifty-nine drive-in campsites .25 mile south of the trailhead as well as three walk-in backpacking sites.
For more information:	Pattison State Park, see Appendix B.

Key points:
- 0.0 Park parking lot.
- 0.2 Underpass under Wisconsin 35.
- 0.3 West end of viewing areas north of Big Manitou Falls.
- 0.4 Bridge over Black River.

Manitou Falls

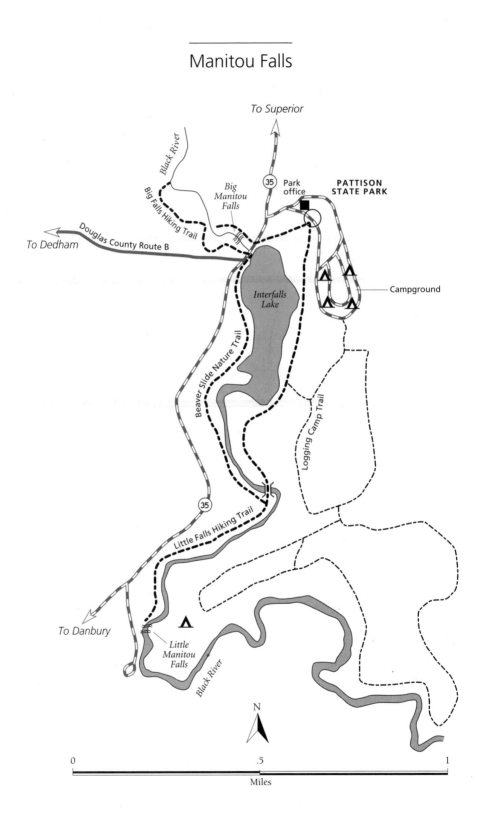

To Superior

Black River

Big Falls Hiking Trail

Big Manitou Falls

35

Park office

PATTISON STATE PARK

Douglas County Route B

To Dedham

Interfalls Lake

Campground

Beaver Slide Nature Trail

Logging Camp Trail

35

Little Falls Hiking Trail

To Danbury

Little Manitou Falls

Black River

N

| 0 | | .5 | | 1 |

Miles

0.9	North end of Big Falls Hiking Trail.
1.4	Bridge over Black River.
2.4	Junction with Little Falls Hiking Trail at bridge.
3.0	Little Manitou Falls.
3.6	Junction with Beaver Slide Nature Trail at bridge.
4.0	Junction with Logging Camp Trail.
4.4	Park parking lot.

The hike: Big Manitou Falls is more than just big; it is a giant. A vertical drop of 165 feet makes it Wisconsin's highest and the fourth tallest waterfall east of the Rocky Mountains. Better yet, another waterfall, the state's eighth highest at 31 feet, is 1.5 miles upstream on the Black River. Combining visits to both these falls with a hike along the park's riverside paths makes a memorable outing.

First decide if you want to pick up a copy of the self-guided tour brochure from the park's office. Then walk west to the entrance of the pedestrian tunnel under Wisconsin 35. As you emerge from the tunnel's west end, a fork in the trail offers a choice. Take the path on the right (west); 100 feet farther on a chasm of air, mist, and falling water appears beyond the railing of the first viewpoint. This is a Big Manitou Falls. Several more observation points, one a platform, offer spectacular views of the waterfall before you reach the west end of this spur and turn around to retrace your steps back to the tunnel.

Just before the tunnel, turn right (southwest) and cross the pedestrian bridge to the southwest shore of the river. Turn right (north) again on a paved path where a series of constructed lookouts stretch along the gorge's crest. The

Little Manitou Falls, one of two outstanding waterfalls on the hike.

second one in, marked with a #5 to correspond with the self-guided tour, offers a good vantage point for viewing the complete top-to-bottom sweep of the waterfall.

Continue west, leaving the constructed viewpoints behind on what is now a broad, gravel path (park maps refer to this as the Big Falls Hiking Trail) that slowly descends past pines and aspens to the river. Here it is a gently gurgling stream, and a trailside bench makes a fine place for a break.

The maintained trail ends at the river. Turn around and walk back to the pedestrian tunnel under the highway and cross to the southeast side. As you emerge from the tunnel, turn right (south) and cross a walkway over the dam that creates Interfalls Lake. This leads to a dirt and gravel path, shown as the Beaver Slide Nature Trail on park maps, that follows the lakeshore south.

Follow that path, first along the lake, then along the Black River to a junction and bridge over the river at mile 2.4. Turn right (southeast), not crossing the bridge, and continue upstream along a charming streamside path, to Little Manitou Falls at mile 3.0. Pause to enjoy the twin torrents of Little Manitou Falls, then return downstream to the bridge junction at mile 3.6. Turn right (north), cross the bridge, and walk north on the east shore segment of the Beaver Slide Nature Trail.

The marshy upper end of the lake appears to your west; at mile 4.0 bear straight (north) as the Logging Camp Trail enters from the right. Follow the path north along the shore of the lake to the park's bathing beach. Continue walking north 200 yards through the picnic area and you will be at the parking lot.

9 Brule–St. Croix Portage

Highlights:	A historic portage trail connecting the Mississippi and St. Lawrence watersheds.
Location:	Northwest Wisconsin, 3 miles northeast of Solon Springs.
Type of hike:	Out-and-back day hike.
Total distance:	4 miles.
Difficulty:	Easy.
Best months:	May–October.
Maps:	Brule River State Forest trail map, North Country Trail segment map, USGS Bennett (inc.) quad.
Permits and fees:	State park car sticker required.
Finding the trailhead:	From Solon Springs, take Douglas County Route A northeast 3.9 miles. After it turns south you will notice a historical marker and sign on the west side of the road. The trailhead is 100 yards farther on the east side of the road, across from the entrance road for a DNR boat launch and picnic area, a good place to park.
Camping:	A county park in Solon Springs has twenty sites.
For more information:	North Country Trail, see Appendix B.

Brule–St. Croix Portage

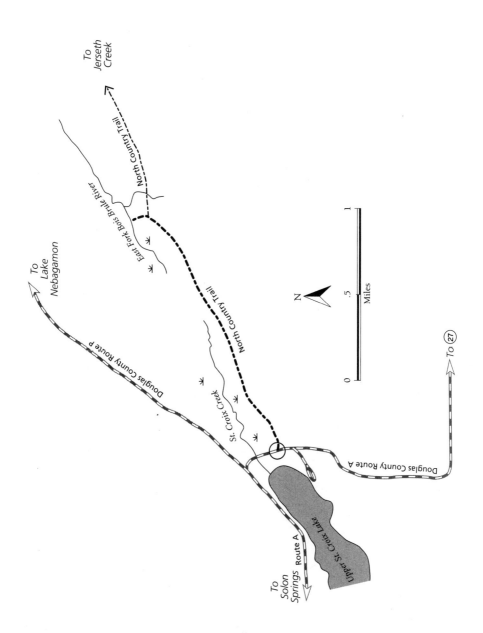

Key points:
- 0.0 County A Trailhead.
- 2.0 Brule end of portage.
- 4.0 County A Trailhead.

The hike: French explorer Daniel Greysolon Sieur duLhut, Duluth's namesake, was the first to make a record of his passage over this trail in 1680. His story mentions cutting through one hundred beaver dams on the Bois Brule River. He may have been the first to leave a written account, but it seems reasonable to believe that he learned of the route from Native Americans who had used it for some time.

Sadly, a recent clear cut mars part of this trail. Normally, that blemish would have warranted dropping the portage trail from this guidebook's list. However, when I stood at the Brule end of the portage I decided to make an exception. I found a powerful sense of place permeating that marshy landing. I wondered who had passed this way, spotted the open water, and happily dropped their loads.

Several stone markers along the trail mention early European pioneers, including another Frenchman, Pierre Le Sueur, in 1693, and Henry Schoolcraft, discoverer of the source of the Mississippi, in 1820. It's the travelers who did not leave a written trip log, the Native Americans, who fascinated me. Who were they? Where did they come from, and where were they going?

Follow the trail east as it leaves Douglas County Route A and makes a short ascent through a pleasant hardwood, pine, and aspen forest in an eroded gully. The North Country Trail continues through the woods on a plateau-like hilltop before entering the cut-over area after .5 mile. That clearing offers views

The author at the Brule end of the portage.

north across the wetland bottom that is the headwaters of both the St. Croix and Brule Rivers.

After crossing the open area the trail reenters woods on a sidehill traverse 15 vertical feet above the wetland. At mile 2.0 a worn path leads left (north) 100 yards, out of the woods and onto grass hummocks. A stream, barely large enough to float a canoe, floats northeast. This is the Brule end of the portage and the hike's turnaround point.

10 Anderson Lake

Highlights:	Quiet lakes in the Rainbow Lake Wilderness.
Location:	Northwest Wisconsin, 6 miles north of Drummond.
Type of hike:	Out-and-back day hike or backpack.
Total distance:	8.2 miles.
Difficulty:	Moderate.
Best months:	May–October.
Maps:	USGS Delta (inc.) quad.
Finding the trailhead:	From Drummond, drive 5.6 miles north on Forest Highway 35 and turn left (west) into a small parking area.
Camping:	This hike is within the Rainbow Lake Wilderness of the Chequamegon-Nicolet National Forest, and camping is permitted along the trail. Campsites must be at least 100 feet away from the trail or water's edge.
For more information:	Chequamegon-Nicolet National Forest, see Appendix B.

Key points:
0.0   Trailhead.
1.5   Bufo Lake spur.
1.7   North Country Trail intersection.
2.8   Turn east for Anderson Lake.
2.9   Anderson Lake.
4.1   North Country Trail intersection.
5.3   Rainbow Lake.
6.5   Anderson Grade intersection.
8.2   Trailhead.

The hike: A first-time visitor to the south end of the Rainbow Lake Wilderness may think the script calls for a mere walk in the woods, but the soundtrack tells another story. The haunting tremolo cry of loons echoes across this pocket-sized preserve, and a map check reveals why: there are a dozen small lakes scattered around this route.

The Anderson Grade, an old railroad grade from the logging era, provides easy access to four of those lakes. Combining that route with a short jaunt

Anderson Lake

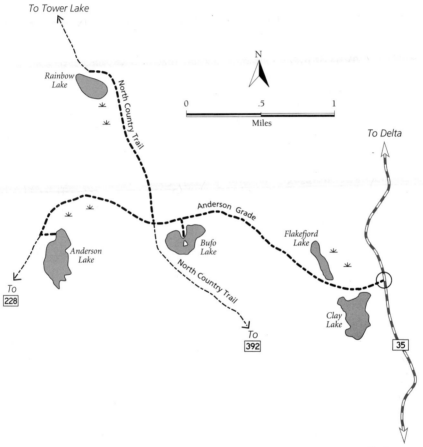

Along the Anderson Grade west of Flakefjord Lake.

on the North Country Trail to Rainbow Lake creates a fine outing, with hardly a mile going by without a new lake to contemplate.

Begin by walking west from the trailhead on the Anderson Grade, Forest Service Trail 502. It's level, fast walking. After little more than 100 yards, Clay Lake appears to the south, and .25 mile after that Flakefjord Lake peeks through the trees to the north.

The old railroad grade enters the woods and more rolling terrain for a mile before coming to an unmarked spur to Bufo Lake at mile 1.5. That spur runs south a short distance to a piney peninsula protruding into Bufo Lake.

Resume walking west on the Anderson Grade. Go straight (west) where the North Country Trail enters from the left (south) at mile 1.7 and splits off to the right (north) 100 yards later.

Follow the Anderson Grade west as it makes a very broad turn to the left around a long wetland. Pay attention as it begins a southwesterly course. At mile 2.8, make a very sharp left turn (east) on a spur of the Anderson Grade and walk east about 100 yards. At that point, a path leads south to the north shore of Anderson Lake, a pleasant place for a break.

When you are ready, return to the Anderson Grade and retrace your steps to the North Country Trail intersection at mile 4.1. Turn left (north) and walk north along that narrow trail to Rainbow Lake at mile 5.3.

Rainbow Lake is another turnaround on this route. Walk south on the North Country Trail, reaching the intersection with the Anderson Grade at mile 6.5. Turn left (east) and follow the old railroad grade back to the trailhead at mile 8.2.

11 Marengo River/Porcupine Lake

Highlights:	A three-day backpacking trip through classic Northwoods terrain, remains of a historic settlement.
Location:	Northwest Wisconsin, 10 miles west of Mellen.
Type of hike:	A point-to-point shuttle hike, a two- or three-day backpacking trip, or a very long day hike.
Total distance:	22.6 miles.
Difficulty:	Difficult.
Best months:	May–October.
Maps:	USFS "The North Country National Scenic Trail," USGS Mineral Lake, Marengo River, Grandview (inc.), and Diamond Lake (inc.) quads.
Finding the trailhead:	From Mellen, drive west 8.7 miles on Ashland County Route GG. Turn right (north) on Forest Road 187 (Mineral Lake Road). Follow Forest Road 187 north and west about 4 miles to the North Country Trail, just south of the Lake Three Campground.
Camping:	This part of the North Country Trail is in the Chequamegon National Forest and camping is permitted along the trail. Campsites must be at least 100 feet away from the trail or water's edge. The Lake Three Campground, with eight drive-in sites, is .1 mile north of the trailhead.
For more information:	North Country Trail Association or Chequamegon-Nicolet National Forest, see Appendix B.

Key points:

0.0   Forest Road 187 trailhead.

1.3   Seitz Lake.

3.0   Trail to Beaver Lake Campground.

6.1   Forest Road 383.

7.4   First overlook.

7.9   Second overlook.

8.1   Remains of Swedish settlement.

8.5   Adirondack shelter.

8.6   Marengo River.

9.1   Third overlook.

9.7   Forest Road 202.

11.2   Pearl Creek.

11.3   Forest Road 378.

13.2   Long Mile Lookout Tower.

15.2   Forest Road 201.

15.5   East Davis Lake.

15.7   Bayfield County Route D, east boundary of Porcupine Lake Wilderness.

16.9   Beaver dam crossing.

19.7   Porcupine Lake.

21.3   Eighteen Mile Creek.

22.6   Forest Road 213, north boundary of Porcupine Lake Wilderness.

Recommended itinerary: A two-night backpacking trip, with the first night near the Marengo River and the second at Porcupine Lake, works well. This would mean 8.6 miles of hiking the first day and 11.1 miles the second. The Marengo River offers brook trout fishing. Nearby are several overlooks and the historic Swedish settlement ruins. Loons frequent Porcupine Lake.

The hike: This hike is a story about woods, very big woods. Along the way there are a few lakes, as well as a handful of viewpoints from rock outcrops, but the overwhelming theme here is the forest. It is a beautiful forest of large, relatively old hardwoods, with a scattering of pines.

There is a mystique to woods this large, and a mere 100 yards into my hike of this route I got a vivid reminder of that. Wolf tracks, tack sharp in mud, and scat not yet cold on a thirty-five-degree morning left my senses racing. The Hell Hole Creek pack was nearby, and if I hadn't been fiddling with my pack straps I might have seen them before they flushed.

Begin your hike by walking west from the small trailside parking area on Forest Road 187. The trail is usually a footpath, but with a design that leaves enough space between trees for an ATV to pass for maintenance purposes. Occasionally, the trail follows an old woods road.

Seitz Lake and its marshy borders come into sight to the north at mile 1.3. The trail continues its run to the west, and at mile 3.0 a sign marks a spur leading south to the Beaver Lake Campground. Stay right (west) at that junction as the trail runs close to Beaver Lake's north shore. Near the lake's northwest corner you pass an old beaver dam before the trail rises into the wooded hills.

The North Country Trail rolls west, bisecting the small drainages that run north-south in this area. Despite that "cross grain" travel the vertical relief

Marengo River/Porcupine Lake (Western)

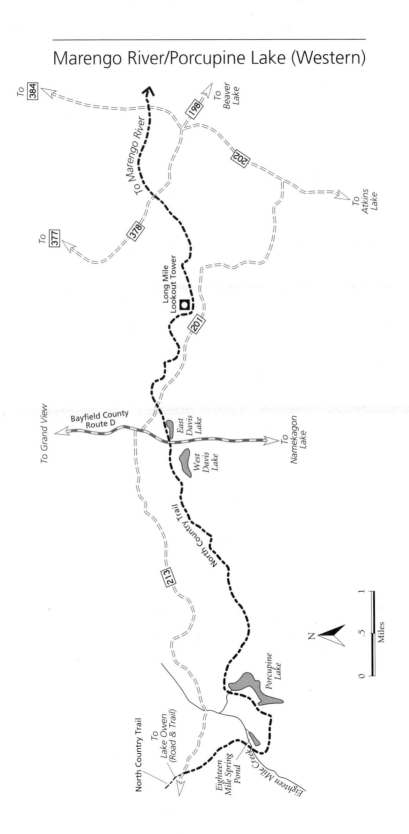

To 384

To Marengo River

198

To Beaver Lake

202

To Atkins Lake

378

To 377

Long Mile Lookout Tower

201

Bayfield County Route D

To Grand View

East Davis Lake

West Davis Lake

To Namekagon Lake

North Country Trail

213

Porcupine Lake

North Country Trail

To Lake Owen (Road & Trail)

Eighteen Mile Spring Pond

Eighteen Mile Creek

N

0   .5   1
Miles

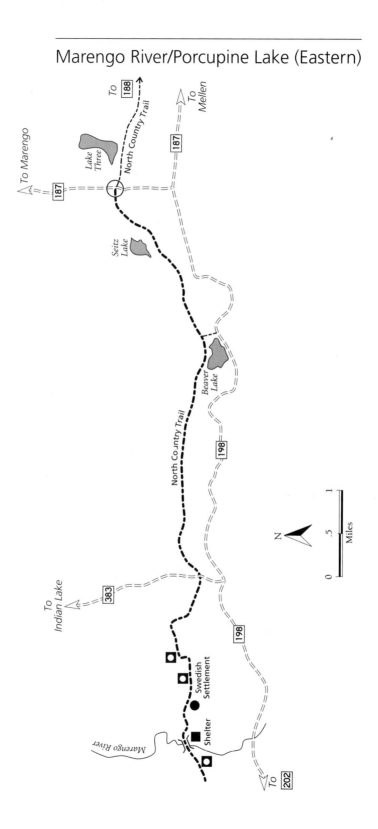

Marengo River/Porcupine Lake (Eastern)

in this section is in the moderate neighborhood of 100-foot gains and losses.

After the trail crosses Forest Road 383 at mile 6.1, the topography becomes more dramatic and the forest notably pleasant. At mile 7.3 the trail reaches the first of three overlooks that mark a 2-mile stretch of trail. A signed spur trail leads 100 feet north where a rock outcrop emerges from the trees, offering long views north to Mount Ashwabay, north of Washburn.

Continue walking west to mile 7.8, where another sign marks another side trail to a viewpoint. This time it is a 140-yard walk to the north to the rock ledge. The views here are northward again but broader than the first overlook. This is the best of the three lookouts in this section.

Resume walking west. As the trail enters a small pine plantation, a marker noting the Swedish settlement appears. To investigate, walk south through the pines to a clearing where old walls and other remains of the settlement endure.

After leaving the settlement area, the trail begins to drop in earnest, some 300 feet, to the Marengo River below. At mile 8.5 a short side trail leads to a three-sided Adirondack-style trail shelter. The trail reaches the Marengo River at mile 8.6, crosses on a wide, sturdy bridge, and ascends steeply on the river valley's west slope.

At the top of that climb, a broad dome of rock rises south of the trail, the third overlook at mile 9.1. This is a pleasant break spot, offering wide views of the upper part of the Marengo River watershed and the wooded hills that line the river valley.

The trail resumes its westward march, passing Forest Road 202 at mile 9.7 and crossing Pearl Creek at mile 11.2 on a bridge. Just after that stream, Forest Road 378 is at mile 11.3.

The next landmark is the Long Mile Lookout Tower at mile 13.2, bordering a stretch of trail where the path takes a northward jog. To the east of the trail, past the closed tower, there is a cluttered but worthwhile view to the east toward St. Peter's Dome. From the tower area, the trail meanders west, roughly paralleling Forest Road 201, before crossing it at mile 15.2. It then runs along the north shore of charming East Davis Lake at mile 15.5 and crosses Bayfield County Route D (paved) at mile 15.7.

County Route D marks the eastern boundary of the Porcupine Lakes Wilderness Area, and a sign there offers a map of the area. The trail shrinks to a narrow footpath and traverses a thick, shrubby forest, a "green tunnel." At mile 16.9 the trail makes a memorable crossing of a beaver dam. This 50-foot-long crossing puts a premium on slow, precise footwork.

The trail continues west through thick, mixed forest. When the woods open into pleasant glades you are within a mile of Porcupine Lake. The path reaches the northern end of the lake, which loons frequent, at mile 19.7, and proceeds south along its western shore.

Pay attention here. Trail markings were poor in this area when I saw it. Do not follow the well-worn paths down the outlet creek. Cross the outlet on a log jam and walk south, ignoring two paths that lead west. Continue walking south and southwest, catching a last glimpse of Porcupine Lake to the east.

The trail is high on a ridge here, and to your northwest another body of

North Country Trail crosses a beaver dam west of West Davis Lake.

water appears, the pond of Eighteen Mile Creek Springs. Your path rounds the south and west side of this marsh, crossing small Eighteen Mile Creek on logs at mile 21.3 and turning north. At mile 21.6 bear left (northwest) as the trail forks. At mile 22.1 turn right (north) at a T intersection. At mile 22.6 the North Country Trail intersects Forest Road 213, marking the end of the hike.

12 Marengo River/ Swedish Settlement

Highlights:	Three overlooks and the remains of a historic Swedish settlement.
Location:	Northwest Wisconsin, 7 miles southeast of Grand View.
Type of hike:	Out-and-back day hike.
Total distance:	4.8 miles.
Difficulty:	Moderate.
Best months:	May–October
Maps:	Chequamegon-Nicolet National Forest map, "The North Country National Scenic Trail," USGS Marengo (inc.) and Grand View quads.
Finding the trailhead:	From Grand view, drive 5 miles south on Bayfield County Route D and turn left (east) on Forest Road 201. Drive 4.1 miles east and turn left (north) on Forest Road 202. Drive 2 miles north to where the North Country Trail crosses the road and turn right (east) into a small parking area.
Camping:	Backpack camping is allowed anywhere along the trail as long as you are 100 feet from the trail or water. Beaver Lake Campground, 6 miles east of the trailhead, has ten drive-in sites.
For more information:	North Country Trail Association, Chequamegon-Nicolet National Forest, see Appendix B.

Key points:

0.0	Forest Road 202 trailhead.
0.6	First overlook.
1.1	Marengo River.
1.2	Shelter spur trail.
1.7	Swedish settlement (Welin farm).
1.9	Second overlook.
2.4	Third overlook.

The hike: This short stretch of the North Country Trail has a lot to offer. Three scenic overlooks offer a steady stream of vistas, and the remains of a Swedish settlement pull in history buffs. A pleasing hardwood forest lines the trail, and native brook trout dimple the surface of the Marengo River.

Begin your outing by walking east from Forest Road 202. A short ascent brings the trail onto a plateau, and .5 mile later, at mile 0.6, the first overlook appears just south of the trail. This rock dome offers broad views of the Marengo River valley to the southeast and a horizon of wooded hills.

After savoring the view, follow the trail east as it quickly drops 200 vertical feet to the Marengo River (at mile 1.1). Cross on a wide and sturdy bridge above the stream. A short .1 mile after the river crossing, a short spur trail runs south to an Adirondack-style, three-sided shelter.

Marengo River/Swedish Settlement

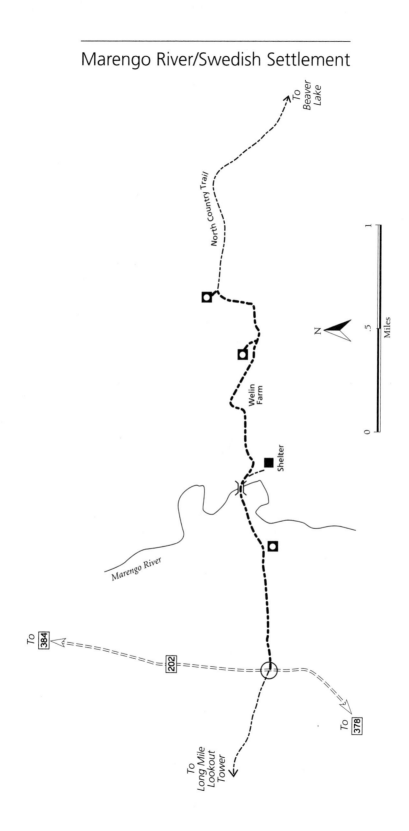

View north from second overlook toward Mount Ashwabay.

After the shelter spur, the trail climbs steadily and at mile 1.7 nears the remains of the Swedish settlement. As the path enters a pine plantation watch for a sign that notes the settlement's location. Walk south of the trail, through the pines, to an old field and the ruins of a constructed wall. Gust Welin and his family homesteaded here around 1900 and nearby were a barn, house, spring house, root cellar, and orchard. The Green Mountain School stood just south of the Welin place, serving the settlers of the Marengo Valley. A brochure available from the forest service office in Glidden explains the history of the settlement.

From the settlement area, continue walking east through a pleasant hardwood forest, until a sign at mile 1.9 announces an overlook. Follow the spur trail 140 yards north to a rock outcrop offering broad, long views to the north, toward Mount Ashwabay and Madeline Island.

Resume your hike going east and at mile 2.4 the sign for the third and last overlook appears. One hundred feet north of the through trail, another rock outcrop provides vistas to the north. The trail continues eastward for another 18 miles, but this is a good place to turn around and retrace your steps to the Forest Road 202 trailhead.

13 Morgan Falls/St. Peter's Dome

Highlights:	A notable scenic waterfall and a viewpoint offering vistas of the Bayfield Peninsula.
Location:	Northwestern Wisconsin, 12 miles west of Mellen.
Type of hike:	Out-and-back day hike.
Total distance:	3.6 miles.
Difficulty:	Moderate.
Best months:	April–October.
Maps:	USFS Morgan Falls and St. Peter's Dome, USGS Marengo Lake (inc.) quad.
Permits and fees:	USFS $3 parking fee.
Finding the trailhead:	From Mellen, drive 8.7 miles west on County Route GG and turn right (north) on Forest Road 187. Drive north and west 4.7 miles and turn left (west) on Forest Road 199. Drive 5 miles and turn right (east) into the trailhead parking area.
Special considerations:	Parts of this trail have rough footing.
Camping:	There are eight drive-in sites at Lake Three, 5 miles southeast of the trailhead.
For more information:	Chequamegon-Nicolet National Forest, Glidden, see Appendix B.

Key points:
- 0.0 Trailhead.
- 0.4 Junction of Morgan Falls Trail and St. Peter's Dome Trail.
- 0.6 Morgan Falls.
- 0.8 Junction of St. Peter's Dome Trail and Morgan Falls Trail.
- 1.4 Snowmobile Trail.
- 1.8 St. Peter's Dome.

The hike: Morgan Falls, plummeting 70 feet down a granite slab, earns mention as the prettiest waterfall in the state. That cascade combines with a notable viewpoint, St. Peter's Dome, to make this an outstanding hike. This trail has its rough spots, but the attractions are worth it. Much of the route, particularly past Morgan Falls, is an eroded jumble, with roots and rocks waiting to trip the careless.

Begin your tour from the southeast corner of the trailhead parking lot where a well-worn trail leads east. Follow that route through a forest of maples and birches to a small stream at mile 0.4, Morgan Creek. Turn right (south) and follow the marked path along the west side of the creek.

Soon the sound of the falls drifts through the woods, and as the valley walls close in you catch a glimpse through the trees of falling water. The drop begins high above you, at the same level as the canopy of the trees, plummets to a pool in a ledge, then descends another 6 feet to the creek bed.

When you are ready, retrace your steps north along the creek to the main trail. Turn right (east), cross the creek on logs, and begin a slow ascent to the southeast. Old foundations, the remains of a Civilian Conservation Corps

Morgan Falls/St. Peter's Dome

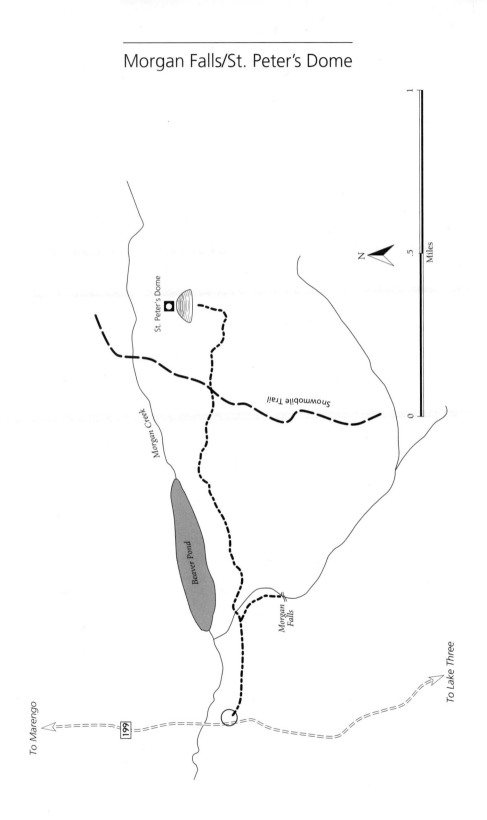

View west, toward Grand View, from St. Peter's Dome.

camp from the 1930s, come into view on the left and shortly after that a spring, encircled in a cistern of stone and mortar. Water, part of a mile-long beaver pond on Canyon Creek, is sometimes visible through the trees to the north.

The trail continues to run east, crossing a charming brook, a miniature Morgan Falls lined with moss and ferns. You will pass another creek, smaller and quieter, as well as a bench. At mile 1.4 stay straight (east) as the path crosses a snowmobile trail. Shortly after the trail hits a T intersection with an old woods road. Turn right (south). A moment later turn left (east) off the old road, following the obvious wear marks up the slope.

Switchbacks ease the trail's ascent as it makes its way to the top of St. Peter's Dome at mile 1.8. A grassy glade appears as the slope levels out, and the trail runs a final 100 yards to the viewpoint, a broad granite dome. Fine views open up to the west and north.

To the west, the Chequamegon Forest seems to stretch forever. Morgan Creek's lake-like beaver pond marks the hike's beginning. As you look north, patches of farms toward Ashland interrupt the woodlands. On a clear day, you can pick out Madeline Island and Mount Ashwabay near Bayfield.

14 Copper Falls

Highlights:	Two waterfalls, numerous cascades, and notable geology.
Location:	Northern Wisconsin, 3 miles north of Mellen.
Type of hike:	Loop day hike.
Total distance:	1.8 miles.
Difficulty:	Easy.
Best months:	April–October.
Maps:	Copper Falls State Park trail map, USGS Mellen (inc.) and Highbridge (inc.) quads.
Permits and fees:	State park car sticker required.
Finding the trailhead:	From Mellen, drive north .5 mile on Wisconsin 13 and turn right (east) on Wisconsin 169. Take that road north and at mile 2.2 turn left (northwest) into the park entrance road. Get a map and park newspaper at the entrance station. Follow the park road north to the trailhead at mile 4.0.
Camping:	Copper Falls State Park has fifty-six drive-in campsites and two backpacking sites.
For more information:	Copper Falls State Park, see Appendix B.

Key points:

- 0.0 Trailhead parking lot.
- 0.3 View of Copper Falls.
- 0.6 Bridge over Bad River.
- 0.9 North Country Trail.
- 1.0 Spur to viewing platform above Brownstone Falls.
- 1.1 Bridge over Tyler's Forks of the Bad River.
- 1.2 Viewing platform for Brownstone Falls and the Devil's Gate gorge.
- 1.8 Trailhead parking lot.

The hike: It is difficult to maintain a brisk pace on Copper Falls' Three Bridges Trail; too many distractions line the path's route. Its well-constructed 1.8 miles offer a constant parade of falling water, charming nooks, and rock canyons. Those canyon walls are part of the rich geological history described in the park's newspaper.

Walk east from the parking lot past the concession building and turn left (north) to cross a sturdy bridge over the Bad River. Follow the broad, constructed trail north to the viewpoint overlooking Copper Falls at mile 0.3. Old pictures show a 30-foot drop, but today the falls is eroding into a rapids, with its largest drop 12 feet.

The path follows the top of the gorge to where Brownstone Falls comes into sight on the other side of the 100-foot-deep chasm. It is a stunner, a 30-foot drop on the Tyler Forks, a tributary of the Bad River that then joins the main stream directly below.

Your route turns west and follows the top of the sheer canyon called Devil's Gate before dropping down stone steps to a bridge over the Bad River. On

Copper Falls

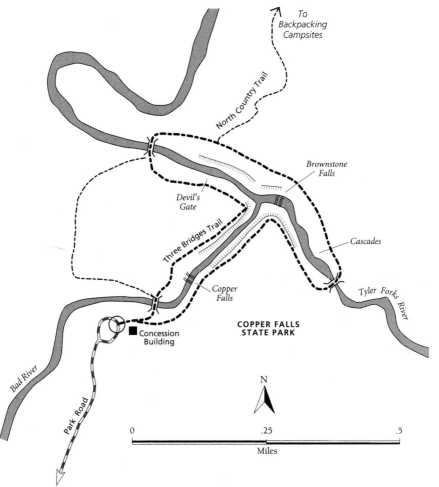

To
Backpacking
Campsites

North Country Trail

Brownstone
Falls

Devil's
Gate

Three Bridges Trail

Cascades

Copper
Falls

Tyler Forks River

COPPER FALLS
STATE PARK

Bad River

Concession
Building

Park Road

To Mellen

N

| 0 | .25 | .5 |
Miles

Looking upstream at Tyler Forks Cascades.

the north side of the river the trail swings east and ascends stone and wood steps to an intersection with a spur trail leading north at mile 0.9. Ignore the spur trail, a segment of the North Country Trail, and continue straight (east) to a spur to the right (south) at mile 1.0.

Take this 100-yard spur to two viewing platforms offering views of Brownstone Falls from above as well as the Tyler Forks Cascades upstream. When you're ready, return to the main trail and continue east to a bridge that crosses the Tyler Forks. After that crossing the path swings west and at mile 1.2 comes to the final viewing platforms. Again, there are views of Brownstone Falls, but the real treat is a view straight down the length of Devil's Gate, a hidden world of rock and water.

The trail swings south and soon the first bridge and the concession building come into sight. The parking lot is just beyond.

15 Potato River Falls

Highlights:	Three spectacular waterfalls.
Location:	Northern Wisconsin, 1 mile west of Gurney.
Type of hike:	Out-and-back day hike.
Total distance:	.5 mile.
Difficulty:	Easy.
Best months:	April–October.
Maps:	USGS Gurney (inc.) quad.
Finding the trailhead:	From Mellen, drive 15.9 miles northeast on Wisconsin 169 and turn left on Cory Road. Take that road west and south 1.7 miles to the parking area.
Camping:	Copper Falls State Park, 13 miles southwest, has fifty-six drive-in sites.
For more information:	Iron County Forestry Department, see Appendix B.

The hike: Potato River Falls, a compact series of drops, has two named features, the Upper Falls and the Lower Falls. The Upper Falls has two 20-foot drops. That cascade starts with a plunge down a bedrock chute, bounces off boulders, and drops again. A few hundred feet downstream, the river spreads out across a black lava shelf and drops another 30 feet at the spectacular Lower Falls.

A system of three viewing platforms eases a tour of the 150-foot-deep, red clay gorge. Walk to the southwest side of the parking lot and you will see the first of these platforms, offering a high view of the lower falls, directly in front of you.

Next walk to the southeast corner of the parking lot where a sign directs you along a path to the Upper Falls. That trail quickly turns into a stairway, descending 130 steps to a viewing deck offering a broad view of the Upper Falls.

Potato River Falls

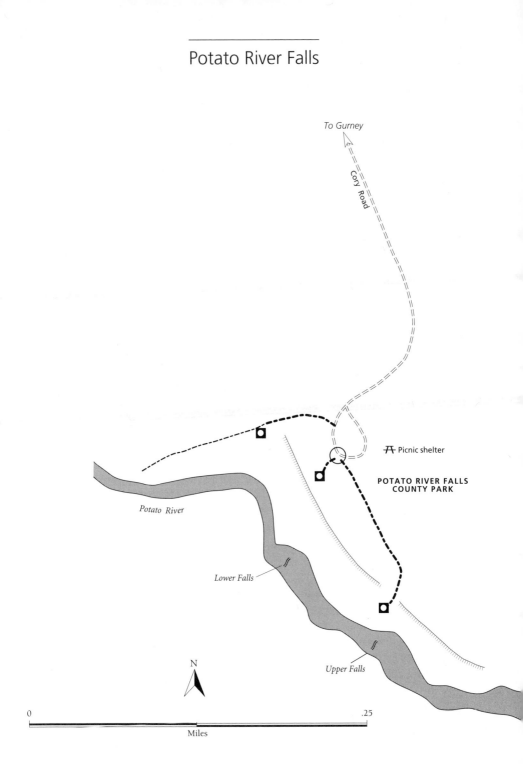

To Gurney

Cory Road

♯ Picnic shelter

**POTATO RIVER FALLS
COUNTY PARK**

Potato River

Lower Falls

Upper Falls

N

0   .25

Miles

Potato River's Lower Falls.

When you are ready, walk back toward the parking lot and cross to the northwest corner. There another sign announces a path to a viewing platform for the Lower Falls. Follow that path downhill 200 feet, halfway down the slope, to the viewpoint. Retrace your steps to return to the parking area.

16 Penokee Range

Highlights:	A remote ridge with an outstanding viewpoint.
Location:	Northern Wisconsin, 10 miles west of Hurley.
Type of hike:	Out-and-back day hike or backpack.
Total distance:	10.6 miles.
Difficulty:	Moderate/difficult.
Best months:	May–October.
Maps:	North Country Trail Heritage Chapter segment map, Uller Ski Trail Map, USGS Saxon (inc.), and Iron Belt (inc.) quads.
Finding the trailhead:	From Hurley, drive 8.9 miles west on Wisconsin 77 and turn right (west) on Iron County Route E. After 2.6 miles stay straight as County Route E turns left (south). The trailhead is about 100 yards from that intersection on the north side of this unnamed road. Park in the county park on the south side of the road.
Special considerations:	Most of this trail segment was originally a ski trail, and footing can occasionally be rough. The two shelters are small cabins built by a local ski club. When I saw them the Scribner Meadow shelter was open but the Smith's Meadow shelter was not.
Camping:	This trail runs through Iron County Forestry lands; camping is permitted along the trail. Campsites must be at least 100 feet away from the trail or water's edge.
For more information:	North Country Trail Association, see Appendix B.

Key points:
- 0.0 Weber Lake Trailhead.
- 1.2 Sullivan Creek.
- 1.9 Vista Spur Junction.
- 2.2 Vista.
- 2.5 Vista Spur Junction.
- 2.8 Tower Road.
- 4.0 Scribner Meadow.
- 5.3 Smith's Meadow.

The hike: Few Wisconsin hikers have heard of the Penokee Range, but thanks to a new section of North Country Trail, that may soon change. This new segment, following the Uller Ski Trail, traverses a remote ridge while passing fine stands of maple trees, hidden nooks and crannies, and a prime viewpoint.

Begin by walking north from Weber Lake on the North Country Trail. The route ascends steadily for .25 mile before leveling out and heading northeast. As the trail begins to skirt a series of rocky knolls on their northern slopes, the ambiance becomes elegant. Hemlocks and oaks accent an open forest of mature maples.

Penokee Range

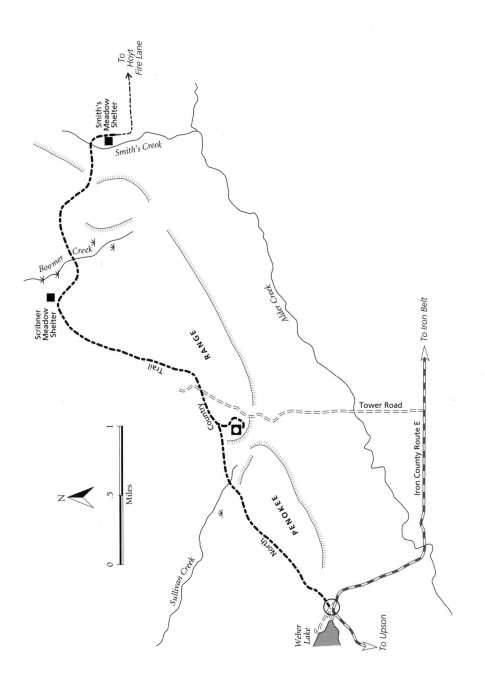

To Hoyt Fire Lane

Smith's Meadow Shelter

Smith's Creek

Boomer Creek

Scribner Meadow Shelter

RANGE

Trail

County Trail

Tower Road

Alder Creek

To Iron Belt

Iron County Route E

PENOKEE

North

Sullivan Creek

N

1

.5

Miles

0

Weber Lake

To Upson

Follow the trail east to Sullivan Creek at mile 1.2 and traverse a series of four bridges across muddy fern gardens. An ascent from the creek brings the trail to a signed intersection for a scenic spur trail at mile 1.9. Turn right (south) on this spur trail, which leads to a worthwhile overlook. Wear marks on this path can be thin but the trail markings are strong as it jogs southeast and finally west. The last 100 yards merge with an ATV trail before you arrive at the overlook at mile 2.2.

A broad dome of rock offers 180-degree views sweeping from the southeast to the northwest. To the south, the long ridge of the Gogebic Range rises across Alder Creek's Valley. Far to the northwest, the Bayfield Peninsula's headlands appear on the horizon.

When you are ready, return to the North Country Trail at mile 2.5 and turn right (east). The trail intersects Tower Road at mile 2.8. Bear left (north) on that old dirt lane for a short distance, then turn right (northeast) off Tower Road at a well-marked spot.

Continue northeast on the North Country Trail. About 1 mile after Tower Road a long descent brings you to the Scribner Meadow shelter, a tiny but functional structure at mile 4.0. Scribner Meadow is a wetland east of the shelter, along the headwaters of Boomer Creek.

From the cabin, follow the trail south then east as it rounds the meadow and ascends to a low gap in a headland among pleasant, old growth hardwoods. From that saddle it descends to cross a branch of Alder Creek and arrives at the Smith's Meadow shelter at mile 5.3. That shelter is a good turn-around spot for the hike.

17 Sandrock Cliffs

Highlights: Walking along the scenic St. Croix River.
Location: Northwest Wisconsin, 5 miles west of Grantsburg.
Type of hike: A loop day hike.
Total distance: 4.4 miles.
Difficulty: Easy.
Best months: May–October.
Maps: National Park Service Sandrock Cliff trail map, USGS Bass Creek (inc.) quad.
Finding the trailhead: From Grantsburg, drive 4.7 miles west on Wisconsin 70 and turn right (north) into the trailhead parking lot just before the bridge over the St. Croix River.
Camping: Seven walk-in campsites are at Sandrock Cliffs, near the northern end of the trail.
For more information: St. Croix National Scenic Riverway, see Appendix B.

Key points:
0.0 Trailhead on Wisconsin 70.
1.3 Trail E Junction.

Sandrock Cliffs

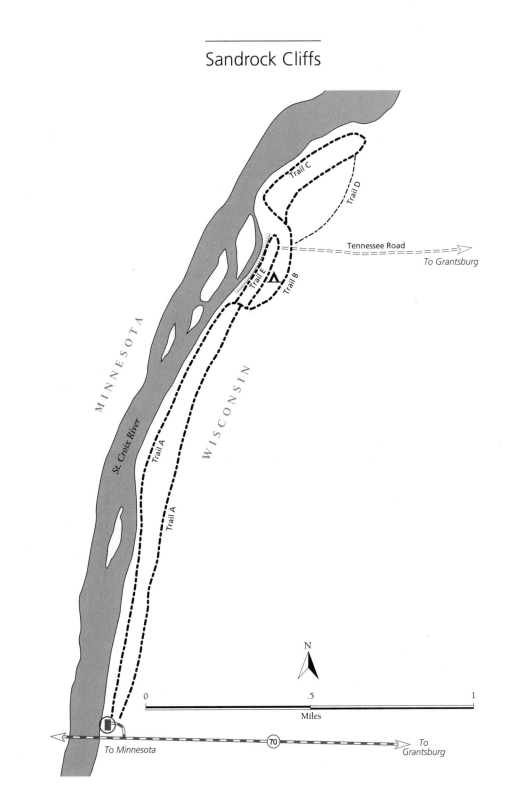

Trail C

Trail D

Tennessee Road

To Grantsburg

Trail E

Trail B

MINNESOTA

WISCONSIN

St. Croix River

Trail A

Trail A

N

0 .5 1

Miles

To Minnesota

70

To Grantsburg

1.6   Trail B Junction.
1.9   Trail C Junction, campground parking lot.
2.4   Trail C and D South Junction.
2.7   Trail C and D North Junction.
2.8   Trail B Junction, campground parking lot.
3.1   Trail A Junction.
4.4   Trailhead on Wisconsin 70.

The hike: The St. Croix River, running swift, clear, and broad alongside this hike's route, is a pristine marvel. Its clean waters support a notably rich and diverse array of freshwater mussels. Above the river, eagles and ospreys patrol and find this stretch pleasant enough to nest nearby. Wolves use the river as a travel corridor, and two packs are in residence just a few miles north of this hike. Species-wise, this is a happening place.

Sandrock Cliff, a low sandstone butte bordering a side channel of the river, is near the northern end of a ski and hiking trail system that bears its name. That trail, a very elongated loop with several smaller loops near the cliffs, has its southern terminus at the Wisconsin 70 trailhead.

Begin your tour by walking north from the northwest corner of the trail-head parking area on a wood-chip-covered dirt road. Ignore the return path coming in from the right (east) and go due north on the outgoing trail.

The broad trail narrows to a four-foot width, running pleasantly through pines in the river's flood plain. The water's edge is a steady 30 to 50 feet to your left (west), and every now and then a path invites you over for a river view.

A series of river islands coincides with the trail's ascent up a minor slope and junction with Trail E at mile 1.3. Turn left (north) and follow this path along the top of the Sandrock Cliffs, pausing to scan the waters below for wood ducks and other notables. Continue on Trail E as it rounds the north end of the plateau and then runs along the east side of the butte's top. It returns south and at mile 1.6 intersects Trail B. Turn left (east) onto Trail B. That trail descends to the north, passing the east side of the uplift and reaching a parking lot that services the walk-in campsites in the area. At the northwest corner of the parking lot, at mile 1.9, take the left (north) choice, Trail C, ignoring the trail on the right.

Walk northwest on Trail C. A short distance farther, bear left (north) as the mowed trail splits. You then emerge from the shade and woods you have been in since the start of the hike and for the next .75 mile walk through open meadows dotted with young trees. The trail quickly reaches the river at a campsite with a fire ring, then runs northeast through the open floodplain.

The trail then makes a broad swing south and begins to run southwest. At mile 2.4 bear right (west) as Trail D enters from the left. This is the last stretch of open meadow; you may want to scan for raptors before you are again among the short sight lines of the forest. Continue south, turning left (south) at mile 2.7, the junction with the outgoing Trail C, reentering shady woods and reaching the parking lot at mile 2.8.

Walk south across the parking lot, pick up Trail B, and follow it southwest to a junction with Trail E, coming in from the right at mile 3.1. Turn

Ferns along Trail A.

left (southwest). One hundred yards later turn left (south) on Trail A's inland return path. That path takes you south through a pleasant woodland setting decorated with giant ferns, to the trailhead at mile 4.4.

18 St. Croix

Highlights:	A pristine river corridor, wildlife, and dozens of lush springs.
Location:	Northwest Wisconsin, 15 miles southwest of Grantsburg.
Type of hike:	Shuttle hike. Long day hike or backpack.
Total distance:	14.1 miles.
Difficulty:	Difficult.
Best months:	April–October.
Maps:	Governor Knowles State Forest Trail Map, USGS North Branch, Rush City, and Randall quads.
Permits and fees:	State park vehicle sticker required.
Finding the trailhead:	From Grantsburg, drive south on Wisconsin 48. Go straight (south) on Wisconsin 87 at mile 4.5 where Wisconsin 48 turns east. Drive another 8.4 miles south on Wisconsin 87 and turn right (west) on Evergreen Avenue. Drive 11.1 miles west to the trailhead. The last .2 mile is a sandy "two track" and the 2 miles before that are gravel.
Special considerations:	The difficult rating reflects the hike's length. Current state forest literature refers to the entire route as the Southern Hiking Trail. State forest maps refer to the segment from Evergreen to Burnett County Route O as the Lagoo Creek Route. Those same maps call the trail from Burnett County Route O to the North Benson Trailhead the Benson Brook Route. Older USGS quads refer to the Southern Hiking Trail as the Sunrise Ferry Hiking Trail.
Camping:	Backpack camping with free permit. Obtain permit from Governor Knowles State Forest, see Appendix B.
For more information:	Governor Knowles State Forest, see Appendix B.

Key points:
- 0.0   Evergreen Trailhead.
- 1.4   Lagoo Creek bridge.
- 3.9   Trail leaves flood plain.
- 4.7   Swinging bridge junction.
- 6.5   Burnett County Route O.
- 8.9   Trail descends bluff.
- 10.3   Benson Brook bridge.
- 11.1   Pleasant Prairie Road.
- 13.4   Trail leaves flood plain.
- 14.1   North Benson Trailhead.

The hike: Before I hiked this route I expected the St. Croix River to be impressive. It is. This is a notably pristine large river, and the National Wild and Scenic Rivers Act protects more than 250 miles of its watershed. Eagles

St. Croix

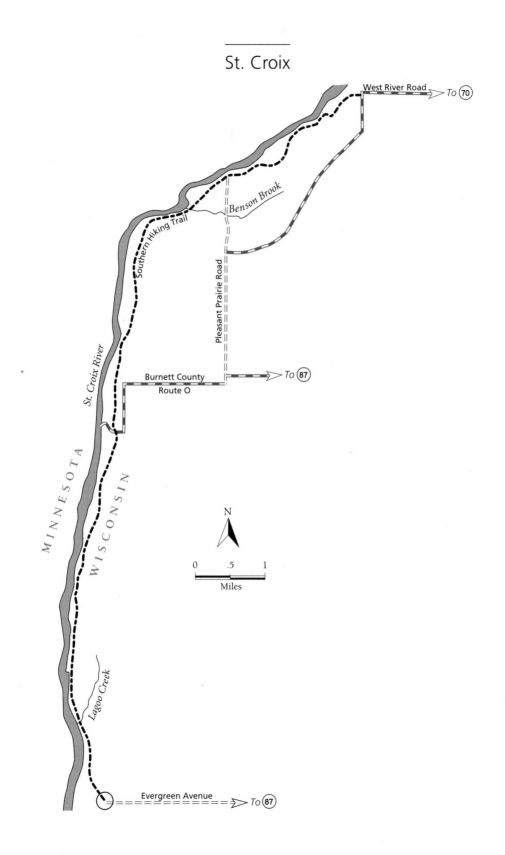

West River Road
To (70)

Benson Brook

Southern Hiking Trail

Pleasant Prairie Road

St. Croix River

Burnett County
Route O
To (87)

MINNESOTA

WISCONSIN

N

0   .5   1

Miles

Lagoo Creek

Evergreen Avenue
To (87)

The Southern Hiking Trail passes through a floodplain forest north of Lagoo Creek.

nest on the river's shoreline, otters romp on the banks, and rare mussels inhabit the riffles.

Any time spent with this great river is a treat, but it is the dozens of springs that line the base of the river valley bluffs that stand out in my memory. Here, springs are like patches of wildflowers, erupting in shady, mossy nooks.

Begin your journey along the St. Croix by walking north and west from the Evergreen Trailhead, following blue blazes through .25-mile long stretch that shows signs of recent logging. Bear with it. The trail enters the woods, and the ambiance improves rapidly as it travels along the crest of the bluff.

To the left of the trail, a spring, the first of a series, gushes from a lush, crater-like hole in the escarpment. More springs and spring runs cross the trail as it makes its way down the bluff onto the river's flood plain and across Lagoo Creek on a wood bridge at mile 1.4.

For the next 2.5 miles the trail runs north, sometimes near the river, sometimes slightly back from the water, across a vast flood plain forest drained by Lagoo Creek. The escarpment runs inland for that distance; when it again nears the river at mile 3.9 the trail ascends the bluff.

Barely .25 mile farther it descends through fern gardens and runs north, past springs and small brooks, just above the flood plain. At about mile 4.7, bear right (north) as a spur trail goes left (west) to a swinging bridge, visible from the junction. That bridge crosses a minor channel of the river to a large grassy island that extends north. Follow the trail north, first traversing the bottom of the slope, then ascending to the top of the bluff. Continue north, walking through hardwood forests, to Burnett County Route O at mile 6.5.

Cross the road. The trail runs west for a short distance, then north along the top of the escarpment. A parade of verdant springs erupts just below the trail to the left. At about mile 8.9 the trail splits. Turn left (northwest), descending the bluff and making a right (north) turn on an overgrown old road, running due north, at the bottom. Both wear marks and trail signs get a little thin for about .25 mile here. Continue due north to where, at the edge of the woods and the bottom of the slope, the trail again becomes clear.

At this point the river curves east and the trail ascends the bluff eastward for .5 mile before descending beside a small brook. A sturdy bridge takes the trail across Benson Brook, there is a beaver dam just upstream, and the trail moves out onto a broad, open flood plain. For the next mile or so the trail traverses open old fields, nearing the river as it passes the end of Pleasant Prairie Road at mile 11.1.

The route continues east along the river another .25 mile, then turns inland through a stretch of scrubby woods. Pleasant older hardwoods return as the path turns back to the river and runs through elegant, shady fern gardens, with the river 30 feet to the left. A slough creek pushes the path inland just before the trail leaves the floodplain and ascends straight up (steps) the bluff alongside a mossy spring run. At the top the trail swings northeast and follows the crest to the North Benson Trailhead.

19 Blue Hills/Devils Creek

Highlights: Two charming creeks, open hardwood forest, and a quiet footpath.

Location: Northwest Wisconsin, 7 miles north of Weyerhauser.

Type of hike: Out-and-back day hike.

Total distance: 4.6 miles.

Difficulty: Easy.

Best months: April–October.

Maps: Ice Age Trail Segment Map #68 or USGS Bucks Lake (inc.) quad.

Finding the trailhead: From Weyerhauser, drive north 6.7 miles on Rusk County Route F to Rusk County Route O. Turn left (west) on Route O and drive 0.3 mile to the marked trailhead. Park on the side of the road.

Camping: Audie and Perch Lake campgrounds have twenty-five drive-in sites, 5 miles north of the trailhead.

For more information: Ice Age Trail and Park Foundation, see Appendix B.

The Ice Age Trail bridges a clear-running branch of Devils Creek.

Blue Hills/Devils Creek

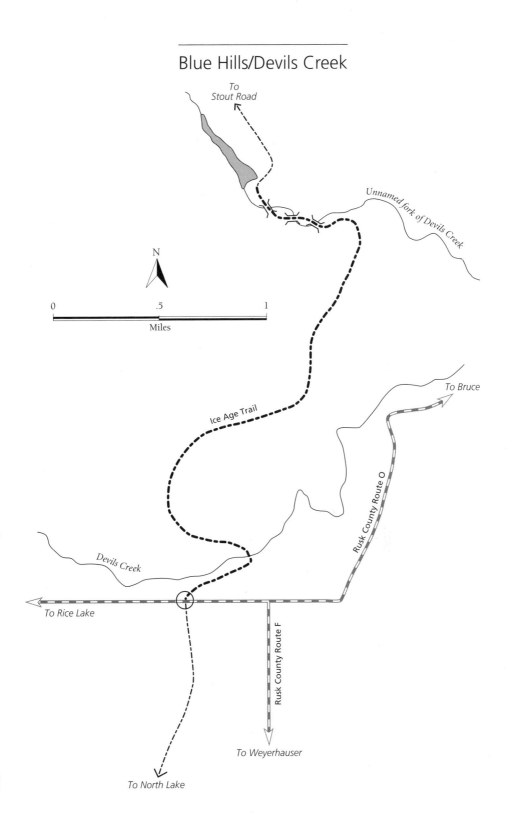

To Stout Road

Unnamed fork of Devils Creek

N

0   .5   1
Miles

Ice Age Trail

To Bruce

Rusk County Route O

Devils Creek

To Rice Lake

Rusk County Route F

To Weyerhauser

To North Lake

Key points:
0.0   County O Trailhead.
0.2   Bridge over Devils Creek.
1.9   First of three bridges over unnamed branch of Devils Creek.
2.3   South end of beaver pond.

The hike: Two creeks mark the beginning and end of this hike. Each is a gurgling gem, tempting you to stay a while and contemplate its secrets.

Walk north from the trailhead and a subtle but beautiful scene unfolds. The path follows the crest of a small ridge, 80 feet above Devils Creek, winding among birches and pines before dropping to a bridged crossing. A steep little ascent takes the trail out of the drainage and into a bluff-top grove of birch trees. The trail continues a slow northward ascent and passes into the open hardwood forest that will characterize most of the hike. For the next mile the path swings northeast through rolling hills until a branch of Devils Creek appears on your right.

This next section, along the creek, is a fine place to pause, picnic, and listen to the stream's song. The creek wanders in a shallow ravine, and the trail reaches the first of a series of three bridges at mile 1.9.

Walk farther upstream; at mile 2.3 the trail nears the outlet of a large wetland, an aging beaver pond. This is a good spot to turn around and retrace your steps south.

20 Escanaba Lake

Highlights:	A loop hike through a beautiful forest and lake setting.
Location:	Northcentral Wisconsin, 15 miles north of Minocqua.
Type of hike:	Loop day hike or backpack.
Total distance:	7.7 miles.
Difficulty:	Moderate.
Best months:	April–October.
Maps:	DNR "Escanaba Lake Ski Trail" map, USGS White Sand Lake (inc.) quad.
Permits and fees:	State park vehicle sticker required.
Finding the trailhead:	From Woodruff drive north 6.4 miles on U.S. Highway 51 and turn right (northeast) on Vilas County Route M. At mile 12.4 turn right (east) on Nebish Lake Road, which becomes gravel at mile 12.5. Drive east to mile 16.2 and turn left (north) into the trailhead parking lot.
Camping:	Backpacking is allowed throughout the forest with a free permit. There are forty-six drive-in sites at Starrett Lake, 3 miles south of the trailhead.
For more information:	Northern Highland State Forest, see Appendix B.

Escanaba Lake

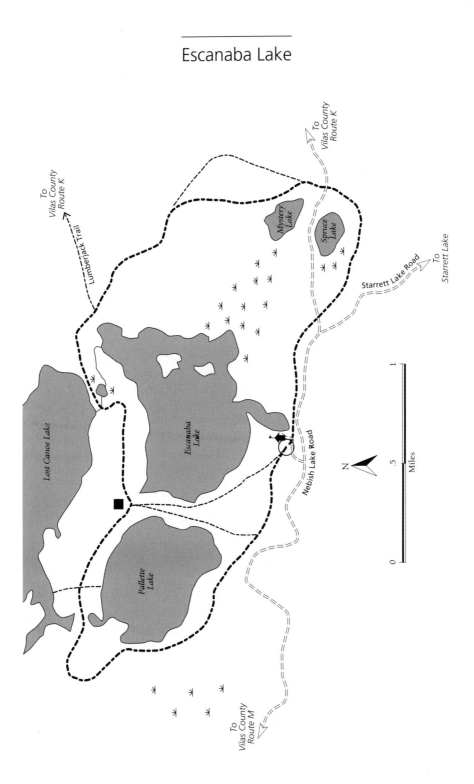

Key points:

- 0.0 Escanaba Lake Trailhead.
- 0.7 Yellow ski trail goes north.
- 2.7 Pallette Lake-Lost Canoe Lake portage trail.
- 3.2 Shelter, junction of green and blue ski trails.
- 4.4 Lumberjack Trail Junction.
- 5.1 Trail splits, take "inner," Mystery Lake Trail.
- 6.0 Trail crosses Nebish Lake Road southward.
- 6.9 Trail crosses Nebish Lake Road northward.
- 7.7 Escanaba Lake Trailhead.

The hike: Cross country skiers know Escanaba Lake as a well-marked ski trail that might just be the most scenic in the state. It loses none of its charm when the snow melts. Mile after mile of this trail dips and rolls through a forest that seems arranged by an artist: a charming combination of maples, birches, and pines, accented with views of Pallette Lake.

From the northwest corner of the trailhead parking lot, walk north on a broad ski trail. After seventy paces turn left (northwest) on a narrower trail, the beginning of the yellow and blue ski loops. Follow this trail west and at mile 0.7 take the green ski trail left (northwest) as the yellow ski loop goes right (north) to Pallette Lake.

From the junction the trail runs west on a low ridgetop and then turns north to round the end of Pallette Lake. Occasional glimpses of the water end as the pathway leaves the lake for .5 mile at its northwest corner. After turning east cross a north-south path at mile 2.7. This is the portage path between Pallette Lake and Lost Canoe Lake, and it is only about 100 yards south to Pallette Lake, a fine spot for a break.

Half a mile east of the portage path are a major intersection and a small trail shelter, complete with fire ring, wood, and a birdfeeder. If for some reason you want to cut your walk short, turn right (south) and the trailhead is .8 mile away.

To continue the hike, turn left (northeast) at the intersection and follow the pathway east. At mile 3.9 you cross a small bridge spanning the outlet creek of Escanaba Lake and follow the southeast shore of Lost Canoe Lake. As it leaves that lake the trail ascends a piney ridge and a few minutes later descends in a tunnel of thick fir trees to the Lumberjack Trail Junction (at mile 4.4). Go straight (south) on the boardwalk and continue to the trail split at mile 5.1. An open, logged area is in sight for a brief moment.

Take the "inside," or "Mystery Lake Trail," to the right (south) at the split and walk south through charming conifers and birch. A bench offers a convenient rest spot and a peek-a-boo look at Mystery Lake through the trees. At mile 5.9 the two trails rejoin and cross Nebish Lake Road at mile 6.0. The trail runs south and then west to round Spruce Lake and its marsh before again crossing Nebish Lake Road at mile 6.9 and reaching the trailhead at mile 7.7.

Options: One alternative would be to turn south from the shelter at mile 3.2, returning to the trailhead for an attractive 4-mile loop hike. Another choice would be to go north from the trailhead to the shelter and do the eastern ski

Bench along trail near Mystery Lake.

loop of 5.5 miles. However, that route leaves out some of the best scenery on this trail system (in the Pallette Lake area). You could also enter the trail system from the north, picking up the Lumberjack Trail at County Route K, 1.5 miles from its intersection with the Escanaba Trail. One option I would not recommend is the "outside" choice, as the trail splits at mile 5.1. The "outside" trail has some open, recently cut areas, and the "inside" or "Mystery Lake Trail" has much more charm.

21 Star Lake

Highlights:	Lake views from a shoreline trail and a "Black Lagoon" bog.
Location:	Northern Wisconsin, just west of the town of Star Lake.
Type of hike:	Loop day hike.
Total distance:	2.5 miles.
Difficulty:	Easy.
Best months:	April–October.
Maps:	Northern Highland-American Legion State Forest hiking map, USGS Star Lake (inc.) quad.
Permits and fees:	State park vehicle sticker required.
Finding the trailhead:	From the village of Star Lake go west .5 mile on Statehouse Road to the trailhead.
Camping:	There are eighteen drive-in sites just east of the trailhead.
For more information:	Northern Highland-American Legion State Forest, see Appendix B.

Key points:
0.0   Trailhead.
0.4   Black Lagoon.
0.5   Nature Trail cutoff.
1.6   Nature Trail rejoins hiking trail.
2.5   Trailhead.

The hike: Few short trails offer such a strong sense of place as the Star Lake Hiking Trail does. Long stretches of windswept lake views and an intimate bog are part of its tour of a narrow peninsula protruding into Star Lake.

Two paths travel this peninsula, the hiking trail marked with brown signs featuring the figure of a hiker, and a nature trail, with its signs bearing the likeness of a hawk. The hiking trail and the nature trail share the same path for much of the route.

From the southern corner of the trailhead parking lot, pass a water pump and walk south, downhill, on a broad footpath. In this area near the trailhead, a jumble of paths can cause minor confusion. Sixty-five paces downhill from the parking lot turn right (southwest) where an interpretive sign explains the

Star Lake

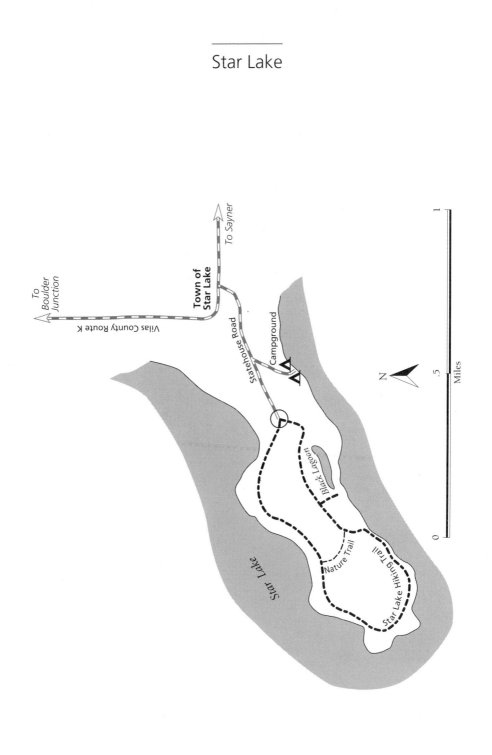

Boardwalk near the Black Lagoon.

role of red squirrels in the forest, a pine plantation dating from 1913.

Continue walking southwest. The trail soon turns into a boardwalk through a shady tamarack bog. At mile 0.4, turn left (south) on a 100-foot-long spur of the boardwalk to view the Black Lagoon, a dark, conifer-ringed pond.

Shortly after the Black Lagoon, the boardwalk segment ends. At mile 0.5

a trail junction appears. Stay left (south) on the hiking trail as the nature trail goes right. Soon after this junction the trail emerges onto the lake shore, first traveling the side of a slope 15 feet above the water, then dropping to the water's edge.

After the confined space of the bog, the vast openness of the lake is an abrupt and pleasing change. The trail weaves its way along the shore, rounds the peninsula's tip, and starts its return to the northeast.

At mile 1.6 stay left (northeast) as the nature trail cutoff comes in from the right. The trail, again the combined route of the nature and hiking paths, continues northeast, near the shoreline. When it finally cuts inland, you are only a few minutes' walk from the trailhead and the end of the hike.

22 Clark Lake

Highlights:	One of the largest stands of virgin forest in the upper Midwest and a quiet, nonmotorized lake.
Location:	Just north of the Michigan border, 5 miles northwest of Land O'Lakes.
Type of hike:	Loop day hike or backpack.
Total distance:	7.6 miles.
Difficulty:	Moderate.
Best months:	April–October.
Maps:	Sylvania Wilderness Trail Map, USGS Black Oak Lake (inc.) quad.
Finding the trailhead:	From Land O'Lakes, drive north 7.2 miles on U.S. Highway 45 and turn left (west) on U.S. Highway 2. Drive 4.1 miles west and turn left (south) on Gogebic County Route 535. Drive 4 miles south and turn left (south) into Sylvania's entrance road. Stop at the A-frame office. Drive south .2 mile and turn right (west) following signs to the boat launch on Clark Lake. Drive west 1 mile and turn left (south). Drive another .3 mile to the boat launch and trailhead.
Special considerations:	This hike travels through an outstanding wilderness area. Treat it with respect.
Camping:	A half dozen designated backcountry campsites border this route. A permit is required between May 15 and September 30 to use them. At other times, self-registration at a trailhead is possible. Forty-eight drive-in campsites are located .5 mile east of the trailhead.
For more information:	Sylvania Wilderness, see Appendix B.

Clark Lake

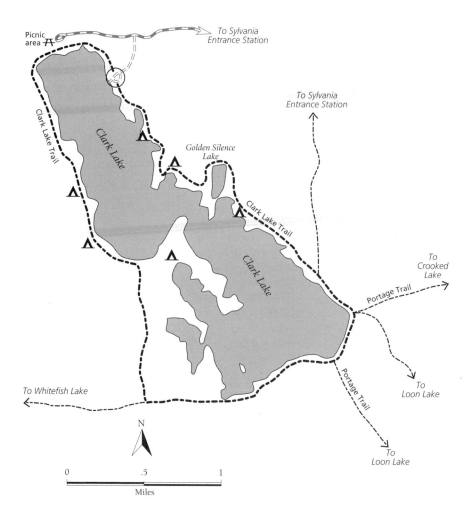

Picnic area

To Sylvania Entrance Station

To Sylvania Entrance Station

Clark Lake Trail

Clark Lake

Golden Silence Lake

Clark Lake Trail

Clark Lake

To Crooked Lake

Portage Trail

To Loon Lake

Portage Trail

To Whitefish Lake

To Loon Lake

N

0   .5   1
Miles

Key points:
  0.0   Trailhead.
  0.9   Golden Silence Lake.
  2.4   Clark Lake east end junction.
  4.3   Turn north on Clark Lake Trail.
  6.9   Beach.
  7.6   Trailhead.

The hike: When hikers stand at the north end of Clark Lake, with its picnic area and boat ramp, they could easily imagine they were at any one of a number of northern lakes. By the time they arrive at the south end of the lake, though, it is obvious they are someplace special, the core of a wilderness area sheltering 17,000 acres of virgin forest.

Paul Bunyan's ax swung hard and wide across our northern forests in the late 1800s, leaving few trees standing. Sylvania is one of the few places that escaped that onslaught, and this hike takes you through notable old growth stands of virgin hemlock, sugar maple, and white pine. Two-hundred-year-old trees are common; a few hardy specimens are 400 years old.

Begin your circuit of Clark Lake on the southeast corner of the boat ramp parking lot where a sign indicates the beginning of the Clark Lake Trail. Follow the trail southeast as it skirts the shoreline, rounding bays and cutting across piney peninsulas. After a little more than a mile, it ducks inland to make its way around aptly named Golden Silence Lake, a placid pond.

Along the way a myth dies that Midwest forests are thick and brushy. Sylvania's forest, like most old growth, tends to be open and park-like under its tall canopy. Below, the ground shows the pleasant lumpiness of fallen trees, aging into mulch and duff.

Clark Lake's southeast corner—pristine water, virgin forest.

Continue following the path southeast and bear right (southeast) at a junction with an old road at mile 2.2. Walk along that old road to a meadow at mile 2.4, the far eastern corner of Clark Lake. Stay straight (southeast) where a portage trail crosses, and 5 feet past that turn right (southwest) on a path that crosses the meadow. That path quickly enters the woods and joins an old road running southwest, near Clark Lake's southern shore. Stay straight (southwest) .25 mile later where another portage trail crosses.

The trail remains close to the lake for almost 1.5 miles before beginning a straight, westward course. Watch for a key, signed intersection at mile 4.3. Turn right (north) on a footpath that is faint at times but features abundant blue blazes.

Walk north, following the path through the forest for a mile, before emerging once again on Clark Lake's shoreline. Another mile of shoreline walking brings you to the picnic area and beach at the north end of the lake at mile 6.9. From there, continue another .5 along the shoreline to the boat ramp and the trailhead at mile 7.6.

23 Deer Island Lake

Highlights:	A quiet trail through one of the largest stands of virgin forest in the upper Midwest. Loons on wilderness lakes.
Location:	Just over the Michigan border from Land O' Lakes, Wisconsin.
Type of hike:	Lollipop. Very long day hike or backpack.
Total distance:	21.2 miles.
Difficulty:	Difficult.
Best months:	May–October.
Maps:	Sylvania Wilderness trail map, USGS Black Oak Lake (inc.) and Land O'Lakes (inc.) quads.
Finding the trailhead:	From the intersection of Vilas County Route B and Airport Road in downtown Land O'Lakes, drive north on Gogebic County Route 539. After .7 mile, go straight (west) where County Route 539 turns right (north) on Fischer Road. Drive west .2 mile and park at the end of the lane.
Special considerations:	This hike travels through an outstanding wilderness area. Treat it with respect.
Camping:	Backcountry camping within the Sylvania Wilderness is only at designated sites. A permit is required between May 15 and September 30 to use them. At other times, self-registration at the trailhead is possible.
For more information:	Sylvania USFS, see Appendix B.

Deer Island Lake

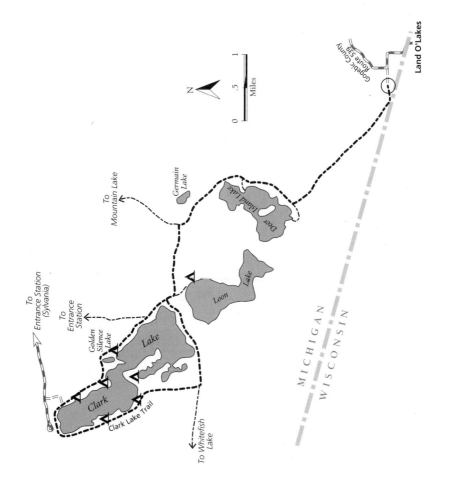

The remote trail and old growth forest east of Deer Island Lake.

Key points:

0.0   Trailhead, Land O'Lakes.
3.2   Deer Island Lake Junction.
5.6   Mountain Lake Trail Junction.
6.8   Clark Lake Junction.
8.7   Clark Lake Trail (turn north).
11.3 Beach and picnic area, Clark Lake.
12.0 Boat ramp, Clark Lake.
12.9 Golden Silence Lake.
14.4 Clark Lake Junction.
21.2 Trailhead, Land O'Lakes.

Recommended itinerary: A multinight stay at the Mallard designated campsite on the north end of Loon Lake works well. That location puts you in excellent position to do the Clark Lake Trail loop as a day trip as well as explore north to Mountain Lake or west to Whitefish Lake. This plan would require a 6-mile backpack on the first and last day.

The hike: Sylvania, with its 17,000 acres of virgin forest and thirty-six named lakes, is no stranger to savvy Wisconsin nature lovers. Most of those folks, however, enter the area from the north, paddling canoes. Few of Sylvania's visitors know of the quiet footpath that enters from Land O'Lakes.

The trail quickly takes hikers into one of the most remote corners of the wilderness, the Deer Island Lake area. For ambitious hikers, that is just the beginning. If you continue walking northwest and round Clark Lake on its loop, you create a prime route. For a brief moment, at the north end of Clark Lake, there are some minor signs of civilization. Other than that this hike is a 21-mile-long walking tour of old growth forest and pristine lakes.

Start by walking west from the Land O'Lakes Trailhead. Follow the path northwest, arriving at a junction with an old woods road just east of Deer Island Lake's south end, at mile 3.2. This is a key intersection and was unmarked when I saw it. Turn right (northeast) and follow the old road north. About 1 mile farther, go straight (north), ignoring a spur that goes left to the north end of Deer Island Lake.

Follow the old road as it swings northwest, offering a last glimpse of Deer Island Lake and arriving at an intersection with the Mountain Lake Trail at mile 5.6. Turn left (west), following another old road to yet another intersection at mile 6.5, north of Loon Lake. Turn right (northwest) and walk to a meadow at the far east end of Clark Lake. Turn left (southwest) there, following a path that enters the woods and joins an old woods road running southwest near Clark Lake's southern shore. Stay straight (southwest), .25 mile later where a portage trail crosses.

The old road remains close to the lake for almost 1.5 miles before beginning a straight, westward course. Watch for a signed intersection at mile 4.3. Turn right (north) there on the Clark Lake Trail, a footpath that is faint at times but features abundant blue blazes.

Walk north, following the path through a forest for 1 mile before emerging once again on Clark Lake's shoreline. Another mile of northward walking brings you to a picnic area. Walk east, past a swimming beach and along a trail that curls south to a boat ramp at mile 12.0. At the southeast corner of the boat ramp parking area a sign marks the Clark Lake Trail. Follow that trail southeast as it skirts the shoreline, rounding bays and cutting across piney peninsulas. After a little more than a mile it ducks inland to make its way around aptly named Golden Silence Lake, a sylvan pond.

Continue following the path southeast and bear right (southeast) at a junction with an old road at mile 14.2. Walk along that old road to the meadow at the far eastern corner of Clark Lake, the same spot you saw at mile 6.8 of your hike. From here, retrace the first part of the hike to return to the Land O'Lakes Trailhead.

24 Hidden Lakes

Highlights:	Quiet lakes, hemlock groves.
Location:	Northern Wisconsin, 15 miles east of Eagle River.
Type of hike:	Loop day hike or overnight backpack.
Total distance:	13 miles.
Difficulty:	Difficult.
Best months:	April–October.
Maps:	Chequamegon-Nicolet Hidden Lakes Trail Map, USGS Anvil Lake (inc.) and Alvin Northwest (inc.) quads.
Finding the trailhead:	From Eagle River, drive 9.3 miles east on Wisconsin 70 and turn right (south) on Forest Road 2178, Military Road. After 2.7 miles turn left (east) on Forest Road 2181, Butternut Lake Road. Drive 4.7 miles east and turn right (east) into the trailhead parking area.
Special considerations:	Although the trail is a well-marked one, it passes many intersections with old woods roads and other footpaths. Remember that only the Hidden Lakes Trail uses white diamond markings. One spot may require wading a small river.
Camping:	The Hidden Lakes Trail is on national forest land, and camping is permitted along the trail. Campsites must be at least 100 feet away from the trail or water's edge. Franklin Lake Campground, adjacent to the trailhead, has eighty-one drive-in sites.
For more information:	Chequamegon-Nicolet National Forest, see Appendix B.

Key points:

0.0   Franklin Nature Trail Trailhead.
0.4   Hidden Lakes Trail Junction.
1.8   Three Johns Lake (north end).
2.7   Forest Road 2140.

Hidden Lakes

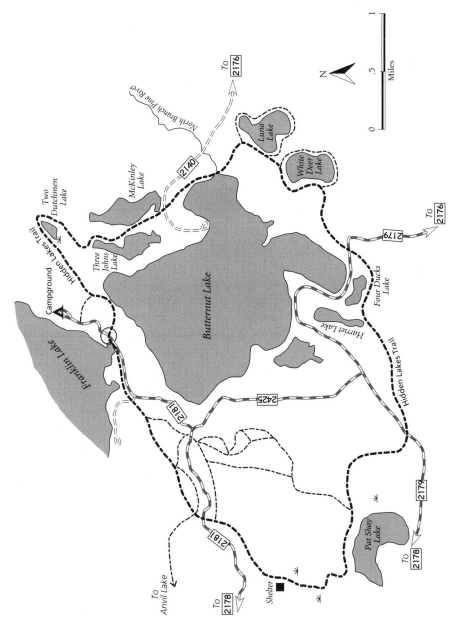

3.8   North Branch Pine River.
4.3   Luna Lake Trail Junction (northeast).
5.3   White Deer Lake Trail Junction (southwest).
6.0   Forest Road 2179.
6.4   Four Ducks Lake.
8.1   Forest Road 2179.
9.7   Pat Shay Lake (northwest corner).
10.3 Trail Shelter.
11.4 Forest Road 2181.
13.2 Franklin Lake boat ramp.
13.3 Franklin Nature Trail Trailhead.

The hike: The Hidden Lakes Trail, the longest loop hike in this guidebook, has no trouble living up to its name. Ten lakes border this route, with eight of them tucked away in quiet corners of the forest. The ambiance is noteworthy. This path meanders past lakes and wanders through hemlock groves with hardly a cabin or building in sight during the entire length of the hike. Its 13-mile length makes it a good choice for an energetic day hike or an overnight backpack.

Begin the loop at the Franklin Lake Nature Trail parking lot. Walk south, following the nature trail loop as it swings east through an ancient grove of hemlock trees. The broad trail passes near the shore of Butternut Lake, turns north, and comes to an intersection (featuring a map), with the Hidden Lakes Trail at mile 0.4. Turn right (northeast) on this narrow, but well-marked path. The trail runs northeast almost 1 mile along a pleasant, low ridge, before rounding the north end of Two Dutchmen Lake. Turning southwest, it runs to the north end of Three Johns Lake, skirts that lake's eastern shore, and crosses Forest Road 2140 at mile 2.7.

Continue walking south, arriving at the North Branch of the Pine River, the outlet of Butternut Lake, at mile 3.8. There is no trail bridge here but the water is only shin-deep. On the south side of the stream, a grassy knoll offers broad views of Butternut Lake and a good break spot.

The trail continues southward and at mile 4.3 intersects the Luna Lake Loop Trail. Bear right (southwest) at this junction as well as at three more in the next mile as your route rounds the northwest shores of scenic Luna and White Deer Lakes.

From the southwest corner of White Deer Lake the Hidden Lakes Trail runs southwest, passing Forest Road 2179 at mile 6. It then passes through spectacular hemlock groves near Four Ducks Lake at mile 6.4 and again near Harriet Lake .25 mile farther west. Pay attention to the white diamond markers here because the trail switches from a path to old woods roads several times.

Resuming its westward march, the trail runs through an extensive section of hardwood forest, crosses Forest Road 2179 again at mile 8.1, and doglegs northwest to Pat Shay Lake. Hemlocks sprinkle the slope leading down to the lake to the south.

From the northwest corner of Pat Shay Lake, the trail runs north, following one of the broad ski trails of the Eagle River Nordic system, as it will for the next 3 miles. The trail travels a narrow isthmus between wetlands and arrives at a three-sided trail shelter at mile 10.3.

Continuing north, the Hidden Lakes Trail crosses Forest Road 2181 at mile 11.4, turns northeast, and arrives at the Franklin Lake boat ramp at mile 13.2. From there it is little more than 100 yards east along Forest Road 2181 to the trailhead at mile 13.3.

25 LaSalle Falls

Highlights:	A thundering cascade in a pristine setting.
Location:	Northeast Wisconsin, 8 miles south of Florence.
Type of hike:	Out-and-back day hike.
Total distance:	2.2 miles.
Difficulty:	Easy.
Best months:	May–October.
Maps:	USGS Florence SE (inc.) quad.
Finding the trailhead:	From Florence, drive 9 miles south on Florence County Route N and another .25 mile south on Florence County Route U. Turn right (west) on Florence County Route C, drive 1.9 miles, and turn right (northwest) on LaSalle Falls Road (dirt). Drive 2.6 miles to a small parking area on the right (north) side of the road.
Special considerations:	Use caution near the waterfall. Be aware that the prime viewing spot is actually an overhang.
For more information:	Florence Natural Resources Center, see Appendix B.

The hike: As you emerge from your car at the LaSalle Falls Trailhead, the first thing you notice is the woods, a mixture of conifers and hardwoods. They are relief for the eyes after driving in through miles of pine plantations and logging debris. Soon you realize that there is a complete lack of road noise in the background.

This walk takes you through a state-designated Wild and Scenic River Corridor. A sign at the small parking area announces the river project and provides a map of the trail. Begin by walking north from the parking area. Constructed wooden steps announce the beginning of a short ascent, and at mile 0.5 you pass a bench and a small creek.

After .8 mile you hear the sound of falling water and find yourself at a fork in the trail featuring a sign that reads END OF DESIGNATED TRAIL. USE CARE NEAR BLUFFS AND WATERFALLS. A bench and boulder also mark this junction. To your right (northeast) a trail leads to a "gorge overlook" that is not noteworthy. Another trail, the portage trail that allows paddlers to bypass the falls, immediately branches east from the gorge trail. Take the left (northwest) fork of the trail, ascend a small ridge, and proceed another .3 mile to the waterfall.

LaSalle Falls

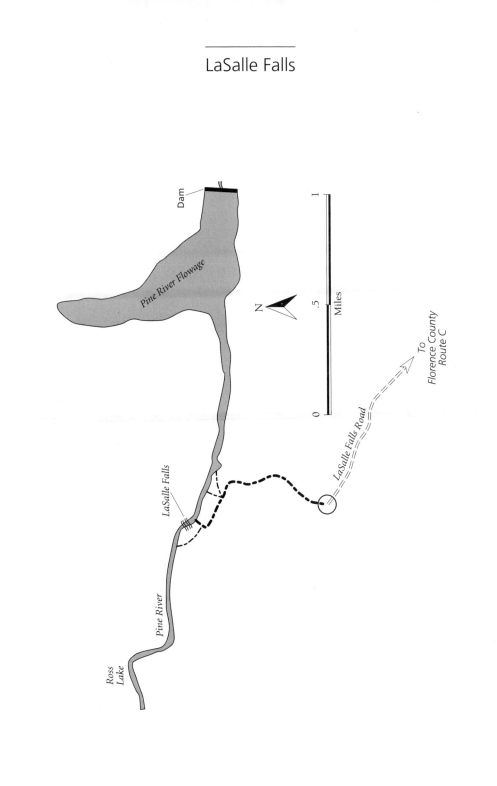

LaSalle Falls, a thundering cascade in a serene setting.

The sounds of falling water increase as you descend the ridge and find several paths leading to your right (north) to the top of the cliff above the falls. Careful investigation reveals one that leads to an overlook directly above the foaming cascade. Be aware that this overlook is more than a sheer drop, it is an overhang. Just to the south of this overhang, a steep scramble down a gully leads you to a spot below the falls' 20-foot drop. A few feet back from the overhang the portage path continues north to the calmer waters above the falls. To return, retrace your steps to the trailhead.

26 Glacial Potholes

Highlights:	Peerless glacial potholes and history.
Location:	Northwest Wisconsin, 1 mile south of St. Croix Falls.
Type of hike:	A lollipop day hike with two stems.
Total distance:	8.9 miles.
Difficulty:	Moderate.
Best months:	April–October.
Maps:	Interstate Park (WI) Hiking Map, Interstate State Park (MN) Map, USGS St. Croix Dalles (inc.) quad.
Permits and fees:	State park vehicle sticker required.
Finding the trailhead:	From the intersection of U.S. Highway 8 and Wisconsin 35 (at St. Croix Falls) drive south .6 mile, then turn right (west) into Interstate Park. Drive 1.5 miles northwest on the park road (get a trail map at the entrance station), then turn right (north) on the road that leads to the north campground and park at the Potholes Trailhead.
Camping:	There are eighty-five drive-in sites in Interstate Park.
For more information:	Interstate State Park, see Appendix B.

Key points:

- 0.0   Pothole Trail parking.
- 0.4   Horizon Rock Trail.
- 0.6   Meadow Valley Trail.
- 1.0   Summit Rock Trail.
- 1.4   Echo Canyon Trail.
- 1.9   River Bluff Trail.
- 2.6   Lake of the Dalles Nature Trail.
- 3.6   Silverbrook Trailhead.
- 4.8   Silverbrook Falls.
- 6.0   Silverbrook Trailhead/ junction with Skyline Trail.
- 7.0   Ravine Trail Junction.
- 7.6   Horizon Rock Trail.
- 8.1   Pothole Trail parking.
- 8.5   Bake Oven pothole, Minnesota Park.
- 8.9   Pothole Trail parking.

The hike: Ten thousand years ago, glacial Lake Duluth rose hundreds of feet above the present level of Lake Superior. Ice blocked the present eastern drainage of the lake near Sault St. Marie. The meltwater of a vast icefield 5,000 feet thick and the size of the state of Minnesota began to flow south past this point.

That incredible current was the source of Interstate Park's famous potholes and rock formations. Giant eddies swirled silt and rocks into the rock in a scouring motion that drilled holes as large as twenty feet in diameter and sixty feet in depth. Riverside cliffs, known as the Dalles of the St. Croix, also owe their shape to the glacial torrent.

Glacial Potholes

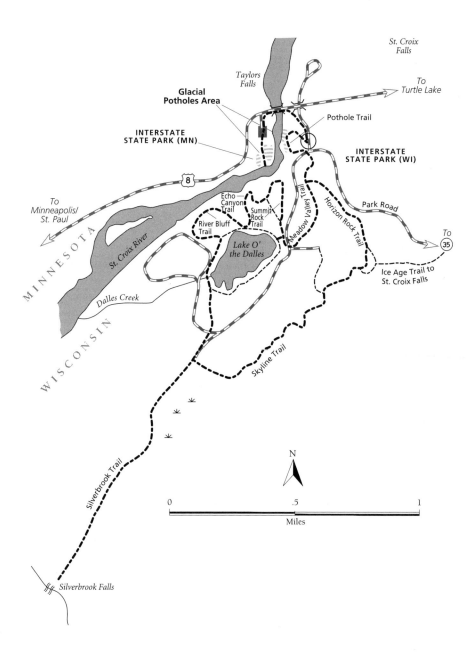

St. Croix
Falls

Taylors
Falls

**Glacial
Potholes Area**

**INTERSTATE
STATE PARK (MN)**

To
Turtle Lake

Pothole Trail

**INTERSTATE
STATE PARK (WI)**

8

To
Minneapolis/
St. Paul

Echo
Canyon
Trail

Summit
Rock
Trail

River Bluff
Trail

Meadow Valley Trail

Horizon Rock Trail

Park Road

To
35

MINNESOTA

St. Croix River

Lake O'
the Dalles

Ice Age Trail to
St. Croix Falls

Dalles Creek

WISCONSIN

Skyline Trail

Silverbrook Trail

N

0   .5   1
Miles

Silverbrook Falls

For sheer variety this hike's route is hard to beat. It starts with glacial potholes and wanders through the intricate topography of the Dalles before heading south to a quiet waterfall. Returning north, it travels through a classic hardwood forest on the Skyline Trail. It then crosses to the Minnesota side of the river for a dramatic finish, a tour of the largest glacial potholes in the world.

From the Pothole Trail parking lot turn right (northwest) and begin walking the Potholes Trail loop in a counterclockwise direction. This rock and gravel path, the westernmost segment of the 1,000-mile-long Ice Age Trail, descends to views of the river gorge and pothole-pocked bedrock. It then loops back to your starting point at mile 0.4.

Walk southeast, crossing the road, and ascend the broad gravel path of the Horizon Rock Trail to the Meadow Valley Trail junction at mile 0.6. Turn right (southwest) on the Meadow Valley Trail and descend rocky switchbacks to the damp hollow below. The transition from a dry, rock-top climate to the moist nook below is striking. Continue walking south, ignoring a spur to the (right) west, until you emerge at a picnic area. Turn right (west), walking 100 yards across a grassy lawn to the park road. Turn right (north), walking 70 yards on the road to the Summit Rock Trail at mile 1.0.

Take the rocky Summit Rock Trail due north, past the Echo Canyon Trail that branches off to the left (west), to a rock outcrop offering broad views north along the river. Continue southwest to a junction with the Echo Canyon Trail at mile 1.4 and turn right (west). That path offers more river vistas before heading south to a junction with the Lake of the Dalles Trail at mile 1.9. Turn right (west) and twenty feet farther turn right (north) again on the River Bluff Trail.

The River Bluff Trail climbs, passing a small pond on the left, to more river views and then descends to the south, emerging onto a grassy flat. Turn east, intersect the Lake of the Dalles nature trail, and turn right (south) on it. At the south end of Lake of the Dalles leave the nature trail and continue walking south through picnic areas to the Pines Group Camp and the Silverbrook Trailhead at mile 3.6.

Follow the Silverbrook Trail, a lane that was the original road from St. Croix Falls to Osceola, as it runs southwest, first on the edge of a marsh, then in woods. A quarter mile before the end a fork swings left, upslope. Ignore it, and take the right (graveled) fork to the end of the trail. Silverbrook Falls, an eighteen-foot drop, is visible through the trees at mile 4.8.

Retrace your steps to the Silverbrook Trailhead, mile 6.0, and turn right (east) to begin the Skyline Trail. That path ascends steeply through the glen of a charming brook, your first taste of the pleasant hardwood forest you will sample for the .5 mile. After climbing to the wooded rim of the valley, the trail winds along the top of the slope. Bear right (north) as the Ravine Trail descends to the left (west) at mile 7.0. In the next half mile bear left (north) as the Skyline Nature Trail and the Ice Age Trail enter from the right. At mile 7.6 the trail arrives at the Ice Age Interpretive Center and the beginning of the Horizon Rock Trail. Follow that path north to your point of origin, the Pothole Trailhead.

A giant glacial pothole along the Minnesota portion of the hike.

From the Pothole Trailhead it is a mere 400-yard walk to the Minnesota park. Two hundred yards north of this point the park road goes under U.S. Highway 8, the bridge to the Minnesota side. Walk north on the road and take note of a well-worn path, beginning at the guardrail that goes up the slope to U.S. 8. Being careful to avoid poison ivy in the area, take that unofficial path to the northwest to the sidewalk along U.S. 8. Walk west across the bridge, taking in the fine views of the Dalles downstream.

Bear left (south) as you leave the bridge, pass the entrance to the tour boat dock, and walk south through the parking lot to the building at its south end. Pick up a map of the Minnesota park there.

South of this point, a system of constructed trails winds through a compact, 100-yard-long area, containing spectacular glacial potholes. One good choice is to follow the self-guided Pothole Trail, which features a tunnel into one of the largest potholes, Bake Oven, at mile 8.5. When you are ready, retrace your steps to the bridge and return to the Wisconsin side and the start of the hike, the Pothole Trailhead.

Options: Any of the numerous small loops that are components of this hike could be eliminated to shorten the distance. Also, cutting out the Silverbrook Falls out-and-back segment would trim off 2.4 miles.

27 Chippewa Moraine Loop

Highlights:	Prime glacial scenery, including seventeen lakes.
Location:	Northwest Wisconsin, 7 miles east of New Auburn.
Type of hike:	Loop day hike.
Total distance:	4.6 miles.
Difficulty:	Easy.
Best months:	April–October.
Maps:	Chippewa Moraine Interpretive Center Trail Map, Ice Age Park and Trail Foundations Chippewa County segment map #66, USGS Marsh-Miller Lake (inc.) quad.
Finding the trailhead:	From New Auburn, drive 7 miles east on Chippewa County Route M and turn left (north) into the Chippewa Moraine Interpretive Center drive. Drive .2 mile north to the center and park.
Special considerations:	An excellent "Hiking Field Trip Guide for Glacial Landforms" handout is available from the interpretive center. Check with the staff there for seasonal wildlife watching opportunities.
Camping:	Morris-Erickson County Park, 5 miles north, has thirty drive-in sites. Check with the staff at the interpretive center for availability of backpacking sites.
For more information:	Chippewa Moraine Interpretive Center, see Appendix B.

Key points:
- 0.0 Trailhead, interpretive center.
- 0.1 Ice Age Loop Trail Junction.
- 0.9 Chippewa County Route M (east crossing).
- 1.4 Ice Age Trail Junction (east).
- 2.9 Esker.
- 3.4 Chippewa County Route M (west crossing).
- 4.4 Interpretive Center spur trail junction.
- 4.5 Trailhead, interpretive center.

The hike: Wisconsin has no shortage of glacial scenery and place names bearing the word *moraine*. The Chippewa Moraine, though, is something special. Here there's an eye-pleasing symmetry to the pattern of rounded hilltops and reflecting lakes. Unlike southeastern Wisconsin's Kettle Moraine, where the glaciers' forward movement formed the moraines, this landscape is a result of glacial ice that had stopped moving. After the glacier's horizontal movement ceased, its surface debris flowed into low spots in the ice. Those accumulations of rock debris formed the hills, called hummocks, and depressions formed by large chunks of ice, thicker spots in the ice sheet, melted to become the kettle lakes.

A loop trail of just under 5 miles meanders through these jumbled hills, passing seventeen lakes along the way. To take the circle tour, begin by

Chippewa Moraine Loop

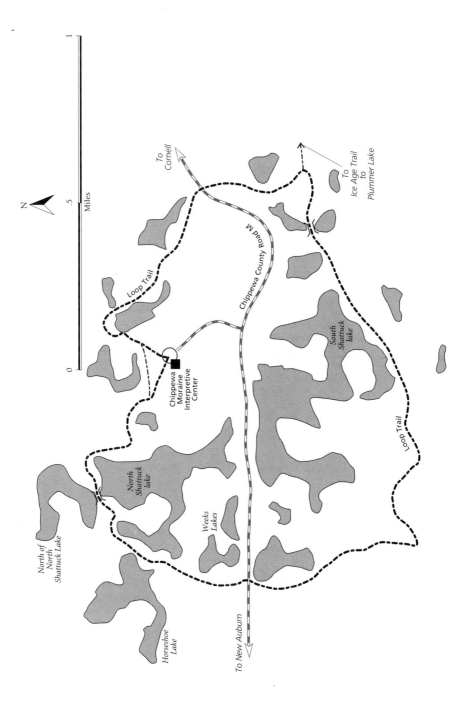

Trailside bench near north end of North Shattuck Lake.

walking northeast from the interpretive center on a short connector trail that drops steeply to a junction with the Loop Trail at mile 0.1. Bear right (north) at that intersection, beginning a clockwise circuit of the loop.

As you walk east on the Loop Trail, the land's inherent beauty is apparent. The trail rounds one kettle lake, passes another, and ascends to a scenic bench above a third. It crosses Chippewa County Route M at mile 0.9, climbs to the top of a moraine, and rolls south, passing between two more lakes. Bear right (southwest) at mile 1.4, an intersection with the Ice Age Trail.

The Loop Trail drops from the intersection's knoll, heading west past small lakes, birch trees, and a .5-mile-long stretch of South Shattuck Lake's shoreline. After a turn north, the path follows the top of a glacial esker, a low ridge of sediment from a glacial stream, at mile 2.9. Still heading north, it crosses Chippewa County Route M a second time at mile 3.4.

Lakes are seldom out of sight. The Loop Trail heads north, passing two of the Weeks Lakes and along an isthmus between Horseshoe Lake and North Shattuck Lake.

A trail bridge crosses a channel between North Shattuck Lake and a body of water known as North of North Shattuck Lake. Just before the bridge, a bench sits under pine trees, offering a fine view of the lakes. The trail swings south, meeting a connector trail leading to the interpretive center at mile 4.4. Bear right (southeast) at that junction and ascend to the trailhead at mile 4.5.

28 Chippewa Moraine/ Plummer Lake

Highlights:	A parade of lakes, twenty-one in 6 miles, and glacial scenery.
Location:	Northwest Wisconsin, 7 miles east of New Auburn.
Type of hike:	Out-and-back day hike or backpack.
Total distance:	12.2 miles.
Difficulty:	Difficult.
Best months:	April–October.
Maps:	Chippewa Moraine Interpretive Center Trail Map, Ice Age Park and Trail Foundations Chippewa County segment map #66, USGS Marsh-Miller Lake (inc.) and Bob Lake (inc.) quads.
Finding the trailhead:	From New Auburn, drive 7 miles east on Chippewa County Route M and turn left (north) into the Chippewa Moraine Interpretive Center drive. Drive .2 mile north to the center and park.
Special considerations:	An excellent "Hiking Field Trip Guide for Glacial Landforms" handout is available from the interpretive center.
Camping:	Backpack camping on county forest land east of the Loop Trail is allowed as long as you are 100 feet from the trail or water. Check with the interpretive center for current regulations and new designated backpacking sites. Morris-Erickson County Park, 5 miles north, has thirty drive-in sites.
For more information:	Chippewa Moraine Interpretive Center, see Appendix B.

Key points:

0.0 Trailhead, interpretive center.
0.1 Loop Trail Junction.
0.9 Chippewa County Route M.
1.4 Ice Age Trail Junction.
2.1 Ice Age Drive.
3.5 Dam Lake outlet.
4.4 Horseshoe Lake (West end).
4.9 Town Line Road.
6.1 Plummer Lake Road.

The hike: Any short walk on the Chippewa Moraine's Loop Trail offers views full of beautiful rounded hills and kettle lakes. Hike the Ice Age Trail east from there and the scenery never lets up, while the trail just keeps getting quieter.

Start by walking northeast from the interpretive center, descending on a connector trail. Bear right (north) at a junction with the Loop Trail at mile 0.1 and swing around the shoreline of a beautiful kettle lake, a first glimpse

Chippewa Moraine/Plummer Lake

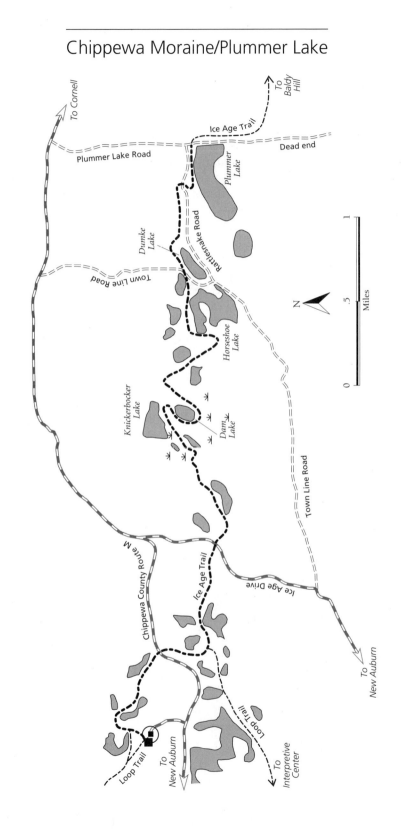

of what is to come. The trail runs east, passing a bench above another lake, and crosses Chippewa County Route M at mile 0.9.

Turning south, the pathway ascends a moraine, passes between two more kettle lakes, and reaches a junction with the Ice Age Trail on the top of a knoll at mile 1.4. Bear left (east), descending to pass three more lakes and a pine plantation before crossing Ice Age Drive at mile 2.1.

The trail skirts the shore of a fine kettle lake .25 mile farther on. A bench under pine trees offers a prime spot for a break and contemplation. Continue walking east as the trail enters a hardwood forest in hilly terrain. A marsh and Knickerbocker Lake are nearby to the north before the trail loops south to Dam Lake, passing the outlet at mile 3.5. Check the marsh south of the outlet for sandhill cranes.

The Ice Age Trail then follows Dam Lake's shore northeast through rolling hills before turning south to Horseshoe Lake, reaching its western end at mile 4.4. This is a quiet and remote stretch of trail. A fisher romped through the woods ahead of me when I was here.

Follow the trail east along Horseshoe Lake's northern shore to Town Line Road at mile 4.9. Continue hiking east, passing Dumke Lake and ascending to a broad, flat plateau, a glacial feature known as an ice-walled-lake-plain. During the glacial era, surface debris covered a rim of stagnant ice surrounding a lake here. Clay and sediment filled the lake, and the ice melted. This left a flat plain, rimmed by the debris and elevated above the surrounding land. A glacial stream drainage, 10 to 40 feet deep, trenches this plain to the northeast.

Resume hiking east. The trail drops from the plateau and follows Rattlesnake Road east for 500 feet. It then parallels the road to its south, following Plummer Lake's shoreline to Plummer Lake Road at mile 6.1. This is a good turnaround spot for the hike.

An unnamed lake along the Ice Age Trail west of Knickerbocker Lake.

29 Jerry Lake

Highlights:	A quiet footpath, one of the best woodland walks in the state.
Location:	North central Wisconsin, 15 miles northwest of Medford.
Type of hike:	Shuttle hike. Long day hike or overnight backpack.
Total distance:	13.1 miles.
Difficulty:	Difficult.
Best months:	April–October.
Maps:	Chequamegon-Nicolet National Forest Ice Age National Scenic Trail Map, Ice Age Park and Trail Foundation, Jerry Lake Segment Map #61, USGS Mondeaux Dam (inc.), Jump River Fire Tower (inc.), and Perkinstown (inc.) quads.
Finding the trailhead:	From Medford, drive north 4.9 miles on Wisconsin 13 and turn left (west) on Taylor County Route M. Drive west 7.6 miles and turn right (north) on Taylor County Route E. Take County Route E north 6.4 miles and turn left (west) on Forest Road 102. Drive 1.6 miles west past the bridge over the North Fork of the Yellow River, turn left (south) at a small parking area for hunters. Park here but do not block the gate.
Special considerations:	The Ice Age Trail is closed during the gun deer hunting season. This is usually, but not exclusively, during Thanksgiving week. Waterproof boots and trekking poles come in handy for wet spots.
Camping:	You can backpack camp anywhere along the trail as long as you are 50 feet off the trail and 75 feet from water. A designated campsite is at Jerry Lake. Mondeaux Flowage, 5 miles east of the trailhead, has sixty-four drive-in sites and pay showers at the concession near the dam.
For more information:	Chequamegon-Nicolet National Forest, Medford, or Ice Age Park and Trail Foundation, see Appendix B for both.

Key points:
- 0.0   Forest Road 102.
- 1.4   Chippewa Lobe Interpretive Loop Junction (eastern).
- 3.1   Chippewa Lobe Interpretive Loop Junction (western).
- 3.9   Forest Road 108.
- 6.9   Forest Road 571.
- 10.1 South Fork of the Yellow River.
- 11.5 Forest Road 572.
- 13.0 Jerry Lake.
- 13.1 Forest Road 571.

Jerry Lake

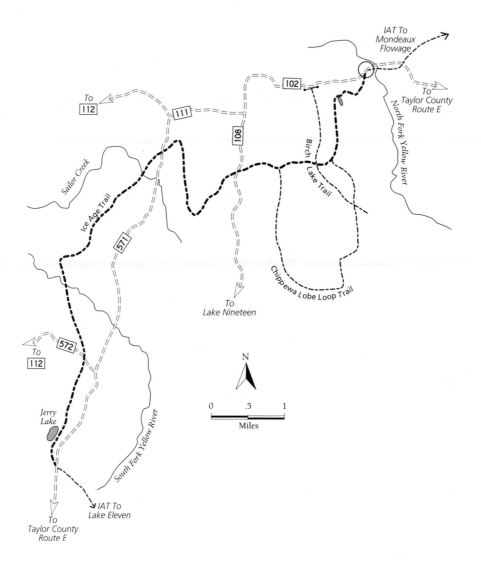

The hike: This stretch of the Ice Age Trail is an undiscovered gem. If you like quiet, woodland walks on narrow, intimate footpaths, push this hike to the top of your list. Mile after mile of soul-satisfying, deep woods ambiance rolls by, while the sight of another hiker is a rarity.

Wolves are raising pups in the area. Bald eagles circle over the rivers, otters leave their tracks below, and sandhill cranes trumpet across the marshes. Hemlock groves, birch stands, hardwood forests, verdant wetlands, and clear-running streams border the trail. What's to dislike?

Begin your hike by walking south from the parking area, past a gate, on a grassy lane. Turn right (west) on the trail, marked with the yellow diamond of the Ice Age Trail, 170 paces south of the gate. A wet stretch, decorated with memorable clumps of moss, announces your arrival at a small pond .5 mile farther.

The trail rounds the pond, enters a hardwood forest, and runs south. At mile 1.4 turn right (southwest) at the junction (eastern) with the Chippewa Lobe Interpretive Loop. Again a footpath, the trail runs through a pleasant stretch of birches and pines, crossing the grassy lane called the Birch Lake Trail, .5 mile farther. A section of open hardwood forest follows before the trail arrives at the Chippewa Lobe Interpretive Loop junction (western) at mile 3.1.

Bear right (west) and follow the Ice Age Trail around the north edge of a wide wetland extending to the south. In June, look for orchids on the edge of the bog. On the northwest corner of the swamp, the trail rises into an upland forest and at mile 3.9 arrives at Forest Road 108.

As you walk west from the road, for a few brief minutes the remains of a thinning logging operation are visible to the north. Pay attention as the trail enters a section of hemlocks. Trail markings are abundant, but wear marks are so thin that without those markings the trail would be hard to follow. This situation repeats itself several times during the hike, solid evidence of the light volume of trail traffic in these parts.

The trail meanders southwest for more than a mile before taking a long, nearly 1.5-mile run north on the top of a low ridge. That northward leg begins in a fine birch stand. Dropping off the ridge, the Ice Age Trail turns to the southwest and crosses Forest Road 571 at mile 6.9.

Follow the trail southwest from Forest Road 571, crossing Sailor Creek on planks at mile 7.5. The trail continues southwest, passing several grassy but passable roads and an ATV trail before arriving at the South Fork of the Yellow River at mile 10.1.

At this point the stream is about 35 feet across, and when I saw it a log provided a dicey but doable dry crossing. That log looked like it might float away with the next high water episode. Without a log, this would be a knee-deep wade under normal conditions and risky in times of high water.

After crossing the river the trail continues south and ascends a low ridge that features the finest hemlock grove of the hike. Continuing a slow rise, the trail meets Forest Road 572 at mile 11.5.

Resuming its southward march, the path ascends slightly through an open hardwood forest and passes a young hemlock grove. A marsh on Jerry

Lake's north end appears and then Jerry Lake itself, a pleasant, large pond. A designated campsite is in the woods a short distance in from the lake's northeast corner, at mile 12.9.

Follow the trail south. A spur trail leads .2 mile east to Forest Road 571. Your route, the Ice Age Trail, reaches Forest Road 571 at mile 13.1, the end of the hike.

30 Chippewa Lobe

Highlights:	A quiet lollipop hike with an outstanding designated campsite on a small backcountry lake.
Location:	North central Wisconsin, 15 miles northwest of Medford.
Type of hike:	A lollipop day hike or overnight backpack.
Total distance:	9.3 miles.
Difficulty:	Difficult.
Best months:	April–October.
Maps:	Chequamegon-Nicolet National Forest Ice Age National Scenic Trail Map, Ice Age Park and Trail Foundation segment map #61, USGS Jump River Fire Tower (inc.), Jump River Fire Tower SE (inc.), Perkinstown (inc.) and Mondeaux Dam (inc.) quads.
Finding the trailhead:	From Medford, drive north 4.9 miles on Wisconsin 13 and turn left (west) on Taylor County Route M. Drive west 7.6 miles and turn right (north) on Taylor County Route E. Take County Route E north 6.4 miles and turn left (west) on Forest Road 102. Drive 3.1 miles west and turn left (south) on Forest Road 108. Drive 1.5 miles south on Forest Road 108 and watch for the trail crossing. Park just off the road.
Special considerations:	The Ice Age Trail is closed during the gun deer hunting season. This is usually, but not exclusively, during Thanksgiving week. Waterproof boots and trekking poles come in handy for wet spots and crossing beaver dams. I found this loop very well marked, with blue diamonds at short intervals. Wear marks are often faint, however, and without those markings this loop would be very difficult, if not impossible, to follow.
Camping:	A fine designated campsite is at the south end of the loop. You can camp anywhere along the trail as long as you are 50 feet off the trail and 75 feet from water. Mondeaux Flowage, 5 miles east of the trailhead, has sixty-four drive-in sites and pay showers at the concession near the dam.
For more information:	Chequamegon-Nicolet National Forest, Medford, or Ice Age Park and Trail Foundation, see Appendix B for both.

Chippewa Lobe

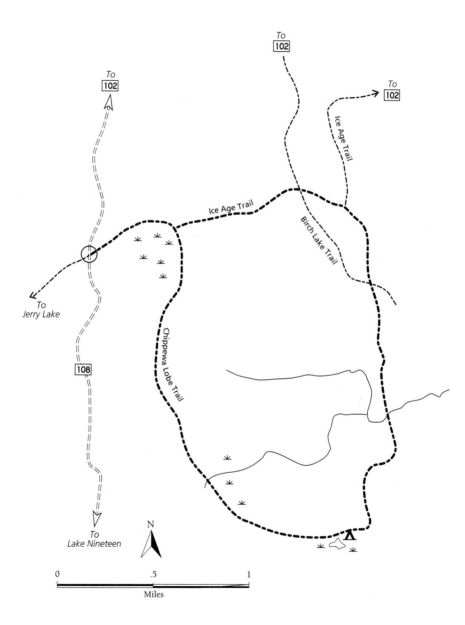

To
102

To
102

To
102

Ice Age Trail

To
Jerry Lake

Ice Age Trail

Birch Lake Trail

Chippewa Lobe Trail

108

To
Lake Nineteen

N

0   .5   1
Miles

Key points:
- 0.0   Forest Road 108 trailhead.
- 0.8   Chippewa Lobe Loop Trail junction.
- 3.0   Constructed trail bridge.
- 3.9   Designated campsite at large beaver pond.
- 4.6   Small beaver dam.
- 4.8   Creek.
- 6.0   Birch Lake Trail.
- 6.8   Ice Age Trail junction.
- 8.5   Chippewa Lobe Loop Trail junction.
- 9.3   Forest Road 108 trailhead.

The hike: If spending a night at a fine backcountry campsite beside a small lake motivates you, this hike is a good choice. Without that inducement, you may find parts of this trail somewhat rough for your tastes, and I recommend the nearby Ice Age Trail as a better choice.

Begin your hike by walking east on the Ice Age Trail from Forest Road 108. This stretch of the trail is a narrow but defined footpath that runs through an upland forest before dropping to round a wetland on its northern border. In June, look for orchids on the edge of the bog.

At mile 0.8 the trail arrives at the Chippewa Lobe Interpretive Loop junction. A large sign announces the project. Turn right (south), following blue diamond markers along the east side of the wetland.

The trail continues south, always well-marked, at times a forest path and sometimes following old roads. A section of old, rotting boardwalk is passable but challenging. Shortly after, at mile 3.0, a sturdy trail bridge crosses over an eastward flowing stream.

On the south side of the bridge a narrow ridge carries the trail between the stream's wetlands before the path swings east. Twenty-foot-tall aspen line the trail for a few hundred yards here.

Doubts about the trail's payoff evaporate as you arrive at a small lake. This body of water, at the south end of the loop, appears to be a very large beaver pond. At its outlet, two beaver dams, the product of generations of work, support that theory.

Cross the outlet on a beefy bridge and you will see an improved campsite, complete with benches and a pit toilet. Wood ducks and herons entertain. Beaver come out at dusk, perhaps to avoid the eagles that circle above from time to time. Their tail-slapping antics punctuate the evening hours.

From the campsite, follow the trail east and north through a pleasant forest, a mix of older hardwoods and much younger pines. At mile 4.6 there is a dicey crossing of a small beaver dam, with a knee-deep soaking waiting if you stumble. Shortly after the trail turns northward and at mile 4.8 crosses a major, eastward flowing creek. The trail makes a crossing on huge, flattened logs.

Continue north as the trail passes through hemlock groves. At mile 6.0 the route crosses a mowed lane, the Birch Lake Trail, that runs south from Forest Road 102. Resume walking north and you meet the Ice Age Trail at mile 6.8.

Turn left (southwest), following the Ice Age Trail's yellow markers. About .5 mile farther you again pass the mowed lane that is the Birch Lake Trail along a charming stretch of pine and birches. A section of open hardwood forest follows before the trail arrives at the Chippewa Lobe Interpretive Loop trail junction at mile 8.5, the same spot as mile 0.8 of this hike. This is the end of the loop section of the hike. To return to Forest Road 108, just walk west on the Ice Age Trail, retracing your steps from the beginning of the outing.

31 Timm's Hill

Highlights:	Wisconsin's highest point, small scenic lakes.
Location:	North central Wisconsin, 10 miles north of Rib Lake.
Type of hike:	Out-and-back day hike.
Total distance:	5.8 miles.
Difficulty:	Moderate.
Best months:	April–October.
Maps:	Ice Age Park and Trail Foundation Segment Map #59, Timm's Hill National Trail Map (Price County Tourism Department, see Appendix B), USGS Timm's Hill (inc.) quad.
Finding the trailhead:	From Rib Lake, drive east 2 miles on Wisconsin 102 and turn left (north) on Taylor County Route C, which becomes Price County Route C. Drive 9.1 miles north. Park on the road's broad shoulder just east of the trail crossing, adjacent to a cemetery.
Camping:	Wood Lake, 10 miles southeast, has eight drive-in sites.
For more information:	Ice Age Park and Trail Foundation, Price County Tourism Department, see Appendix B.

Key points:
- 0.0 Trailhead on County Route C.
- 0.2 Ski Trail Junction.
- 0.9 Ski Trail Junction.
- 1.2 Otter Lake.
- 1.4 Ski Trail Junction.
- 2.1 Rustic Road 62.
- 2.9 Timm's Hill summit.

The hike: Timm's Hill, at 1,951 feet above sea level, is the highest natural point in Wisconsin. The hill is the namesake of the Timm's Hill National Scenic Trail, a 10-mile-long spur of the Ice Age Trail. This hike follows the last 3 miles of that path, along roller coaster–like ski trails, past small scenic lakes, to the summit.

Begin your walk where the Timm's Hill National Scenic Trail crosses Price County Route C, just west of the cemetery. Hike north, following red paint

Timm's Hill

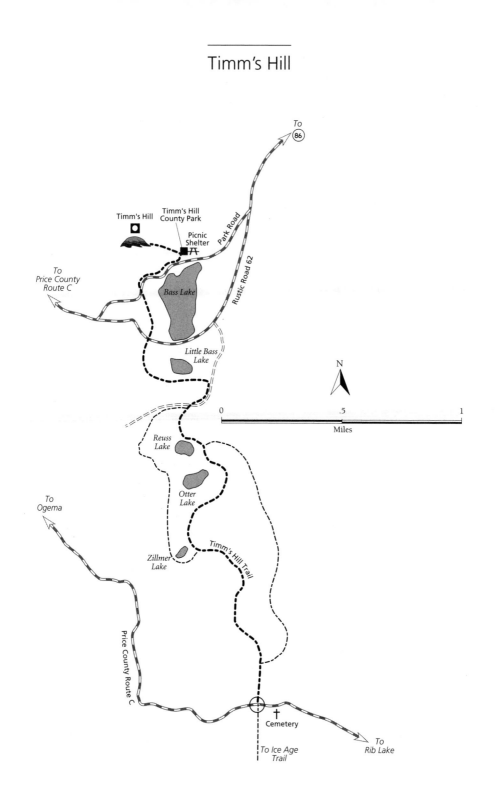

blazes, at first along a shallow drainage and then up a slope. At mile 0.2, go straight (north) where a ski trail enters from the right.

After that junction, the broad trail ascends through a stretch of young aspen. Don't be discouraged, because the scenery improves soon. The trail then enters an older hardwood forest, sprinkled with pine trees, and takes on the character of a rowdy ski trail, not blinking at steep drops and climbs. Bear right (north) at mile 0.9, following the red blazes, at another ski trail intersection. Zillmer Lake appears through the trees to your left as you pull away from the intersection.

The trail ascends and descends a few more hills, passes Otter Lake on your left, and reaches another ski trail junction at mile 1.4. Turn left (northwest) where you see Reuss Lake to the left of the trail and follow the trail as it swings around to the north. At about mile 1.6 bear right (east) as the trail joins a dirt road that runs east for a short distance before swinging north. At mile 1.8 turn left (west) where the trail leaves that road.

Walk west, following the trail as it passes to the south of Little Bass Lake and swings north to meet Rustic Road 62 at mile 2.1. Cross the road and proceed north on a slope above Bass Lake, notably larger than the other lakes along the route. About .25 mile farther, turn right (north) on a paved park road, part of Timm's Hill County Park.

That road dips to the shores of Bass Lake and passes a fine, small swimming beach. One hundred and fifty feet east of the beach, watch for a boardwalk that extends to a small island.

The park road swings north from the lake to a parking area and picnic shelter at the eastern base of Timm's Hill. The summit and its observation

Bass Lake, at the base of Timm's Hill.

tower are several hundred yards to the west, 150 feet above the waters of Bass Lake. Ascend steps from the picnic shelter, following white blazes west, up the hill to the tower.

The view from the top is of wooded hills and forest on all sides, with Timm's Lake and Bass Lake nearby in the foreground. Retrace your steps to return to County Route C.

32 Wood Lake

Highlights:	A quiet lake, marsh and woods, and an old logging camp.
Location:	North central Wisconsin, 6 miles east of Rib Lake.
Type of hike:	Loop day hike.
Total distance:	2.8 miles.
Difficulty:	Moderate.
Best months:	April–October.
Maps:	Ice Age Park and Trail Foundation Taylor County segment map #58, USGS Wood Lake (inc.) quad.
Finding the trailhead:	From Rib Lake, drive east and north 4 miles on Wisconsin 102 and turn right (east) on Wood Lake Avenue. Drive 3.2 miles to Wood Lake County Park and another .3 mile to the park's picnic area.
Camping:	There are eight drive-in sites, adjacent to the trailhead, at Wood Lake County Park (715–748–1460).
For more information:	Ice Age Park and Trail Foundation, see Appendix B.

Key points:
   0.0   Trailhead, picnic area.
   0.6   Wood Lake Creek bridge.
   1.6   Ice Age Trail Junction (East).
   2.1   Camp Four Logging Camp.
   2.4   Ice Age Trail Junction (West).
   2.8   Trailhead, picnic area.

The hike: Wood Lake is one of those quiet, out-of-the-way spots that grow on you. This hike's route begins beside the clear, spring-fed lake waters, continues past an extensive beaver pond, and leads to the remnants of an historic logging camp.

In addition to the trail's attractions, the car campground at the trailhead makes Wood Lake a great choice for families or others looking for a weekend camping spot. It's at the end of a dead-end road, next to a nonmotorized lake, and features a small playground and swimming beach.

The Wood Lake Trail, a loop route, begins on the south side of the picnic area next to the swimming beach. Walk south on the trail, beginning a counterclockwise circuit of the lake. As the trail rounds the lake's south end, it

Wood Lake

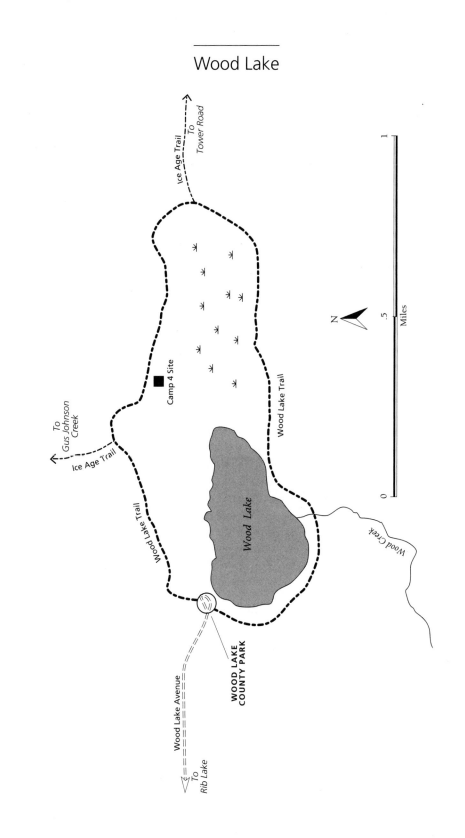

The trail passes a marshy beaver pond east of Wood Lake.

passes stands of birch trees and Wood Creek, the lake's outlet, at mile 0.6.

Continue walking east as the trail follows an old logging railroad grade and begins its run along the south shore of an extensive marsh, enhanced by beavers, east of Wood Lake. Near that marsh's eastern end, the trail swings north on an old woods road and meets the Ice Age Trail at mile 1.6. Walk straight (north) at that intersection as the trail, now combined with the Ice Age Trail, rounds the eastern end of the marsh and begins a hilly, up-and-down passage west.

At mile 2.1 the trail arrives at a small clearing, the site of Camp 4. An interpretive sign describes the logging camp as active from 1906 to 1916, with two bunkhouses lodging eighty men apiece. A piece of metal debris, perhaps part of a wood burning stove, carries the date 1886.

From Camp 4, follow the trail as it heads north, then west, through an open park-like hardwood forest. Turn left (south) at mile 2.4 where the Ice Age Trail goes north.

Continue walking west along the Wood Lake Trail, through woods featuring an increasing number of pine trees, arriving at the trailhead at mile 2.8.

33 Ed's Lake

Highlights:	A quiet birch and hardwood forest.
Location:	Northeast Wisconsin, 7 miles west of Wabeno.
Type of hike:	Loop day hike.
Total distance:	4.6 miles.
Difficulty:	Easy.
Best months:	April–October.
Maps:	Chequamegon-Nicolet National Forest trail map, USGS Roberts Lake (inc.) quad.
Finding the trailhead:	From Wabeno, drive 0.9 mile west on Wisconsin 32 and turn left (west) on Wisconsin 52. At mile 3.7 go straight (west) on Forest County Route W as Wisconsin 52 goes left (south). Take County Route W west to mile 9.6 and turn right (north) into a parking area with a signed trailhead.
Camping:	These trails are on national forest land, and camping is permitted along the trail. Campsites must be at least 100 feet from the trail or the water's edge. Ada Lake, 8 miles south of the trailhead, has nineteen drive-in sites.
For more information:	Chequamegon-Nicolet National Forest, Laona Ranger District, see Appendix B.

Key points:
0.0   Trailhead.
0.3   Birch Ski Trail.
1.5   Trail shelter near Ed's Lake.
2.0   Intersection with "Long Birch Ski Trail"; go east on old railroad grade.
2.2   Turn off old railroad grade on signed ski trail heading south.
2.6   Intersection with "Maple Ski Trail"; turn northeast.
3.1   Intersection with "Long Birch Ski Trail."
4.6   Trailhead.

The hike: Ed's Lake Trail is a classic walk in the woods on a cross-country ski trail that works well as a hiking trail. Along the way the route passes picturesque hemlock and birch groves, a small lake, and railroad grades left over from the logging era. Note that these trails have directional signs for guiding ski traffic. The first half of this hike will go with the flow of those directional signs on the Birch Trail, and the second half will go "backwards" on the Maple Trail.

Begin by walking north from the County W trailhead to an intersection at mile 0.3 that features a trail map. Ignore the incoming Maple Trail and turn left (north) on the Birch Trail. After a short, winding ascent, a series of birch groves validates the name before the trail heads northwest past a fine stand of hemlocks to Ed's Lake.

A three-sided trail shelter, complete with picnic table and fire ring, sits amid pines near the lake's southeast shore. Ed's Lake, a .5-mile-long pond

Ed's Lake

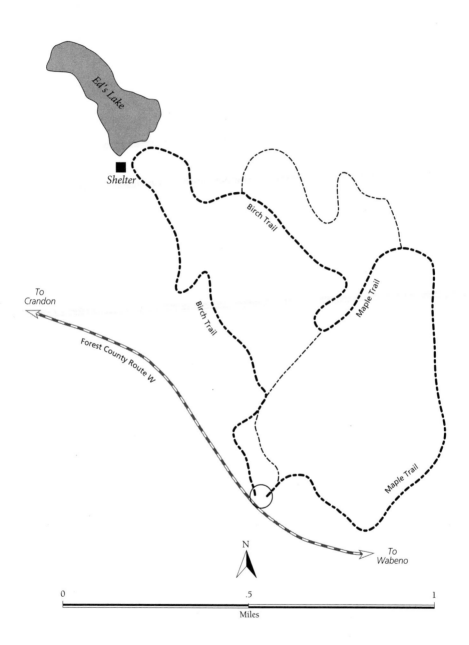

Ed's Lake

Shelter

Birch Trail

Birch Trail

Maple Trail

Maple Trail

To
Crandon

Forest County Route W

N

To
Wabeno

0   .5   1

Miles

Along the beginning of the Birch Trail.

with marshes at either end, fades from sight as the trail swings north and east to an intersection in a small clearing at mile 2.0. Ignore the longer option of the Birch Trail that goes north. Go straight (east) on the shorter version of the Birch Trail along an old railroad grade. Pay attention at mile 2.2 as the ski trail leaves the railroad grade. Bear right (south) here to the next intersection at mile 2.6. Turn left (northeast) on another old railroad grade and your hiking route is now going "backwards" on the Maple Trail.

About .5 mile farther on the railroad grade trail you are following curves to the east and a compact series of three intersections appears. First, ignore the old railroad grade (actually the same one you left at mile 2.2) that approaches as a sharp left turn (from the west). Second, pass the longer option of the Birch Trail as it too approaches as a sharp left turn from the west. Take a ninety-degree turn to the right (south) at mile 3.1, following the Maple Trail.

This is a pleasant stretch of trail, wandering through a hardwood forest sprinkled with pines and birches. The trail heads steadily south before swinging west to the trailhead. Just before the trailhead the "incoming" ski trail enters from the right. Go straight (south) and soon you will be at the parking lot.

34 Jones Spring

Highlights:	A quiet area with a pleasant mixture of woods and open springs and wetlands.
Location:	Northeast Wisconsin, 5 miles southwest of Townsend.
Type of hike:	Loop day hike or backpack.
Total distance:	9.2 miles.
Difficulty:	Moderate.
Best months:	April–October.
Maps:	Chequamegon-Nicolet National Forest Jones Spring Map, USGS Reservoir Pond (inc.) quad.
Special considerations:	Use caution during hunting season. All trails on this hike are ski trails that use a system of colored circles (red, yellow, orange, white) in blue diamond plastic blazes for trail markings.
Finding the trailhead:	From Townsend, take Oconto County Route T south and west 5.4 miles and turn right (west) on to Fanny Lake Lane (dirt). Park at the trailhead at mile 6.1.
Camping:	These trails are on national forest land, and camping is permitted along the trail. Campsites must be at least 100 feet from the trail or the water's edge. Fanny Lake has five campsites, and there is a three-sided shelter is between Upper and Lower Jones Lakes. Boot Lake, 1 mile east of the trailhead, has thirty-five drive-in campsites.
For more information:	Chequamegon-Nicolet National Forest, Lakewood Ranger District, see Appendix B.

Key points:
  0.0   Trailhead on Fanny Lake Lane.
  0.3   Junction A. Yellow Trail enters from south.
  0.4   Junction B. Red Trail goes north.
  1.8   Junction with parking spur north of Mary Creek.
  1.9   Bridge over Mary Creek, west of Jones Spring Impoundment outlet.
  2.0   Junction with parking spur south of Mary Creek.
  3.5   Junction with parking spur west of the southernmost Jones Springs Pond.

Jones Spring

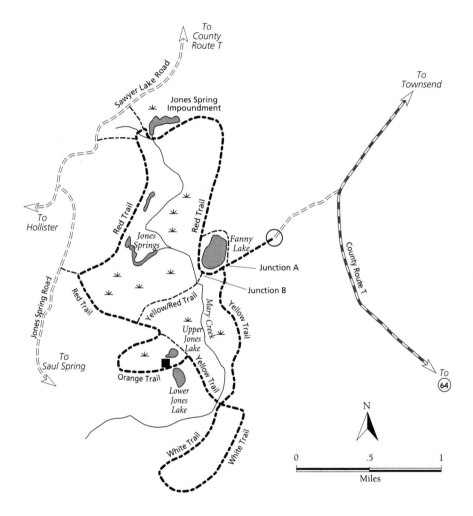

To
County
Route T

Sawyer Lake Road

Jones Spring
Impoundment

To
Townsend

To
Hollister

Red Trail

Red Trail

Jones
Springs

Fanny
Lake

Junction A

Junction B

Jones Spring Road

Red Trail

Yellow/Red Trail

Mary Creek

Yellow Trail

County Route T

Upper
Jones
Lake

To
Saul Spring

Orange Trail

Yellow Trail

Lower
Jones
Lake

To
64

White Trail

White Trail

N

0   .5   1

Miles

4.2 Cutoff Junction.

5.2 Shelter.

5.3 Yellow Trail Junction.

6.0 White Trail Junction.

7.7 White Trail Junction.

8.9 Junction A.

9.2 Trailhead on Fanny Lake Lane.

The hike: Walking at Jones Spring has a steady rhythm to it and it goes like this: woodland scene, broad marsh views, then forest scene again. It is an alternating pattern of habitats that makes for an enjoyable and interesting hike. The various forest stretches are intimate, while the marsh and lake segments offer long sight lines and opportunities to scan for wildlife.

Begin by hiking southwest from the trailhead on a broad footpath to Fanny Lake. Stay straight (southwest) on this wide trail, ignoring a trail entering from the right (north). Go straight (southwest) again as the Yellow Ski Trail enters from the left at mile 0.3.

Walk west along the south shore of Fanny Lake, a picturesque .25-mile-long pond lined with birch trees and five pleasant designated campsites. At the lake's southwest corner, at mile 0.4, bear right (north) on the Red Ski Trail.

That trail runs north nearly a mile, then swings southwest to climb a low ridge paralleling Jones Spring Impoundment, a marshy pond. Before stepping out from the cover of the woods, scan the open wetland for sandhill cranes and other wildlife. Then continue west along the trail as it passes the pond's outlet on a berm and bear left (west) at mile 1.8, where a spur trail goes right to a parking area on Sawyer Lake Road.

Fanny Lake's north shore.

Cross a bridge over Mary Creek and bear left (southeast) where a second spur trail goes right to a second parking area on Sawyer Lake Road. Follow the Red Ski Trail south, cruising along a low ridge, a good vantage point to look for fauna, just west of the marshes that border Jones Springs. The trail turns southwest and at mile 3.5 reaches another junction with a parking spur trail in a small clearing that goes west to Jones Spring Road. Ignore the spur and turn left (south), following the trail as it turns southeast and runs through a hardwood forest to a junction with the Yellow Ski Trail at mile 4.2.

Bear right (south) following the Yellow Ski Trail to a junction at mile 4.3, where a right (southwest) turn takes you onto the Orange Ski Trail. Follow that trail as it swings south, then east to arrive at a three-sided trail shelter at mile 5.2. This shelter sits on a pleasant knoll among pine and birch trees, halfway between tiny Upper and Lower Jones Lakes.

From the shelter, walk north to a junction at mile 5.3 and turn right (east) on the Yellow Ski Trail. Proceed southeast on that trail, crossing marshy Mary Creek on a culvert, to an intersection with the White Ski Trail at mile 6.0. Turn right (south), following the White Ski Trail through pine woods and open fields. That loop swings around and returns to the same intersection at mile 7.7. Turn right (northeast) and follow the Yellow Ski Trail as it meanders north past pines and birches, arriving at Fanny Lake at mile 8.9. Turn right (east) and retrace your steps from the first part of the hike to the trailhead at mile 9.2.

35 Long Slide Falls

Highlights:	A short walk to a waterfall with a 50-foot drop.
Location:	Northeast Wisconsin, 6 miles north of Pembine.
Type of hike:	Out-and-back day hike.
Total distance:	.4 mile.
Difficulty:	Easy.
Best months:	April–October.
Maps:	USGS Pembine (inc.) quad.
Finding the trailhead:	From Pembine, drive north 5.9 miles on U.S. Highway 141 and turn right (east) on Morgan Park Road. Drive southeast on that road and turn right (south) at mile 7.5, at the signed road for Long Slide Falls. Park at the trailhead at mile 7.8.
Special considerations:	Use caution near the top of the falls. There are many slanting rock ledges.
For more information:	Marinette County Extension Office, see Appendix B.

Key points:
- 0.0 Trailhead.
- 0.1 Top of falls.
- 0.2 Bottom of falls.

Long Slide Falls

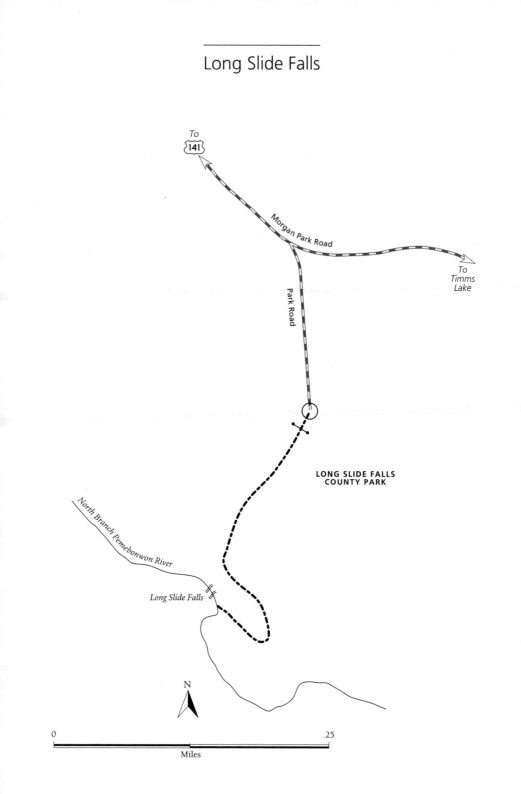

To [141]

Morgan Park Road

To Timms Lake

Park Road

LONG SLIDE FALLS
COUNTY PARK

North Branch Pemebonwon River

Long Slide Falls

N

0 .25
Miles

Looking upstream at Long Slide Falls.

The hike: Long Slide Falls is a short walk for a large payoff, a 50-foot-high, multitiered drop in a shady rock gorge setting. If you are motoring past on U.S. Highway 141 it is well worth the brief detour to view it.

From the parking area walk south on a broad, gated dirt road, which turns into a well-worn path. Continue on this path; at a point 150 yards from the parking area you arrive at the top of a bluff. The North Branch of the Pemebonwon River, and the falls, are below you.

The best viewing, from the bottom of the falls, involves a little more walking. Turn left (east) and walk along the edge of the escarpment through a jumble of short paths. The trail you want follows the top of the bluff for 50 yards, then begins a gradual descent to the southeast, to the valley floor.

Part of the way down the trail turns back to the west, continuing in that direction to the base of the falls.

36 Mead State Wildlife Area

Highlights:	Notable spring birdwatching, nesting ospreys, and a heron and cormorant rookery.
Location:	Central Wisconsin, 18 miles east of Marshfield.
Type of hike:	Lollipop day hike.
Total distance:	6.1 miles.
Difficulty:	Moderate.
Best months:	April–August.
Maps:	George W. Mead Wildlife Area map, USGS Big Eau Pleine Reservoir quad (inc.)
Finding the trailhead:	From Milladore, drive north 3.5 miles on Portage County Route N. Turn right (east) and drive 1 mile east on Portage County Route H. Then turn left (north) on Plum Lane and take it north 1.3 miles to the trailhead.
Special considerations:	This route follows obvious but unmarked lanes and dike roads. Note fall closure dates (September to December) on the refuge. Avoid hunting seasons. Bring binoculars, and perhaps a camp chair, to comfortably spend time with the ospreys, herons, and cormorants.
For more information:	George W. Mead Wildlife Area, see Appendix B.

Key points:

0.0 Plum Lane Trailhead.
0.9 Junction T.
1.9 North end of Four Oaks Flowage.
3.1 North end of Townline Reservoir, rookery.
3.6 Lone tree marks junction of two dike roads, turn south.
5.2 Junction T.
6.1 Plum Lane Trailhead.

The hike: This is a classic spring bird hike, mixing hardwood forests and open marsh habitat. A wide variety of birds are present here in mid-April, but two features are notable. At the far end of the hike, a dike runs between a heron and cormorant rookery and an active osprey nesting platform. Each of these ongoing shows is about a hundred yards offshore, and parking yourself in between for a sojourn with parents and young is well worthwhile.

From the northeast corner of the Plum Lane Trailhead, follow a gated lane northeast through a hardwood forest. This lane shows signs of occasional mowing and has some pea gravel on its surface. It runs north for .5 mile before swinging east, arriving at a key intersection I call Junction T at mile 0.9.

A small field borders a grassy lane running due north. Ignore that grassy lane and bear right (east), following the heavier wear marks and pea gravel of the lane you have been following. To the east .5 mile the lane leaves the woods and dry ground, turning north and becoming a dike road traveling among broad wetlands.

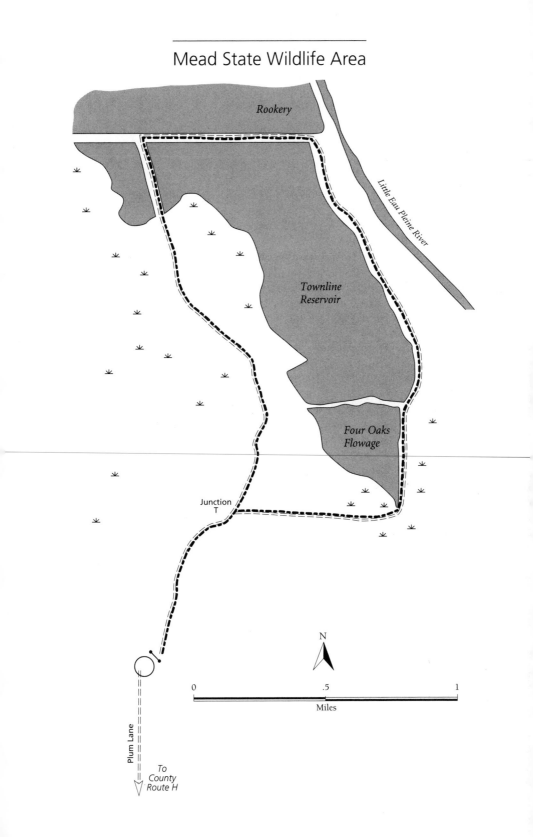

Mead State Wildlife Area

Rookery

Little Eau Pleine River

Townline
Reservoir

Four Oaks
Flowage

Junction
T

N

0   .5   1

Miles

Plum Lane

To
County
Route H

Walk north, with the wide pool known as Four Oaks Flowage on your left. In April, herons and ducks seem to be moving in every corner of the marsh. The primeval bark of sandhill cranes reaches across the water.

At mile 1.9 you will reach the north end of Four Oaks Flowage, a dike running east-west. Go straight (north), continuing on the obvious dike road. A huge expanse of water, the flowage called Townline Reservoir, stretches west and northwest. Swallows swoop for insects near its surface.

Another dike running east-west appears at mile 3.1; this one holds the highlight of the trip. Turn left (west), walk 100 yards or so and look north. A cormorant and heron rookery thrives on platforms perched on poles emerging from the water, safe from raccoons and other land-based raiders. To the south several active osprey nest platforms are in sight. Parents of all three species come and go constantly, with fresh food for the family. The Little Eau Pleine River runs nearby to the east. During my visit, an eagle patrolled the river corridor.

When ready, walk west on the dike to a lone tree at mile 3.6. That tree marks an intersection with another, newer dike that runs south. Turn left (south) and follow that newer dike. The open waters of the flowage give way to more vegetated marsh, and finally, a little more than .5 mile south from the lone tree, dry land. The lane, grassy with a few pebbles now and then, runs southeast and then south through young woods.

At mile 5.2 this grassy lane reaches Junction T, the intersection you saw at mile 0.9 of the hike. Turn right (southwest) and retrace your steps from the first part of the hike to reach the Plum Lane Trailhead at mile 6.1.

Western Upland

Wisconsin's huge glaciers ground to a halt short of the southwestern portion of the state. As a result, the landscape there shows what the region looked like before the great ice sheets bulldozed it and rounded off the sharp corners. Steep stream valleys dissect the western upland, and the 200-mile-long gorge of the Mississippi River runs the length of it.

That great river is a vital migration route for birds, with tundra swans and pelicans among the notables. Other large rivers, the Chippewa, Black, and Wisconsin, add to the rich web of wildlife habitat here. River otters romp, great blue herons stalk, and eagles nest along the current's flow.

Hiking routes here meander along the rivers, wander through flood plain forests, and climb the steep, wooded hillsides for sweeping views of the river valleys from bluff-top prairies.

37 Chippewa River

Highlights:	An extensive floodplain forest lining the mighty Chippewa River, notable birdwatching.
Location:	Western Wisconsin, 5 miles west of Nelson.
Type of hike:	Out-and-back dayhike or overnight backpack.
Total distance:	12.4 miles.
Difficulty:	Moderate.
Best months:	April–October.
Maps:	Tiffany State Wildlife Area map, USGS Wabasha and Ella quads.
Permits and fees:	State park vehicle sticker required.
Finding the trailhead:	From Nelson, drive north and west 4.1 miles on Wisconsin 35 and turn right (north) into the trailhead, a riverside boat landing.
Special considerations:	This hike traverses a floodplain environment. High water levels could be a factor between March 15 and May 1. Depending on conditions, it may be necessary to make a few minor fords to follow this route. Use caution during hunting season.
Camping:	Backpacking permit available from DNR, Alma, see Appendix B.
For more information:	DNR, Alma, see Appendix B.

Key points:
- 0.0 Trailhead at Wisconsin 35 boat ramp.
- 1.2 Cross railroad tracks.
- 3.4 Cross sandy, dry channel (intermittently dry or wet).
- 5.5 Small, narrow clearing.

Chippewa River

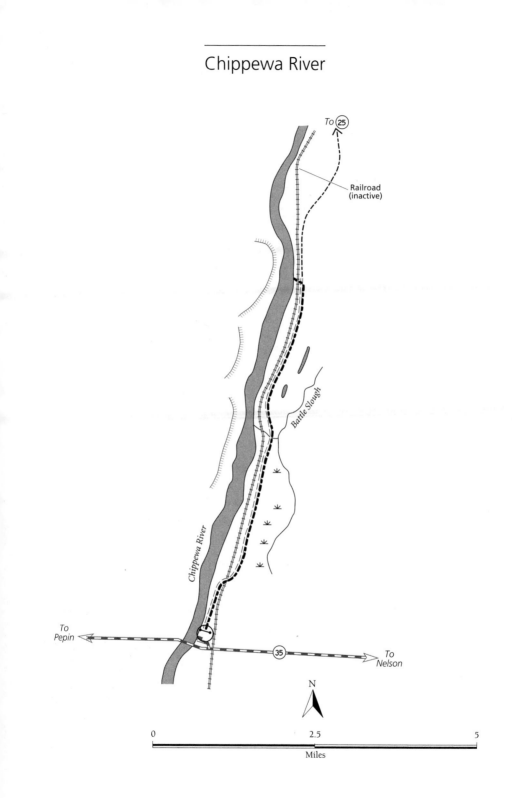

6.1   Path to river.
6.2   Bank of river.

The hike: It takes a while to grasp the size of this place. Tiffany State Wildlife Area, a big chunk of land on a big river, extends 12 miles along the east bank of the Chippewa River, just above its confluence with the Mississippi River. In addition to the east river bank, large sections of the bluff-lined west bank are also state property.

After coming to grips with the scale of the landscape, another impression sinks in. This place feels remote. For almost 7 miles, no road reaches the river on the west bank. On the east bank, Wisconsin 25 parallels the river and the hike's route, but it is almost 2 miles away and its presence is hardly noticeable.

This hike's route follows a gated dirt road that shows signs of occasional mowing but is at times grassy and lumpy. It tends to run a little inland from the river but is totally within its flood plain. From time to time narrow paths, some deer trails, some created by hunters, offer an opportunity to approach the riverbank to the west.

Begin your hike by walking north from the trailhead, passing through a floodplain savannah of widely spaced trees and tall grass. A half mile later the road pulls away from the river, enters an oak forest, and at mile 1.2 jogs east slightly and crosses an overgrown railroad line. These railroad tracks parallel your route throughout the hike. They offer an alternate route, but the spacing of the track's ties makes it awkward walking.

Continue walking north through a landscape that alternates between oak forest and the open edge of wetlands to the east. At mile 3.4 the lane crosses

The floodplain forest near Battle Slough offers excellent birdwatching.

a side channel that connects the main river with Battle Slough. I saw this spot during dry conditions in the fall and found a dry wash with a sandy bottom. At other times this may be a ford.

After this wash the road swings west for a short stretch before resuming its progress north. The tall bluffs lining the west bank of the river come into view, a vivid contrast to the flat bottomland you are walking.

Beaver sign is abundant. During my visit, ospreys and an eagle cruised the river corridor while turkey vultures rode the thermals rising from the south-facing bluffs. In the woods, a flashy pair of pileated woodpeckers entertained. A flock of snow geese passed overhead.

At mile 5.5 the road widens into a small, narrow opening in the woods. This is apparently the turnaround spot for mowing. North of here the lane becomes noticeably more overgrown, but not enough to discourage walking. Watch for a narrow but well-worn path leading west to the river at mile 6.1. Orange flagging marked this trail when I was there.

Turn left (west) and follow this path 150 yards, first across the railroad tracks, then on to the riverbank. The Chippewa River runs swift and wide here, with 500-foot-tall bluffs rising steeply from the opposite shore. This is a good place to turn around for the hike back to the trailhead.

38 Trempealeau River

Highlights:	Outstanding wildlife viewing opportunities at the confluence of the Trempealeau and Mississippi Rivers.
Location:	Trempealeau National Wildlife Refuge, western Wisconsin, 28 miles northwest of LaCrosse.
Type of hike:	Out-and-back day hike.
Total distance:	5.9 miles.
Difficulty:	Easy.
Best months:	March–November.
Maps:	Trempeauleau NWR Map/Brochure, USGS Winona East and Trempealeau quads.
Finding the trailhead:	From Centerville, drive west 3.3 miles on Wisconsin 35, turn left (south) on West Prairie Road for 1.2 miles, then turn right (south) into the refuge. Continue south on the refuge road for 1 mile before turning left (east) on a gravel lane for .3 mile. At that point turn right (south) onto another gravel lane where a sign directs you to the boat landing, a mere .2 mile farther. Park at the boat landing.
Camping:	Perrot State Park, 4 miles east of the trailhead, has ninety-eight drive-in campsites.
For more information:	Trempealeau National Wildlife Refuge, see Appendix B.

Trempealeau River

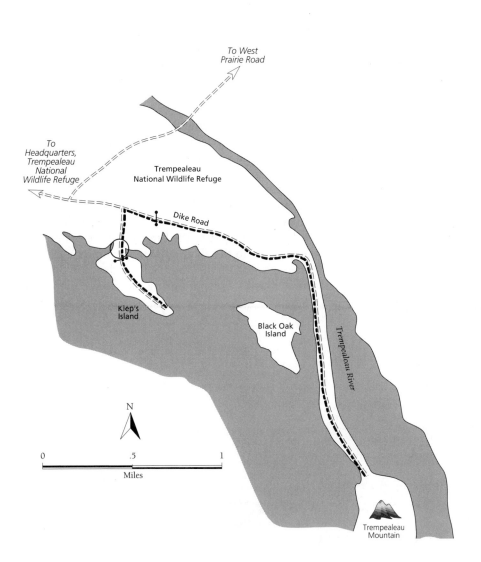

To West
Prairie Road

To
Headquarters,
Trempealeau
National
Wildlife Refuge

Trempealeau
National Wildlife Refuge

Dike Road

Kiep's
Island

Black Oak
Island

Trempealeau River

N

0   .5   1
Miles

Trempealeau
Mountain

Key points:
- 0.0 Boat landing.
- 0.4 South end of Kiep's Island (turn around).
- 1.1 Intersection of boat landing road with Dike Road (turn east).
- 3.4 South end of Dike Road (turn around).
- 5.7 Intersection of Dike Road with boat landing road (turn south).
- 5.9 Boat landing.

The hike: Halfway down the Dike Road a family of otters let me know I was in the right place. All four of them were splashing in a puddle by the riverbank, having such a good time they didn't notice me for ten minutes. Finally spotting me, they ambled up the dike's slope. Each in turn stopped to stare at me for a moment before scooting down the other side and heading for Black Oak Island.

Frolicking otters made my day, but they are only one of many reasons to walk here. This place, a national wildlife refuge since 1936, offers hikers a pleasant combination of broad sight lines on dike roads and intimate woodland scenes. Three railroads built dikes here in the late 1800s to hold their tracks. Those railroad dikes unintentionally worked to shield the refuge area from siltation and pollution from the two rivers. Today, the refuge is an important resting area for migratory birds.

This hike's trailhead, the boat ramp area, is a staging area for bald eagles in early March. They gather there, anticipating the breakup of the upper Mississippi's ice cover and their return to the river's fishing grounds.

Start your walk by continuing south on the dirt road you drove in on, past the gate, onto Kiep's Island, a warbler hotspot during the spring migration.

The Dike Road borders Trempealeau's wildlife-rich marsh.

Note the osprey nesting platform to the northeast and continue walking the lane to the island's southeast corner, at mile 0.4. Look to the southeast and you can see the almost 400-foot rise of Trempealeau Mountain, your walk's next goal. A new dike continues south across the lagoon at this point, but it is barren and unattractive, so you will turn around here and walk north.

Continue walking north, past the boat ramp, to the intersection of the boat ramp road and Dike Road at mile 1.1. Turn right (east) and follow Dike Road past the gate and into an area of low, sandy ridges and open oak forest. A mile later, the lane emerges into the open near a marshy pond on its north side, turns south, and rises a few feet to run on the crest of a dike.

The broad, open space of the refuge's main lagoon opens to the southwest, with Black Oak Island .25 mile away. Paralleling the dike to the east, and the reason for its existence, the Trempealeau River runs quiet and brown.

Continue walking south on the Dike Road. To the southeast Brady's Bluff and other heights in Perrot State Park come into view. As the dike doglegs southeast toward Trempealeau Mountain the sight lines to the west across the lagoon are very long. Pelicans were in the far reaches of the lagoon during my September visit, with a sprinkling of ducks near Black Oak Island. An osprey patrolled the river.

At mile 3.4 the Dike Road bumps up against the island of Trempealeau Mountain, a good place to turn around. Retrace your steps on the Dike Road to return to the boat ramp trailhead.

39 Perrot Ridge

Highlights:	Broad, scenic views of the Mississippi River and a prairie full of rare plants.
Location:	Western Wisconsin, 15 miles northwest of La Crosse.
Type of hike:	Loop day hike.
Total distance:	3.9 miles.
Difficulty:	Difficult.
Best months:	April–October.
Maps:	Perrot State Park trail map, USGS Trempealeau quad.
Permits and fees:	State park vehicle sticker required.
Finding the trailhead:	From Trempealeau, take the Perrot State Park Road west 3 miles to the Brady's Bluff (West) trailhead.
Camping:	Perrot State Park has eighty-seven drive-in sites .5 mile north of the trailhead.
For more information:	Perrot State Park, see Appendix B.

Key points:
0.0   Brady's Bluff West Trailhead.
0.5   Brady's Bluff summit, intersection with Brady's Bluff East Trail.
1.2   Intersection with Park Road.

Perrot Ridge

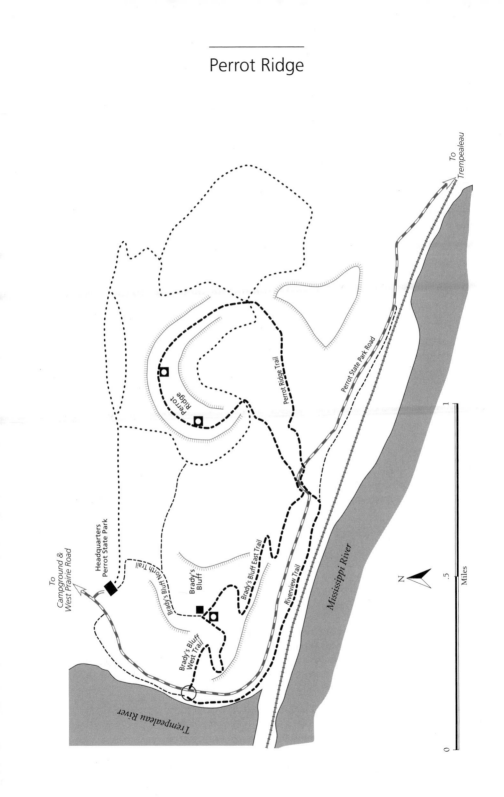

1.3 Perrot Ridge Trailhead.
1.6 Intersection with bike/ski trail.
1.8 Summit of Perrot Ridge.
2.1 Intersection with bike/ski trail.
2.8 Intersection with Park Road.
2.9 Riverview Trail.
3.9 Brady's Bluff West Trailhead.

The hike: Location matters and this hike has it. Make the effort to make two 500-foot climbs to the heights of Perrot State Park, and your reward will be views of the Mississippi River that are among the best in Wisconsin.

Others before us favored this spot. Early Native Americans were here as long as 7,000 years ago, and hundreds of Indian mounds, some the work of the famous Hopewell Culture, dotted the area at one time. European presence began with Nicholas Perrot, who wintered here in 1685, the beginning of a French vanguard that led to the building of a fort in 1731. The story of the human history of this area is the subject of an exhibit in the park's nature center. It is a work in progress. Our understanding of many parts of the history is incomplete.

Begin your hike by walking east from the parking area, across the park road, to the marked trailhead of the Brady's Bluff West Trail. The trail immediately ascends a beautiful ravine and then doubles back above its south wall, a mossy sandstone cliff, before continuing a relentless climb to the top. Wood and stone steps ease the way, and several lookouts provide distraction. The path reaches the summit, containing a shelter and the junction with the Brady's Bluff North and East Trails, at mile 0.5.

Broad views stretch along the river bluffs to Winona in the west and the mouth of the Black River to the east. After savoring the views, walk east through the bluff-top dry prairie, a state natural area that features more than one hundred plant species. Long views linger as the path, the Brady's Bluff East Trail, descends to the first trees and then a beautiful oak forest. Turn left (east) at mile 1.2 and walk one hundred paces on the park road to the trailhead of the Perrot Ridge Trail.

Turn left (northeast) and walk up the Perrot Ridge Trail, at this point a grassy jeep road ascending through scrubby woods. Pause and turn around for the views across the river of the Minnesota bluffs and the mouth of the Big Trout Creek Valley as the lane climbs a large, sloping meadow. Pay attention at mile 1.6 as the Perrot Ridge Trail jogs right (northeast) on a bike/ski trail for a short distance. About .1 mile, after joining the bike/ski trail, turn left (north) as the Perrot Ridge Trail climbs steps to continue its climb to the bluff's summit.

The path tops out in a rocky scramble and continues north, an airy, open ridgewalk. Your route continues along the ridge top for .5 mile, but trees soon clog the view, only relenting for one last vista at the crest's end. The Perrot Ridge Trail drops from its namesake, and at a saddle you go straight (south) where the bike/ski trail crosses your path.

Continuing its descent to the southwest, the trail passes through a pleasant, open woodland and down a fern-filled drainage. A jeep road now, the

139

The trail descends Brady's Bluff's open ridgetop.

trail meets the park road at mile 2.8, the site of a Civilian Conservation Corps Camp in the 1930s.

Turn right (west) and walk the park road until you are opposite the trailhead of the Brady's Bluff (East) Trail. There, at mile 2.9 of the hike, turn left (west) and pick up the beginning of the Riverview Trail. At first this is a wide grassy lane, but it soon turns into a well-trod, but sometimes root-filled, path.

Continue walking west, sometimes on the water's edge, but always near the river. The shoreline and the trail swing north where the Trempealeau River joins the Mississippi River. Another .25 mile of walking will complete your loop, bringing you to the parking area where the hike started.

40 McGilvray Bottoms

Highlights:	The vast, wooded flood plain of the Black River, historic road and bridges.
Location:	Western Wisconsin, 10 miles north of La Crosse.
Type of hike:	Out-and-back day hike.
Total distance:	5.2 miles.
Difficulty:	Easy.
Best months:	April–October.
Maps:	Van Loon State Wildlife Area map, USGS Galesville (inc.) quad.
Finding the trailhead:	From Trempealeau, drive east 7.2 miles on Wisconsin 93 and turn left (north) on Amsterdam Prairie Road. Drive north 1.7 miles and turn left (west) into the signed parking area. A box on the bulletin board holds maps.
Special considerations:	Use caution during hunting seasons. This is a floodplain environment, and high water could be a factor between March 15 and May 1.
Camping:	Perrot State Park, 10 miles west, has ninety-eight drive-in sites.
For more information:	DNR La Crosse, see Appendix B.

Key points:
0.0   Trailhead on Amsterdam Prairie Road.
1.6   Bridge 6, turn north on jeep road.
2.6   Jeep road ends, turn around.

The hike: Alexander McGilvray began a ferry service across the Black River at this site in 1854, but the log drives of the second half of the 1800s blocked operations for months at a time. The first attempt at a solution, construction of bridges on "McGilvray's Road," lasted only until the spring floods of 1895 took out several of the wooden spans.

The next round of construction saw the erection of five steel bridges of the bowstring-arch-truss type around 1908. Part of their design was an unusual hook-clip, invented by Charles Horton, that eliminated the need for rivets and bolts. These five bridges, along with one at Amnicon State Park near Superior and two others, are the only existing examples of this configuration in the state.

Two other bridges, one the main channel structure dismantled in 1948, added to the total, and locals nicknamed the route "Seven Bridges Road." Today, it is a pleasant walking route, and McGilvray Bottoms's official name is the Van Loon State Wildlife Area.

Begin your outing by hiking west from the trailhead, down a short slope, on the gated lane that is McGilvray's Road. At the bottom of this incline is the first bridge and the beginning of the vast flood plain ecosystem your route traverses.

McGilvray Bottoms

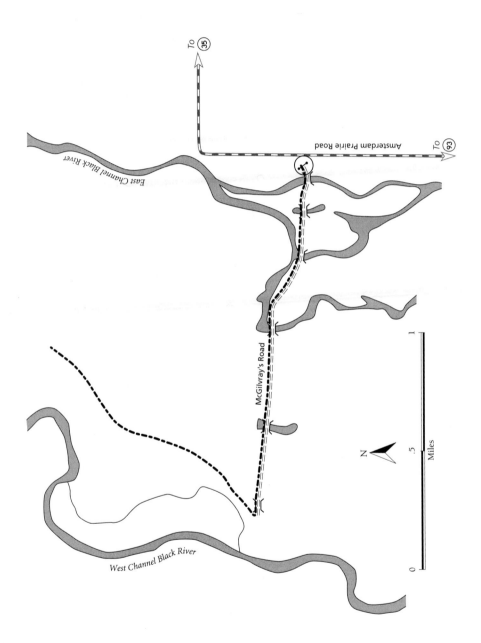

A mosaic would be an apt description of the flood plain. Part of the variety comes from its components: river channels, sloughs, hardwood forests, and wetlands. Within those commingling parts, the seasonal ebb and flow of water levels changes the entire landscape. Surging river channels that may threaten to knock out a bridge in the spring can be dry, sandy walking routes in the fall. And sometimes there is the big change, the kind of epic flood that knocked out the 1895 bridges and rearranged river channels at will.

Continue walking west and within .25 mile pass the second and third bridges. The road has been running due west, and at this point it angles slightly northwest before running due west again. Scenery between the river channels varies between open hardwood forest and expansive wetlands.

The route, an elevated old road, is also an excellent viewing platform to scan this rich ecosystem for wildlife. Turkeys and grouse inhabit the hardwoods while herons hunt frogs in the marshes. Beaver and otters swim the river channels.

Crossing the fourth and fifth bridges takes you over channels that hold water even in a dry fall. At mile 1.6 you reach the sixth bridge. Twenty yards

The fourth bridge on McGilvray Road, passing through the flood plain of the Black River.

past that span turn right (north) on a grassy jeep road that runs northeast. This lane shows up as a broken line on the map at the trailhead bulletin board.

This old road, little more than tire ruts at times, runs northeast through open woods and an occasional meadow-like opening. One pleasant mile from the McGilvray Road it disappears into a jumble of faint paths. This is a good spot to turn around and walk back to the trailhead.

41 Rush Creek Bluff

Highlights: Notable views of the Mississippi River from a little-known, bluff top prairie.
Location: Southwestern Wisconsin, 25 miles north of Prairie du Chien.
Type of hike: Out-and-back day hike.
Total distance: 2 miles.
Difficulty: Difficult.
Best months: April–October.
Maps: USGS De Soto (inc.) and Lansing (inc.) quads.
Finding the trailhead: From Ferryville, drive north 2.5 miles on Wisconsin 35 and turn right (north) on Rush Creek Road. After driving .4 mile look for a grassy jeep road leading east (the beginning of the hike). Park on the west side of Rush Creek Road.
Special considerations: Confidence in your route-finding ability is a requirement for this hike. The difficult rating reflects that.
For more information: La Crosse DNR, see Appendix B.

Key points:
0.0 Trailhead.
0.6 Top of bluff, turn southwest.
1.0 Goat prairie viewpoint.

The hike: If you are willing to walk up a tall bluff, wade through some thorn bushes, and navigate a faint path, there is a reward here: a broad river view and solitude. The thorns aren't horrendous, but this is not a good place for bare legs.

From the Rush Creek Road, walk east, uphill, on a grassy lane through old fields. This old road quickly swings north and then east, beginning a long side-hill ascent of a wooded south slope. Continue walking uphill, keeping the drainage to your right (south). As the top of the bluff nears, the slope broadens and the road swings to the south. At mile 0.6, the top of the slope, ignore a path that goes south (straight) and turn right (southwest) on a rutted jeep road.

Your route has been through an older, predominantly oak, woodland that tends to be quite open under its canopy. As the jeep road heads southwest

Rush Creek Bluff

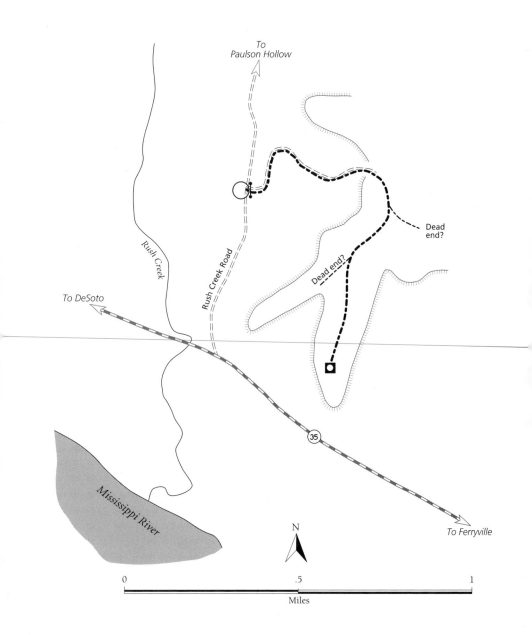

To Paulson Hollow

Dead end?

Dead end?

Rush Creek

Rush Creek Road

To DeSoto

35

To Ferryville

Mississippi River

N

0   .5   1
Miles

View from Rush Creek Bluff looking south along the Mississippi River.

and then south it becomes overgrown, until little but a faint path is evident. This is the stretch with the thorn bushes. Stay straight (south) at a fork in the path, as a spur goes right (southwest).

Continue walking south on the faint path until you see the woods ending in front of you. Hawks perch in the trees on the edge of the prairie, and a slow approach can be worthwhile.

The transition from woodland to prairie, and the broad open space of the river valley, is abrupt. Among the jumbled grasses of the prairie, the path is again faint but visible. Walk a short distance left (south) and forward 100 yards, descending slightly to the best viewpoint. From this south-pointing promontory, a broad swath of prairie sweeps north, spilling down the steep slopes below. Watch for hawks riding thermals rising from the south slope of the open bluff just to the north. Iowa's river bluffs fill the western horizon while the broad Mississippi River curls out of sight to the south. This is the hike's turnaround point.

42 Wyalusing State Park

Highlights:	Broad views of the confluence of the Wisconsin and Mississippi Rivers from tall bluffs, Native American mounds, notable birdwatching, wildflowers, and hardwood forests.
Location:	Southwest Wisconsin, 4 miles south of Prairie du Chien.
Type of hike:	Loop day hike.
Total distance:	8.2 miles.
Difficulty:	Moderate.
Best months:	April–October.
Maps:	Wyalusing State Park trail map, USGS Bagley (inc.) and Clayton (inc.) quads.
Permits and fees:	State park car sticker required.
Finding the trailhead:	From Prairie du Chien, drive 7.2 miles southeast on U.S. Highway 18 and turn right (southwest) on Grant County Route C. Take that road southwest 3.1 miles and turn right (west) on Grant County Route X. Drive 1.3 miles and turn right (north) on the park entrance road. Drive north 1.8 miles and turn left (west) on Sentinel Ridge Road. After .4 mile, turn left (south) on Long Valley Road, and after .6 mile turn left again where a sign says SOUTH PICNIC AREAS. Take that road south 1.3 miles to the Homestead Picnic Area, the trailhead.
Special considerations:	Parts of the Sentinel Ridge and Bluff Trails are not for acrophobics.
Camping:	Wyalusing State Park has 110 drive-in sites.
For more information:	Wyalusing State Park, see Appendix B.

Key points:

0.0 Homestead picnic area trailhead.
0.9 Boat Landing.
2.2 Indian Trail Junction.
2.6 Bluff Trail.
3.5 Connector trail descends to Wisconsin River.
3.9 Old Immigrant Trail.
4.4 Walnut Springs Trail.
6.7 Mountain bike trail junction.
7.0 Park entrance road, Turkey Hollow Trail.
8.2 Homestead picnic area trailhead.

The hike: Of this entire 8-mile loop, there is only a 1 mile stretch of trail that I think of as halfway commonplace. Every other mile of trail on this route possesses something special, a telling scene of time and place, that I would gladly return to see.

Begin your tour by walking to the west side of the Homestead Picnic Area. Look for a sign, the trailhead of the Sugar Maple Nature Trail, announcing

Wyalusing State Park

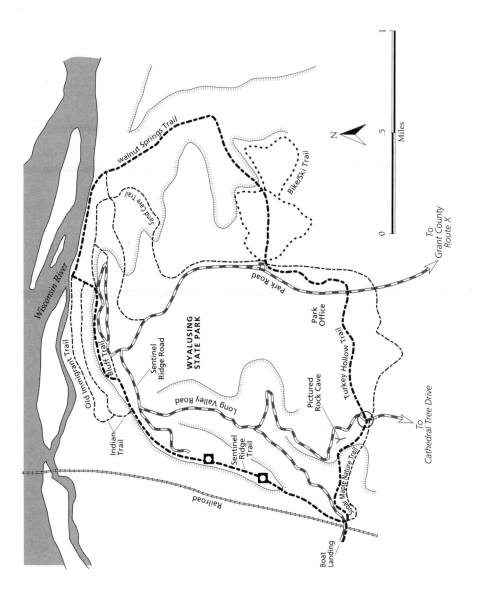

that Pictured Rock Cave is .4 mile away. The trail, three feet wide, eroded, and root-filled, descends through a beautiful open forest of maples and oaks to the short spur to the cave. Turn right (east) to view this charming spot, a mossy sandstone overhang with a small, seasonal waterfall.

Return to the main trail and continue the descent, emerging on the park road that leads to the boat landing at mile 0.8. Turn left (west) on the road, walk 30 yards, and you will see the Sentinel Ridge Trail on your right (north). Two reasons justify a delay. First, this area is a top spot for birdwatching, especially colorful warblers, during the spring migration. Also, the .1-mile walk west to the boat landing is worthwhile, a chance to commune with a Mississippi River slough.

Next, walk north on the footpath that is the Sentinel Ridge Trail. It quickly begins a serious ascent, one of two 500-foot climbs on this hike. Wooden steps, views from rock outcrops, and a charming forest setting ease the gain in elevation. The path reaches the top of the bluff and passes a long series of Native American burial and effigy mounds, views over the Mississippi River Valley, and a monument to the extinct passenger pigeon.

Continue walking north and east on the Sentinel Ridge Trail, going straight (east) as the Indian Trail crosses at mile 2.2. At mile 2.6 turn left (north) on the Bluff Trail where a sign points to Treasure Cave. The Bluff Trail runs precariously east, below a band of cliffs. This stretch, a state natural area, is notable for its black walnut and other hardwoods as well as spring wildflowers. A steep set of steps, more ladder than stairs, leads up to the cave. Continue east and at mile 3.5 turn left (north) to descend to the Wisconsin River, on an unnamed connector trail.

Looking northwest at the confluence of the Wisconsin and Mississippi Rivers from the Sentinel Ridge Trail.

The narrow path switchbacks steeply downhill past a small rock overhang and reaches the Old Immigrant Trail, at riverside, at mile 3.9. Turn right (east) and follow this old wagon road along the river. Massive boulders dot the woods uphill to your right. A bench offers a spot to linger beside the river before the trail turns inland, meeting the Walnut Springs Trail at mile 4.4.

Turn left (east) at that intersection and follow the Walnut Springs Trail southeast as it enters a large ravine. Sandstone walls accent the forest scene. The trail crosses the gravel creek bottom several times, an easy, short hop in normal conditions.

About .5 mile into the ravine, the trail turns southwest and enters a large side drainage. The trail settles down into a steady ascent and emerges into open old fields at the top of the plateau.

Pay attention at mile 6.7 where a mountain bike trail intersects the Walnut Spring Trail you are following. Continue straight (southwest) where a bike trail enters first from the left, then another from the right. Then turn right (west) where the trail splits and another bike trail goes left (southwest).

Continue west on the Walnut Springs Trail, passing through meadows and patchy woods, to a marked trailhead bordering the park entrance road at mile 7.0. Two segments of the Turkey Hollow Trail, an elongated loop, lead south from here. Take the one on the right (nearest the park road). This trail runs south before swinging west to cross the park entrance road. It arrives at the Homestead Picnic Area, the hike's end, at mile 8.2.

43 Berghum Bottoms

Highlights:	A remote walk along the Wisconsin River at the base of tall bluffs.
Location:	Southwest Wisconsin, 8 miles east of Bridgeport.
Type of hike:	Out-and-back day hike.
Total distance:	5.4 miles.
Difficulty:	Difficult.
Best months:	April–October.
Maps:	USGS Wauzeka (inc.) quad.
Finding the trailhead:	From Bridgeport, drive south 1.5 miles on Wisconsin 35 and turn left (east) on Grant County Route C. Drive 7.1 miles east and turn left (north) on Winklers Lane, a graded dirt road. Follow Winklers Lane north and east. At a residence about .75 mile after leaving County Route C, bear right (northeast) following a sandy lane along a fence line. The lane continues across a long field. Park at the end of that field, 2.7 miles after leaving County Route C.
Special considerations:	Confidence in your route-finding skills is a requirement for this hike, and the difficult rating reflects that. Use caution during hunting season.
Camping:	Wyalusing State Park, 15 miles southwest, has 110 drive-in sites.

Berghum Bottoms

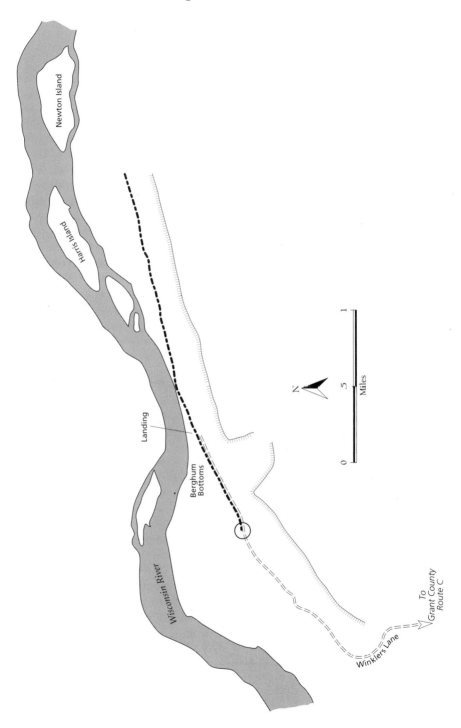

Newton Island

Harris Island

Landing

Berghum Bottoms

Wisconsin River

Winklers Lane

To
Grant County
Route C

N

Miles

0   .5   1

For more information: Wilson Nursery DNR, see Appendix B.

Key points:
  0.0   Trailhead.
  1.0   Landing on river.
  1.5   Wisconsin River swings north.
  2.7   Ravine. Turnaround point.

The hike: Berghum Bottoms, a remote stretch of river front land at the base of wooded bluffs, is one of those diamonds in the rough that a guidebook author hesitates to write up. What first caught my eye was the lack of a paved highway along the south side of the river, a rare situation in these parts.

Better yet, the Lower Wisconsin State Riverway owns 5 miles of shoreline here, as well as 1 mile inland, to the top of the bluffs and beyond. The quiet lane you drive in on is the only intrusion. When you get out of your vehicle you sense the isolation of this swath of north slope woodlands and floodplain forest. It is possible to drive a mile farther, past the starting point of the hike, along that lane. The setting is so pleasant, though, that it makes more sense to walk that mile than drive it.

Don't be overly intimidated by the difficult rating of this hike. That grade reflects the need to find a narrow path and the lack of markings. The basic direction of the route is simple and easy to describe. Walk east, with the bluffs rising to your right (south) and the river and its floodplain forest to the left (north). Keep to the base of the bluff, neither ascending to the south nor venturing onto the flood plain to the north. Use the lane, a path, and old woods roads along this route to travel to the eastern end of the property.

Begin your outing by walking east from the parking area along the lane. The lane immediately begins to traverse the bottom of the bluff's slope, offering a strong hint of this outing's ambiance. At this point, the river is a full .5 mile north, and the floodplain forest spreads out to your left. To your right, a rich oak-maple forest thrives on the shady north slope.

At the .5-mile mark, a large drainage enters from the north. The woods turn to brush for a brief moment, but as you continue east the slope and its charming forest return.

The lane splits 1 mile from the parking area. Take the right branch down to a landing on the river, a good place to pause and soak in the Wisconsin River views. Floodplain forests and wooded bluffs line the river to the east. Downstream, to the west, the river curls around a bend. Raptors and waterfowl cruise the river corridor.

Walk 120 feet inland from the water's edge. Scan the east side of the lane for a narrow but well-defined path that leads into the woods. Follow that trail east 200 feet to an old road that leads east along the base of the bluff. This old road, sometimes obvious and sometimes just a hint of its old self, is the core of your route east. Vegetation or erosion obscure it temporarily in a few places. In those spots, walk east on faint paths or through the open forest, and the old road quickly reappears.

The river runs at the bottom of the bluff for the first .5 mile after the landing, then curves north, and the floodplain forest returns. At a spot 1 mile

152

from the landing, the path and old road swing south 100 yards to avoid a gully before winding back north.

At mile 2.7 the route reaches a notable washout at the mouth of a ravine. This is a good turnaround spot. You could continue on, but the end of the state property, marked by a sign, is near. That property line runs south from a point between the river islands known as Harris and Newton.

44 Kickapoo River

Highlights:	A quiet, deep valley and headland along a fabled Wisconsin river.
Location:	Southwest Wisconsin, 2 miles north of Wauzeka.
Type of hike:	A lollipop day hike with a 1-mile off-trail segment.
Total distance:	7.3 miles.
Difficulty:	Difficult.
Best months:	April–October.
Maps:	USGS Wauzeka (inc.) quad.
Finding the trailhead:	From Wauzeka, drive east 1.8 miles on Wisconsin 60 and turn left (north) on Wisconsin 131. After driving north 1.1 miles turn left (west) into a gravel and grass parking area.
Special considerations:	Confidence in your route-finding ability is a requirement for this hike. The first 3.7 miles of this hike follow obvious but unmarked lanes. The mile that follows that stretch is off-trail. Use caution during hunting season.
For more information:	Viroqua DNR, see Appendix B.

Key points:
- 0.0 Trailhead.
- 1.6 Junction T Intersection with lane from top of bluff.
- 2.2 Junction with old railroad grade.
- 3.7 Leave railroad grade, ascend drainage to east.
- 4.3 Drainage splits, turn right (south).
- 4.8 Top of bluff, join lane to descend.
- 5.5 Junction T Intersection with lane at base of bluff (same spot as mile 1.6).
- 7.1 Trailhead.

The hike: This state-owned wildlife area, stretching from the banks of the Kickapoo River to the bluff tops, is a quiet spot that could stand a few more visitors. The setting, a quiet C-shaped valley, offers a pleasant sense of isolation due to the tall bluffs surrounding it. In the center of that C is a 300-foot-tall bluff, rounded by the Kickapoo River on three sides, that defines this hike. This hike's route rotates around the base of this headland on two of its sides, past river bottom sloughs, steep forested slopes, and sandstone cliffs before crossing the top of the ridge on its return.

153

Kickapoo River

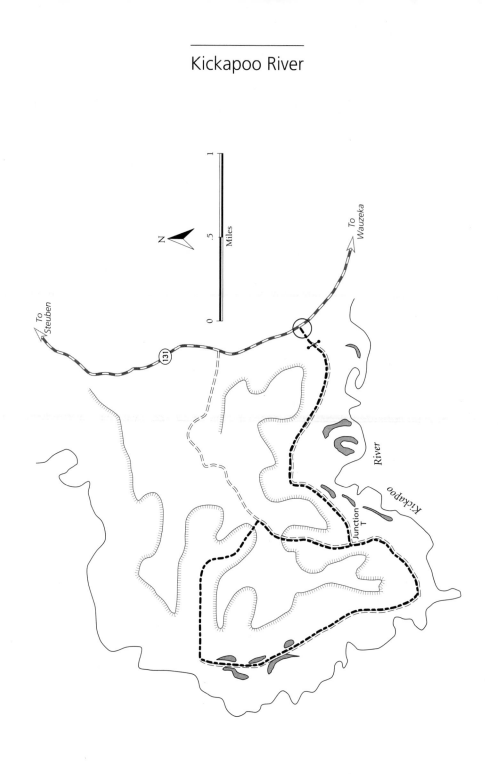

Most, but not all, of this hike consists of easy walking on unmarked but mowed lanes. A little over 1 mile of "off-trail" walking, largely on old woods roads, is necessary to complete the loop portion of this route. The navigation of that segment is straightforward: follow a drainage uphill.

Start your outing by walking west from the trailhead on a grassy lane. After a short drop to cross a small drainage, the lane wanders west, hugging the bottom of the steep, wooded slope. Watch the woods for flocks of wild turkeys in this area. On chilly mornings, they seem to seek the first direct sunlight on the south slope. To the left of the lane, the river and its sloughs lie below. At mile 1.5 two car-size boulders, droppings from a large cliff above, mark your approach to an obvious, key intersection.

That important junction, which I call Junction T for identification purposes, is at mile 1.6. Here, an old dirt road ascends a drainage to the right (north). Later in the hike, you will be descending that road from the top of the bluff on your return.

Turn left (south), and follow a faint two track, on the edge of the woods, through an old field. The wear marks become more obvious and the lane continues to the far southwest corner of the bluff at mile 2.2. What appears to be another lane but is actually an old railroad grade leads north from here. Before heading north, take a moment to walk 100 yards south toward the river to visit a clear, flowing spring. A low rock wall suggests that a spring house was once here.

Walk north on the old railroad grade among the wildlife-rich sloughs and wetlands of the flood plain. At mile 3.7 what had been pleasant passage on a mowed route ends in a jumble of brush and tall grass. Fortunately, it doesn't matter. Your return route, the mouth of a large drainage, beckons to the east.

Marshes and sloughs line the old railroad grade.

Follow a faint old road east into the wooded drainage that you will follow uphill for the next segment of the hike. Beautiful, older maple trees inhabit the north slope to your right. The ravine floor has open, pleasant woods, and for the next .6 mile it doesn't matter whether you walk on the remains of that road, follow the dry creek bed or follow your own route. Each option has a mix of smooth going and occasional rough footing.

At mile 4.3 the drainage splits into two large branches. Ignore the one that goes straight (east) and turn right (south). As you ascend the ravine the bearing goes from due south to slightly southeast. At first there is 100 yards of eroded gullies and streambed, but then an old road appears, offering an easy climb to the bluff top. This road steadily ascends the right (southwest) slope of the ravine until it emerges into an open field on the bluff top.

Cross that open field 100 yards to the southeast and you are also crossing a large spur ridge of the bluff top. Just before you hit the opposite slope, and woods, you will bump into a dirt and grass lane oriented on a southwest/northeast axis. This point is mile 4.8 of the hike. Turn right (southwest) on the lane, which soon turns south and descends from the top of the bluff to Junction T at mile 5.5. At Junction T, turn left (east) and retrace your steps from the first part of the hike to the trailhead.

Options: The first 3.7 miles of this hike follows obvious but unmarked lanes. That segment makes a fine out-and-back route for anyone who doesn't want to do the off-trail portion of the recommended hike.

45 Pine Cliff

Highlights:	Scenic cliffs dotted with notable pine trees
Location:	Southwest Wisconsin, 5 miles north of Dodgeville.
Type of hike:	Out-and-back day hike with small loop at end.
Total distance:	6.1 miles.
Difficulty:	Moderate.
Best months:	April–October.
Maps:	Governor Dodge State Park trail map, USGS Pleasant Ridge (inc.) quad.
Permits and fees:	State park vehicle sticker required.
Finding the trailhead:	From Dodgeville, drive 3.5 miles north on Wisconsin 23 and turn right (east) on the park entrance road. Drive .3 mile northeast on the entrance road, stopping to get a trail map at the park office, and turn right (southeast) on Cox Hollow Road. Follow that road a little less than 2 miles to the trailhead, the park concession at Cox Hollow Lake's dam.
Special considerations:	Pine Cliff State Natural Area extends between mile 0.5 and mile 1.0 of this hike. Treat it, and its notable plants, well.
Camping:	Governor Dodge State Park has 269 drive-in sites within a mile of the trailhead.

Pine Cliff

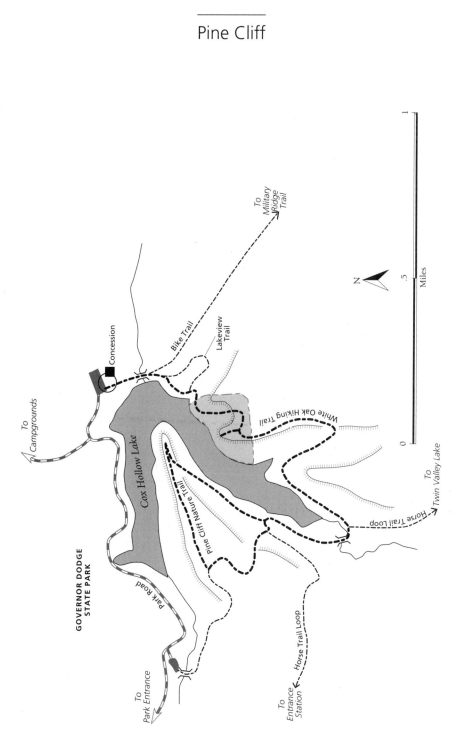

For more information: Governor Dodge State Park, see Appendix B.

Key points:
- 0.0 Trailhead at concession.
- 0.2 Split from bike trail, Lakeview Trail.
- 0.4 Lakeview Trail (return) Junction.
- 0.8 Promontory, Pine Cliff State Natural Area.
- 2.1 Horse Trail junction.
- 2.5 Pine Cliff Nature Trail Junction South.
- 3.2 Pine Cliff Nature Trail Junction North.
- 3.6 Pine Cliff Nature Trail Junction South.
- 6.1 Trailhead at concession.

The hike: Many families find Governor Dodge State Park, with its two lakes and miles of trails, an ideal place for a camping vacation. Two of those trails, the White Oak Hiking Trail and Pine Cliff Nature Trail, are near the top of the list of park attractions. Combined, they tour a state natural area: Pine Cliff, much of the south shore of Cox Hollow Lake, and miles of oak-hickory forest. This wide variety of terrain and views had no trouble holding my interest throughout the hike.

Begin your hike from the concession by walking south on the paved bike trail across the lake's outlet and up a small slope. At mile 0.2 turn right (southwest) on the White Oak Trail and a moment later right (south) again as the Lakeview Trail goes left. Follow the wide White Oak Trail south to mile 0.4, where the Lakeview Trail's broad return trail enters from the south at a small creek. Turn right (west) on the White Oak Trail, which now becomes a path.

Shortly after this intersection, you catch your first glimpse of craggy sandstone in the deep shade of huge white pines. It is a scene that seems to be from much farther north and the beginning of the Pine Cliff State Natural Area, a relic community of white, red, and jack pines. Ancient trees aren't the only stars in this show. The moist, north-facing sandstone cliffs harbor an abundance of mosses, lichens, and ferns.

The trail rounds the first outcrop, heads southwest in a shady hollow, and climbs above the cliffs. It swings north onto the next cliff top, a notable promontory. An arrow marks the trail's turn west, but a short side trip north is worthwhile. One hundred yards north the end of the spur ridge towers above the lake's waters, visible through the pine trees hugging the cliff.

Return to the White Oak Trail. It quickly turns south in a descent to the next creek, then swings north, rounding the next spur ridge at a lower level and running southwest along the lake's southernmost arm. At mile 2.1 a horse trail enters from the south and joins the White Oak Trail for about .5 a mile. Bear right (west), crossing the open, marshy valley, a good place to scan for birds.

This wide dual-purpose trail swings northeast for a bit. Where it makes a sharp, 180-degree turn inland to climb the hillside, turn right (north) at mile 2.5 on the Pine Cliff Nature Trail. This trail meanders along the lakeshore, offering views from the water's edge, then ascends to a high point near the tip of the peninsula.

Looking across Cox Hollow Lake at the Pine Cliff Nature Trail's peninsula.

The rocky high point contains another pine relic community where the main trail makes a sharp turn west, an opportunity for exploration. East of that sharp turn a rock plateau rises. Walk east, staying in the middle of the spur ridge, and a route up the low rise of rock reveals itself.

Return to the main trail, ascending steps as it rises on its westward path, then contine to an intersection, the Pine Cliff Nature Trail North Junction, at mile 3.2. Turn left (southeast). The trail rises slightly to the ridge's summit, winds southwest a bit, and then descends the ridge's south slope. It intersects the horse trail (mile 3.6) just 100 feet west of the Pine Cliff Nature Trail South Junction you saw at mile 2.5.

Turn left (east) on the horse trail. For a short distance it goes northeast, then it does a 180-degree turn to head southwest. Retrace your steps of the first part of the hike to return to the trailhead.

Options: By altering the second half of the hike you can form a 4.8-mile loop, which includes 1 mile of road walking. Do this by staying right (west) at the Pine Cliff Nature Trail North Junction at mile 3.2 of the hike. Continue west .6 mile on the segment of the nature trail that leads to the Enee Point Picnic Area. From there, walk the Cox Hollow Road east 1 mile to the trailhead, the park concession.

46 Ferry Bluff

Highlights:	Broad views of the Wisconsin River Valley from a riverside bluff.
Location:	Southern Wisconsin, 5 miles southwest of Sauk City.
Type of hike:	Out-and-back day hike.
Total distance:	.8 mile.
Difficulty:	Easy.
Best months:	April–October.
Maps:	USGS Mazomanie (inc.) quad.
Finding the trailhead:	From Sauk City, drive 6.4 miles west on Wisconsin 60 and turn left (south) on Ferry Bluff Road. Take that road southeast to mile 7.5, a riverside trailhead.
Special considerations:	Ferry Bluff is closed from November 15 to April 1 to protect wintering raptors. The viewpoint at the end of the trail is atop a sheer cliff.
Camping:	Devil's Lake State Park, 15 miles north, has 500 drive-in sites.
For more information:	Tower Hill State Park, see Appendix B.

Key points:
0.0   Trailhead.
0.4   Viewpoint at end of trail.
0.8   Trailhead.

Ferry Bluff

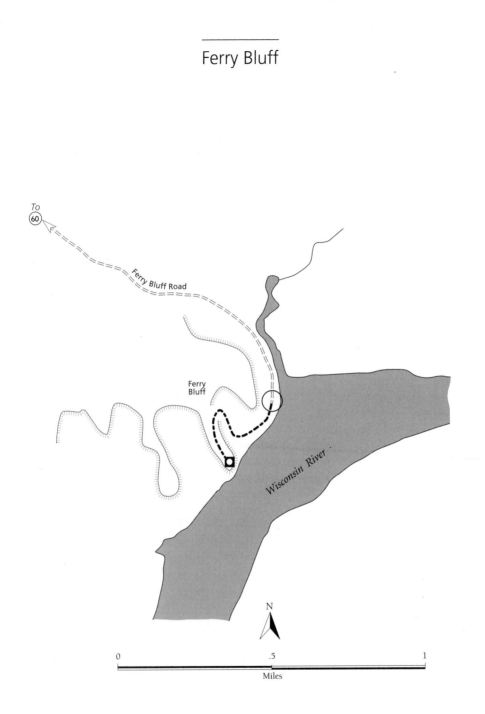

To
60

Ferry Bluff Road

Ferry
Bluff

Wisconsin River

N

0   .5   1
Miles

View from Ferry Bluff looking southwest along the Wisconsin River.

The hike: Ferry Bluff features a memorable view of the Wisconsin River Valley. Two hundred feet above the river, a wide sandstone ledge offers broad vistas, stretching to Blue Mounds, 15 miles to the south, and beyond.

Moses and Persis Laws operated a ferry boat landing near the base of the bluff during the late 1800s. Today it is a well-known canoe landing, and the short hike to the bluff-top vistas is a popular one.

From the riverside trailhead walk south on a smooth, constructed trail. When the trail nears the base of the sandstone cliffs it veers inland and begins a steady climb. The trail continues uphill to the north and then swings south to the top of the bluff. The trail continues south toward the river. A few steps farther the clutter of trees and shrubs drops away and a sweeping panorama greets you.

47 Blackhawk Ridge

Highlights:	A quiet trail system featuring hardwood forests and bluff top views of the Wisconsin River valley.
Location:	Southern Wisconsin, 20 miles northwest of Madison
Type of hike:	Out-and-back day hike. A lollipop with a second stem.
Total distance:	8.3 miles.
Difficulty:	Moderate.
Best months:	April–October.
Maps:	Lower Wisconsin State Riverway, Black Hawk Unit map, USGS Black Earth (inc.) quad.
Finding the trailhead:	From Sauk City, drive southeast .5 mile on U.S. Highway 12 and turn right (south) on Wisconsin 78. At mile 5.8 turn left (east) on Dunlap Hollow Road and at mile 6.3 turn left (north) on a dirt road for Cedar Hills Campground. Drive uphill through the private campground to the signed trailhead.
Special considerations:	Trail maps appear at several intersections on this system. However, these trails do not feature names or markings. I assigned a series of letter designations to intersections to avoid confusion.
Camping:	Cedar Hills Campground (608–795–2606), a private facility, is directly south of the trailhead and has forty drive-in sites.
For more information:	Lower Wisconsin State Riverway, see Appendix B.

Key points:

0.0	Trailhead at Cedar Hills Campground.
1.2	Junction A.
1.3	Spur junction. Spur to viewpoint.
2.2	Junction B. Wachter Road trailhead.
2.4	Junction C. Trail goes north.
2.7	Junction D. Trail descends.
2.9	Junction E. Near saddle.
3.1	Meadow viewpoint.
3.3	Junction E. Near saddle.
3.5	Junction D.
3.7	Junction F. Rope swing.
4.1	Junction G; turn west.
4.4	Junction B; turn south.
7.1	Junction A; turn south.
8.3	Trailhead at Cedar Hills Campground.

The hike: In July 1832, Fox-Sac warriors led by Chief Black Hawk ambushed pursuing soldiers on the north end of this state property. That well-executed maneuver gave 1,200 starving Fox and Sac children, women, and elders enough time to escape across the Wisconsin River.

Today, Blackhawk Ridge has a quiet trail system featuring fine views of the Wisconsin River Valley. A private campground at the trailhead offers prime

Blackhawk Ridge

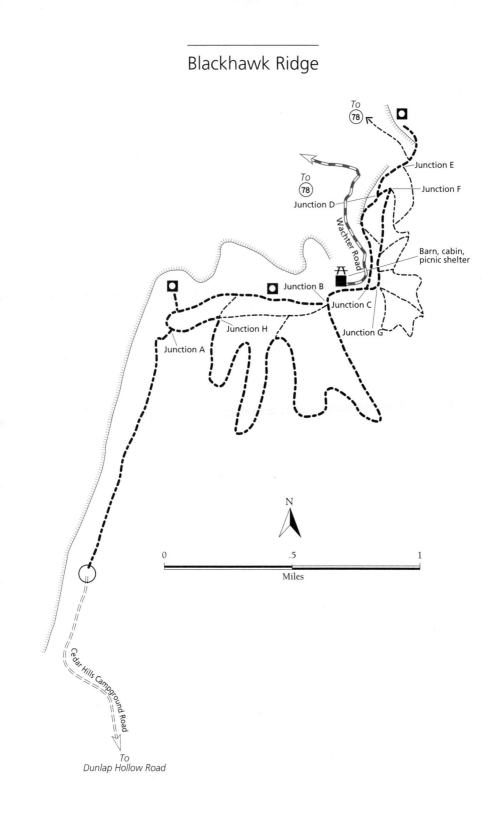

To ⑦⑧

To ⑦⑧

Junction D

Junction E

Junction F

Wachter Road

Barn, cabin, picnic shelter

Junction B

Junction C

Junction H

Junction G

Junction A

N

0   .5   1
Miles

Cedar Hills Campground Road

To
Dunlap Hollow Road

bluff-top campsites, a good base camp for exploring the trails.

Begin your hike by walking north on a gated old woods road along the crest of the bluff. About 1 mile north the trail swings around the western edge of a meadow, turns east, and intersects a north running connector trail at mile 1.2 (Junction A). Turn left (north) on this trail, entering an oak forest. Almost immediately, turn left (west) again on a trail that quickly loops around to an intersection with a viewpoint spur trail at mile 1.3.

Turn left (northwest) and walk a short distance to a fine lookout, offering long views north to the Baraboo Hills above Devil's Lake. When ready, return to the main trail and walk east, passing another viewpoint offering similar views .5 mile later. At mile 2.2 the trail emerges from the oak forest into open old fields near a barn and other structures at the end of Wachter Road. Bear left (northeast) at Junction B, walk to an obvious log cabin, and turn right (east). Walk east from the cabin and shortly after turn left (northeast) at mile 2.4 (Junction C).

Follow this trail north on the top of the slope that descends to the west. At mile 2.7 (Junction D) the trail splits. Bear left (north) as the trail descends and swings east to Junction E at mile 2.9. Turn left (northeast), quickly dropping to a saddle. Go straight (northeast), following a path uphill, where the maintained trail turns left.

This path is slightly overgrown and there are a few briar bushes ahead, but the reward is a broad view of the Wisconsin River Valley, the best of the hike. Follow the path uphill and bear left (northeast) as the path splits. Another split appears as the slope begins to level out. Bear left (north) again at this second split and walk north 100 yards to an open meadow near the top of the bluff's slope. Broad views stretch north and west to Ferry Bluff and beyond.

Return to the maintained trail and retrace your steps to Junction D. Turn left (northeast), walk a little over 100 yards, and turn right (south) at Junction F, at mile 3.7. Before going on, look for a narrow path leading north a short distance to a great rope swing dangling from a high tree branch. After checking out the swing, walk south from Junction F. Hike south through meadows studded with pine trees, going straight where a connector trail enters from the right, then two more from the left. At mile 4.1, Junction G, turn right (west) returning to the barn and other buildings at the end of Wachter Road.

Walk west through the buildings and turn left (south) at Junction B. This trail leads through old fields at the edge of woodlots, across the bluff's plateau-like top. About a mile after Junction B, ignore a connector trail coming in from the north and bear left (west), beginning another swing to the south.

The trail runs south through an oak forest, meanders north before one last, smaller surge to the south, and finally turns north to Junction H at mile 6.7. Turn left (west), following the broad trail through the woods. A short distance farther, bear left (south) at a small triangular intersection, arriving at Junction A at mile 7.1. From there, retrace your steps south to the trailhead.

Central Sandy Plain

Ten thousand years ago, Wisconsin's mighty glaciers stopped north and east of the Central Plain and began to melt. That water formed Glacial Lake Wisconsin. When the lake drained, it left a flat landscape that was a mixture of wetland and low-lying oak savannahs and pine barrens. Here and there, sandstone buttes and mesas, once islands in the glacial lake, punctuate the plain.

Today this is a remarkably quiet landscape, teeming with wildlife. Huge swaths of public land, anchored by the 150 square miles of the Central Wisconsin Conservation Area, cover most of the plain. Large parts of the central sand area are de facto wilderness. Hikers who explore the nooks and crannies of the Central Plain will find the same quiet ambiance that has drawn eight packs of wild timber wolves to raise pups here.

48 Wildcat Mound

Highlights:	A scenic ridge walk through the home turf of an active wolf pack followed by a crossing (dry) of a wildlife-rich marsh.
Location:	West central Wisconsin, 20 miles east of Black River Falls.
Type of hike:	Shuttle hike. Overnight backpack or long day hike.
Total distance:	13 miles.
Difficulty:	Difficult.
Best months:	April–August.
Maps:	Black River State Forest map, BRSF skiing and hiking trails map, USGS Hatfield Southeast and Warrens West quads.
Finding the trailhead:	From Millston, drive 4.7 miles east on Jackson County O. Turn left (north) on Smrekar Road and after another .7 mile turn right (east) into the Smrekar trailhead parking lot.
Special considerations:	The Dike Seventeen Wildlife Refuge (the last 2.8 miles of the hike) is closed from September 1 to December 15. That segment, pleasant and full of birds in early April, can be mercilessly hot in the summer. A compass is helpful for the short (.5 mile) off-trail portion at the north end of the Wildcat Trail. Water is scarce on the ridge ski trails. Note that all directions for walking on ski trail segments of this hike are in the direction of signed ski traffic except for the 1 mile of "backwards" travel on the North Trails.
Camping:	Backpack camping is allowed throughout the forest (except refuge) with free permit. Pigeon Creek Campground, 3 miles west of the trailhead, has thirty-eight drive-in sites.
For more information:	BRSF, see Appendix B.

Wildcat Mound

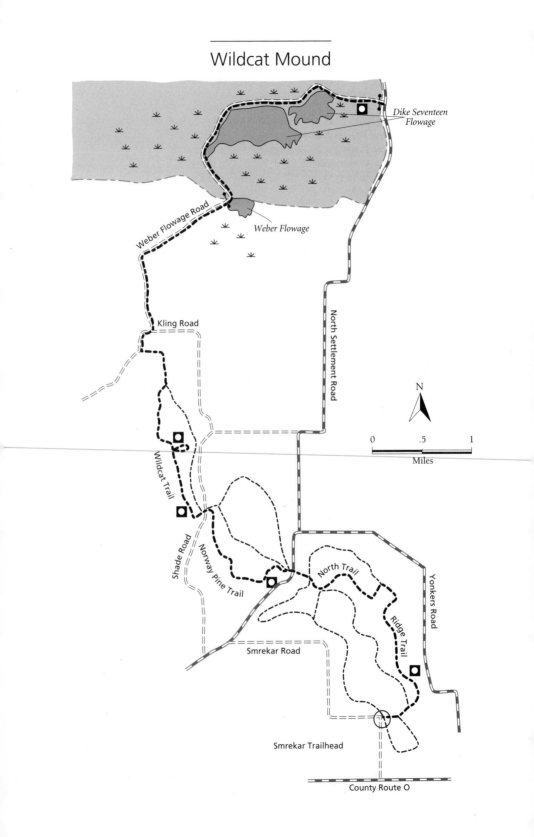

Dike Seventeen Flowage

Weber Flowage Road

Weber Flowage

Kling Road

North Settlement Road

N

0 .5 1
Miles

Wildcat Trail

Shade Road

Norway Pine Trail

North Trail

Yonkers Road

Ridge Trail

Smrekar Road

Smrekar Trailhead

County Route O

Key points:

   0.0   Smrekar parking lot.
   0.4   Ridge Trail Junction.
   2.2   North Trail Junction.
   3.2   Connector Trail Junction.
   3.4   North Settlement Road, Wildcat parking lot.
   3.7   Norway Pine Trail Junction.
   5.6   Wildcat Trail Junction/Shale Road.
   8.1   North end of Wildcat Trail.
   8.8   Kling Road Junction With Weber Flowage Road.
 10.8   Weber Flowage gate.
 13.6   Dike Seventeen Observation Tower parking lot.

The hike: Wisconsin wolf biologists made an interesting observation in the mid-1990s: The southernmost breeding pack of wild timber wolves in the lower forty-eight states was here, in the Wildcat Mound area. Unlike the Yellowstone wolves that garnered so much publicity, these wolves didn't require a multimillion-dollar federal transplant program to persuade them to migrate. They walked in on their own. Wolves prospered in the area, and by 2000 biologists counted eight packs in the central Wisconsin forest. This hike will take you through the home turf of the "pioneer" pack, the Wildcat Mound grouping.

From the south side of the Smrekar parking lot, walk east on a broad cross country ski trail toward the Ridge Trail. At mile 0.4 go straight (east) on the Ridge Trail as the Central Trail turns north. You ascend steadily through open oak forest for .2 mile before gaining the ridgetop and sampling the ambiance that will characterize much of the first half of this hike. Here, from a vantage point 200 feet higher than the trailhead, scenic views appear through openings in the trees. Benches enhance the viewpoints, and sandstone outcroppings appear by the side of the trail.

At mile 1.9 the trail plunges off the crest. At mile 2.2 make a hard left (south) going "backwards" on the North Trail. Ignore a sign that announces DO NOT ENTER for ski traffic purposes but be aware that mountain bikes use these trails. After a mile of contouring the lower slopes of the ridge, turn right (north) on the connector trail that soon takes you past North Settlement Road and the Wildcat parking lot.

Ascend the Norway Pine Trail on its "out" leg, left (west), and a bench with a view rewards you at the top of the climb. A half mile farther the ski trail plunges to the right (north) and a distinct but narrow path ascends to the west. This path takes you to a charming knoll and returns you to the main ski trail .25 mile later.

At mile 5.6 the ski trail dips to cross Shale Road. Take the Wildcat Ski Trail to the left (west) on the other side. The ascent, bench, and scenic view pattern repeats itself again and the ski trail swings north. As it rounds Wildcat Mound at mile 6.7, a scenic side trail shoots eastward .2 mile on a spur ridge. It leads to a fine view southward showing much of the ridgeline you just traveled.

Continue north on the Wildcat Trail to mile 8.1 of the hike, the northernmost point of the ski trail where it swings definitively east and a little south to begin its return route to the Shale Road crossing. This spot is in open oak forest after a small downhill drop and features an arrow and skier sign. Your next destination is the junction of Kling Road and the Weber Flowage Road; getting there requires a short and simple exercise in off-trail navigation. Proceed due north; at 130 yards you will find a faint woods road leading north. Follow that faint road north through thickening brush, and after .4 mile you will intersect another, more distinct, brushy road. Turn left (west) on this road. You will turn right (north) on Kling Road, a maintained sandy dirt road, .1 mile farther. Follow Kling Road north then east .25 mile and turn left (north) onto the Weber Flowage Road.

Follow the Weber Flowage Road north and east 2 miles through open oak and pine forest, with abundant grouse and wild turkey, to the small parking lot and gate at Weber Flowage. Round the gate and 100 yards farther on step into the wide open expanse of the Dike Seventeen Wildlife Refuge. Note Saddle Mound, a prominent hill on the east, northeast horizon; under its east end you will see the observation tower near North Settlement Road and the end of the hike.

A grassy road leads northwest through meadows thick with tall grass. As it swings north and northeast it becomes a dike road with wetlands and abundant wildlife on either side. Osprey, northern harrier, great blue heron, and sandhill cranes are often present here. A mile after the Weber Flowage gate the road turns east and follows the northern shore of Seventeen Flowage. Be sure to ascend the observation tower for a broad view of the wetlands recently crossed as well as the ridge that began your walk.

Looking south from Dike Seventeen tower at the Wildcat Mound ridge.

Options: You can start at Dike Seventeen and hike south, reversing the route. Another option would be to use the ski trails to create a very elongated loop hike. The ski trails described are part of three loop systems that allow you to return south from the Wildcat system to the Smrekar parking lot with a minimum of backtracking.

49 North Bluff

Highlights:	A wildlife-rich wetland and a high view from North Bluff.
Location:	Central Wisconsin, 2 miles west of Babcock.
Type of hike:	Out-and-back day hike.
Total distance:	7 miles.
Difficulty:	Easy.
Best months:	April–October.
Maps:	Swamp Buck Hiking Trail Map from Sandhill State Wildlife Area, USGS Quail Point Flowage (inc.) quad.
Finding the trailhead:	From Babcock, drive .8 mile southwest on Wisconsin 80 and turn right (north) on Wood County Route X. After .8 mile on County Route X, turn left (west) into the entrance area of Sandhill State Wildlife Area. Drive 1 mile on the Trumpeter Trail (a graded dirt road) and turn left into the parking area for the Swamp Buck Hiking Trail. Trail maps are in a box at the trailhead.
Special considerations:	Use caution during hunting season.
For more information:	Sandhill State Wildlife Area, see Appendix B.

Key points:
- 0.0   Trailhead.
- 0.8   Gravel road crossing.
- 1.5   Bridge over ditch.
- 2.6   Trail uses Trumpeter Trail road dike.
- 2.9   Trail crosses Trumpeter Trail road-eastern base of North Bluff.
- 3.5   Top of North Bluff.

The hike: Sandhill State Wildlife Area's abundance of wildlife and open sight lines make this one of the best wildlife viewing spots in the state. As its name indicates, sandhill cranes are a frequent visitor here, but they are far from the only attraction. Wood ducks, heron, teal, and geese are among the seasonal visitors. Otter, beaver, and timber wolves are present all year.

Start your hike by walking south from the trailhead on a gated dirt road. One aspect of the trail's layout is worth noting, a pattern that repeats itself often during the hike. The trail is in the oak and pine woods, but just barely. This routing allows a hiker to scan the open marsh and pond just to the west for birds and other wildlife while remaining hidden in the cover of the trees.

North Bluff

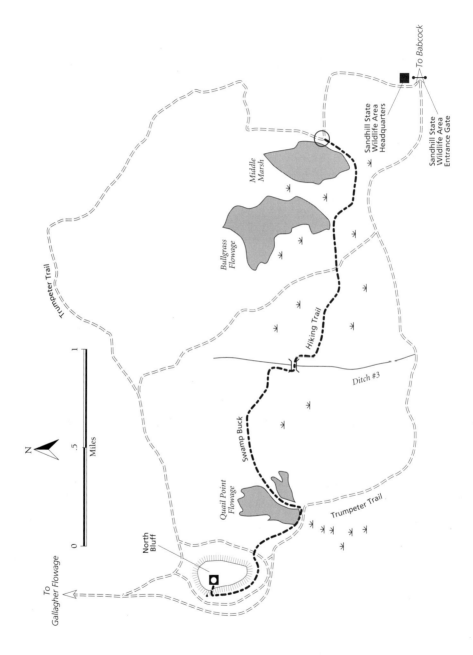

To Babcock

Sandhill State Wildlife Area Headquarters

Sandhill State Wildlife Area Entrance Gate

Middle Marsh

Bullgrass Flowage

Trumpeter Trail

Hiking Trail

Ditch #3

Swamp Buck

Quail Point Flowage

Trumpeter Trail

North Bluff

To Gallagher Flowage

N

0   .5   1

Miles

Continue walking south as the trail emerges from the woods and swings west, rounding the south end of the pond on a dike. As you reenter the woods, a sign points you northwest on a wide, grassy trail. At mile 0.8 the trail arrives at a gravel road. Go straight (west) here.

Past the road the trail becomes more of a path, with occasional wood chips in wet spots. About .5 mile after the gravel road the trail reaches a drainage ditch running in a north-south direction. Approach the ditch slowly to improve your odds of seeing muskrat or other wildlife. A sign points you north on a wide, grassy path on top of the dike bordering the ditch, and at mile 1.5 a bridge takes you to the west side of the ditch. The trail continues north on the ditch's west side for a bit, then turns west, taking boardwalks across wet spots.

As the trail emerges onto dry ground in an oak savannah, a sign points you west onto a grassy dirt road. About .25 mile farther the road swings south (ignore a skier sign pointing northwest here), eventually emerging from the woods on a dike heading southwest and intersecting the Trumpeter Trail Road at mile 2.6. Check the broad marsh to the west, Quail Point Flowage, for sandhill cranes.

Turn right (west), crossing the marsh on a dike. As you reach dry ground, a trail sign points right (north) onto a path. That path heads northwest, nears the road again, and then swings north across a field. At mile 2.9 it turns west and crosses the Trumpeter Trail Road as it runs along the base of North Bluff.

On the west side of the road the trail turns southwest in an ascending traverse of the south end of the ridge. It levels out as it reaches the bluff's west side and runs north to a small picnic area. There a trail rising from a

Boardwalk trail west of ditch #3.

172

parking area to the west leads steeply to the top of the bluff. Turn right (east) and ascend to the top.

An observation tower rises above the trees, offering sweeping views of the central plain. South Bluff's wooded slopes rise 3 miles south and Sugarloaf Mound and other buttes appear 15 miles west. To the southwest, the marshes and woods of the Central Wisconsin Conservation Area seem to stretch forever.

50 Lone Rock

Highlights:	A quiet, isolated sandstone bluff offering long views.
Location:	Central Wisconsin, 5 miles south of Adams/Friendship.
Type of hike:	Out-and-back day hike.
Total distance:	6.2 miles.
Difficulty:	Moderate to the base of the rock, difficult to the top.
Best months:	April–October.
Maps:	USGS Adams (inc.) quad.
Finding the trailhead:	From Adams/Friendship, drive 3 miles south on Wisconsin 13 and turn right (west) on Adams County Route F. Go 1.5 miles west on County Route F and turn left (south) on 14th Drive. Drive 1.2 miles south and turn right (west) into the parking area at the trailhead.
Special considerations:	Use caution during hunting season. The entire walk traverses a state natural area. Treat it well.
Camping:	Roche a Cri State Park, 8 miles north, has forty-one drive-in sites.
For more information:	DNR, Friendship, see Appendix B.

Key points:
- 0.0 Trailhead.
- 1.6 Newer snowmobile trail heads south.
- 1.8 Bridge.
- 2.7 North end of Lone Rock.
- 3.0 Intersection west of south end of Lone Rock.
- 3.1 Ascent route.

The hike: Lone Rock is an outing with a story line I like. The walk in, through pleasant oak-pine woods, is just long enough to build suspense. When the sandstone bluff finally comes into sight there is a sense of reward, of compensation for curiosity and effort. The hidden route to the top, and the long views, add to that sentiment.

Most remarkable about those views, stretching across the forested flats and buttes of central Wisconsin, is that little that is made by humans is in sight. Bluffs and mounds in Black River State Forest, some 40 miles away, show on the northwest horizon.

Lone Rock

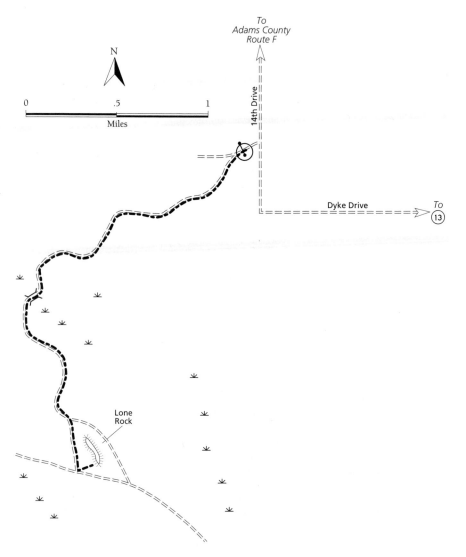

N

0   .5   1
Miles

*To
Adams County
Route F*

14th Drive

Dyke Drive   *To* (13)

Lone
Rock

Sandstone spire along ascent route up Lone Rock.

The route to Lone Rock is a marked snowmobile trail that makes for fast walking. From the trailhead, walk west past a gate on a wide grassy trail that was once a road. Just past the gate there is a split. An orange arrow points to the choice on the right, a lane going west. Ignore that arrow and take the choice on the left (southwest). This road displays the orange markings of a snowmobile trail.

Follow this road west and south through the forest, along narrow, low fingers of dry land amid wetlands. At mile 1.6 there is a notable change in your route as it turns south. At that point, the older road becomes a newer snowmobile trail, more of a winding lane.

At mile 1.8, amid a westward jog, the snowmobile trail crosses a new wood bridge over a small creek. Resuming its southward march, the trail crosses a power line, and at mile 2.7 the sharp north end of Lone Rock looms above the trees. As the butte comes into sight, there is a split. Ignore an arrow pointing left (east) to the snowmobile trail. Bear right (due south) on a lane that travels the bottom of Lone Rock's western slope. A pine plantation lines this lane to the right (west).

At mile 3.0 this lane stops at a T intersection with a dirt road, apparently untraveled by vehicles, running east-west. This point is west and a little south of the south end of Lone Rock. A lane runs northeast from this point, up the slope and through the open oak woods to the butte.

Follow the lane up to 100-foot-high cliffs. At the base of the cliffs, turn right (southeast) and walk 200 feet to a break in the walls that shows the wear marks of an impromptu path. This break, a charming, 30-foot-wide canyon, offers a way to the top that is little more than steep walking. One or two spots require high steps. There is no serious danger on the ascent route, only above, on the cliff tops.

Lone Rock's plateau-like top is pretty darn neat. A path leads around the circumference, with notable viewpoints on the west side and south end. The north end narrows to a catwalk, with sheer drops on either side. Rattlesnake Mound fills a good part of the eastern horizon, and Quincy Bluff is prominent to the southwest. Sandhill cranes bugle in the marsh below Quincy Bluff, and hawks ride the thermals rising from the promontories. When you're ready, hike back along the route you came in on to return to the trailhead.

Eastern Moraines and Lake Michigan Plain

Two glaciers, the Green Bay Lobe and the Lake Michigan Lobe, scoured Eastern Wisconsin, leaving plains and low hills in much of their path. The rock debris at what was the boundary between the two ice sheets, the tumbled topography of the Kettle Moraine country, holds renowned samples of glacial landscape forms: kames, eskers, moraines, and kettles. Marshes in the low spots offer valuable habitat for sandhill cranes, beaver, and waterfowl.

To the east, the long swath of Lake Michigan's shoreline runs north to the Door County Peninsula, where dolomite bedrock shows in coastal headlands. There lake effect climate nurtures remnant boreal forests and rare orchids. All of Lake Michigan's shoreline, Wisconsin's East Coast, is a vital migration route for raptors, shorebirds, and songbirds.

Hikers can walk the roller coaster-like terrain of the Kettle Moraine or scan for mergansers along Door County's rocky shores. Point Beach's 6-mile-long strand makes a fine walking venue for a Lake Michigan treat, a moonrise glistening on the water.

51 Eagle Bluff

Highlights:	Door County's highest bluff and a fine shoreline ramble.
Location:	Northeast Wisconsin, 2 miles west of Ephraim.
Type of hike:	Loop day hike.
Total distance:	2.1 miles.
Difficulty:	Difficult.
Best months:	April–October.
Maps:	Peninsula State Park trail map, USGS Ephraim (inc.) quad.
Permits and fees:	State park vehicle sticker required.
Finding the trailhead:	From Ephraim, drive 1.4 miles southwest on Wisconsin 42 and turn right (northwest) on Shore Road. Drive north on Shore Road to mile 2.9 and turn right (north) into the Eagle Bluff trailhead and parking area.
Special considerations:	Parts of this trail are steep and rough. Stay on the trail, both for safety reasons and to protect the fragile bluff ecosystem.
Camping:	Peninsula State Park has 469 drive-in campsites 2 miles west of the trailhead.
For more information:	Peninsula State Park, see Appendix B.

Eagle Bluff

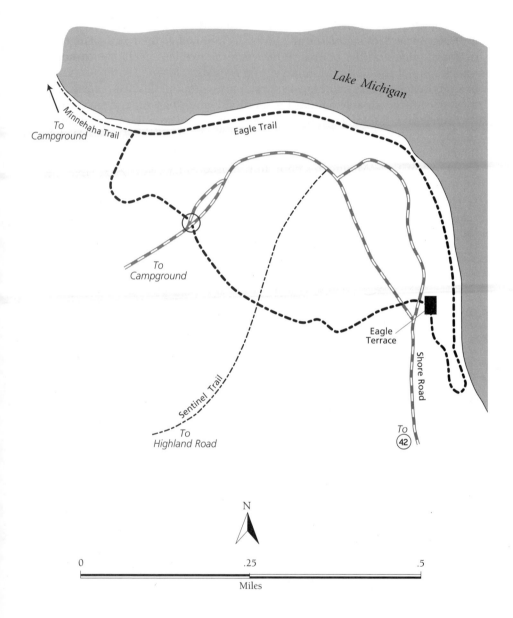

Lake Michigan

To Campground

Minnehaha Trail

Eagle Trail

To Campground

Sentinel Trail

To Highland Road

Eagle Terrace

Shore Road

To 42

N

0   .25   .5

Miles

Key points:
- 0.0 Eagle Bluff Trailhead.
- 0.2 Minnehaha Trail Junction.
- 1.5 Eagle Bluff Trail crosses Shore Road.
- 1.9 Sentinel Trail intersection.
- 2.1 Eagle Bluff Trailhead.

The hike: Peninsula State Park's Eagle Bluff Trail is a small package with a large impact. In its 2-mile length, it loops above and below the cliffs of Door County's highest bluff and samples the shoreline of Eagle Harbor. For a finale, it strolls through charming grassy glens in a beech-maple forest with birch trees scattered throughout.

Start your hike at the signed trailhead at the north end of the Eagle Bluff parking area. The trail, steep and rough at times, switchbacks its way down the slope to the north, passing birch trees, ferns, and a cliff band. At mile 0.2 the Minnehaha Trail enters from the left (west). Turn right (east) and begin a 1-mile-long traverse at the bottom of the bluff.

As the trail heads east the steep slope of the bluff above becomes a dolomite cliff. Because of the curve of the shoreline and cliff here, as well as vegetation, you never quite see the cliff as a whole here. Rather, a series of smaller scenes develops: small caves and hollows, arches, shady nooks, and a flowing spring.

Eventually the cliffs end, the slope lessens, and the trail turns west to make its ascent. Before you start up, sample the shoreline just to the east. It's rocky but welcoming and a good place to practice the fine art of Lake Michigan gazing.

Lake Michigan shoreline at the south end of the Eagle Bluff Trail.

From the shore the trail swings west and then north, ascending past rock bands to Eagle Terrace. This constructed terrace was a quarry around 1900 and later a tourist site. Ascend the steps on its west side and continue west across the parking lot to Shore Road beyond at mile 1.5.

The trail is now on the plateau-like top of the headland and continues west through a pleasant hardwood forest. Go straight (northwest) as the Sentinel Trail crosses at mile 1.9 before returning to the Eagle Bluff Trailhead at mile 2.1.

52 Deathdoor Bluff

Highlights:	A quiet viewpoint for sunset vistas.
Location:	Northeast Wisconsin, 3 miles north of Ellison Bay.
Type of hike:	Out-and-back day hike.
Total distance:	.5 mile.
Difficulty:	Easy.
Best months:	April–October.
Maps:	USGS Ellison Bay (inc.) quad.
Finding the trailhead:	From Ellison Bay, drive north on Garrett Bay Road. At mile 2.3 turn left (west) on Door Bluff Road then immediately turn right (north) at the county park sign. This road becomes gravel as it enters Door Bluff County Park. Park at the turnaround at mile 3.5.
Special considerations:	Be careful near the sheer cliff at the viewpoint.
Camping:	Peninsula State Park, 12 miles south, has 469 drive-in sites.
For more information:	Door County Parks, see Appendix B.

Deathdoor Bluff, a perfect sunset spot, overlooks Lake Michigan.

Deathdoor Bluff

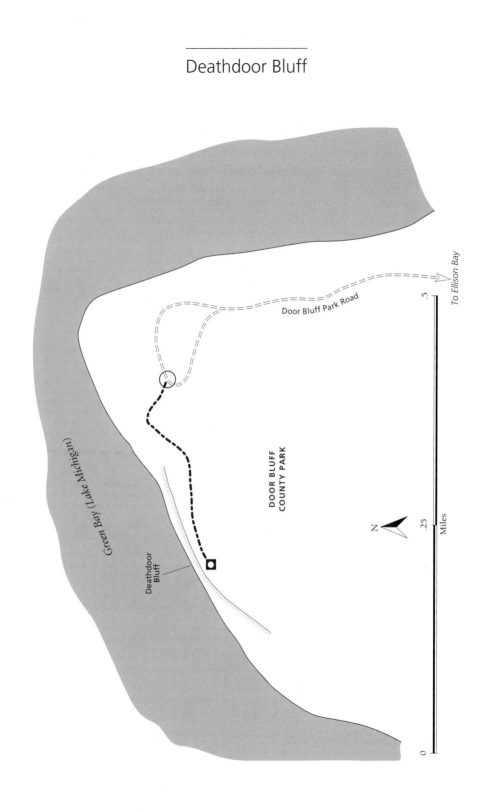

Key points:

    0.0   Trailhead.

    0.2   Deathdoor Bluff viewpoint.

The hike: Deathdoor Bluff is a classic place to be at sunset. Better yet, the short walk back to the trailhead makes lingering to the end of the show, and a twilight retreat, reasonable.

A rough, well-worn trail starts at the northwest corner of the parking loop. Follow this path northwest, first level, then descending, for ninety paces. At that point you will find yourself on the top of a small cliffband. Turn left (southwest) on a trail that soon ascends to the west. Numerous exposed roots and rocks demand your attention as you walk up this slope. To your north a steep slope becomes a cliff and an opening in the trees offers splendid north and west views across Green Bay to the Michigan shore, some 20 miles away.

53 Rock Island

Highlights:	A remote island park and lighthouse.
Location:	Northeast Wisconsin, 55 miles north of Sturgeon Bay.
Type of hike:	Loop day hike or backpack.
Total distance:	5.2 miles.
Difficulty:	Moderate.
Best months:	June–October.
Maps:	Rock Island State Park trail map, USGS Washington Island Northeast (inc.) quad.
Finding the trailhead:	Rock Island is in the far northern end of Door County. From Gills Rock, take the Washington Island Ferry (800-223-2094). On Washington Island drive north, then east about 7.5 miles on Door County Route W to Jackson Harbor. Turn left (north) on Indian Point Road .1 mile then right (east) into the Rock Island ferry parking lot.
Special considerations:	If not arriving by private boat, the only way to Rock Island is on the passenger ferry Karfi. That service (920-847-2252) runs several times a day between late May and early October, connecting Washington Island's Jackson Harbor and Rock Island. Motor vehicles are prohibited on Rock Island.
Camping:	Rock Island has thirty-five walk-in campsites within .5 mile of the dock. Five designated backpack campsites are 1 mile from the dock, along the island's southeast corner.
For more information:	Rock Island State Park, see Appendix B.

Rock Island

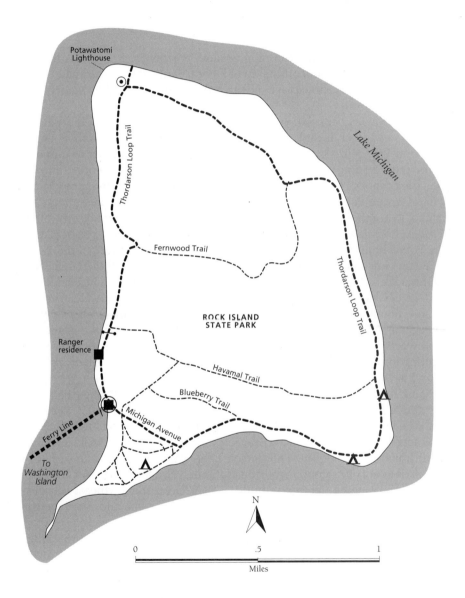

Potawatomi
Lighthouse

Lake Michigan

Thordarson Loop Trail

Fernwood Trail

Thordarson Loop Trail

ROCK ISLAND
STATE PARK

Ranger
residence

Havamal Trail

Blueberry Trail

Ferry Line

Michigan Avenue

To
Washington
Island

N

0   .5   1
Miles

Key points:
- 0.0 Dock.
- 0.3 Gate.
- 0.7 Fernwood Trail Junction West.
- 1.5 Potawatomi Light House.
- 2.4 Fernwood Trail Junction East.
- 3.7 Havamal Trail Junction.
- 4.5 Blueberry Trail Junction.
- 5.2 Dock.

The hike: State maps and common wisdom portray Rock Island as the end of the line. A small island off the tip of Door County, it is the ultimate weekend getaway and a prime place to watch the moon rise from a watery Lake Michigan horizon.

Turn the clock back 300 years and travel patterns, as well as the way humans viewed Rock Island, were significantly different. Both Native Americans and Voyageurs saw Rock Island not as the end but rather as a middle point in the trading route known as the Grand Traverse. This course allowed freighter canoes to travel from what is now Door County to Upper Michigan's Garden Peninsula. The string of islands in between, including Rock Island, guaranteed that the longest open water crossing would be only about 5 miles. Rock Island was an important rendezvous point for fur traders. Both the Potawatomi and the French had intermittent villages here in the 1700s.

Begin your tour of the island at the boat dock on its southwest side. Next to the dock is a significant distraction, the spectacular boathouse and great hall of Chester Thordarson. Thordarson, an Icelandic-born electrical inventor, bought most of Rock Island in 1910. The building, with its mythological carvings, is a notable relic of the Thordarson era on the island and well worth a visit. It is also a great place to duck out of the weather while waiting for the ferry back to Washington Island. Thordarson's heirs sold the island to the state in 1964 and it became a state park.

Walk north from the dock along the Thordarson Loop Trail past a ranger residence and up a short hill to a large, arching gate at mile 0.3. Continue walking north on the broad trail, entering the fine hardwood forest that will characterize much of the loop. Bear left (north) at mile 0.7 at the Fernwood Trail Junction (West). The Thordarson Loop Trail resumes its course north and arrives at Potawatomi Light House at mile 1.5. This stone structure, built in 1858, replaced a lighthouse built in 1836. Scan the northeast corner of the lighthouse clearing for a path that leads down stone and wood steps to the rocky beach below.

When ready, proceed to the southeast corner of the lighthouse clearing where the trail begins its run to the east. A small cemetery is nearby. After about .25 mile, an opening in the trees offers a long view to the north. On a clear day, Michigan's St. Martin Island and Garden Peninsula are easily seen.

The trail comes to the Fernwood Trail Junction (East) at mile 2.4. Turn left (northeast) and descend a short slope on a path with an abundance of rocks and roots. Shortly after the trail reaches the top of the cedar-lined shoreline cliffs and turns south, along the top of the bluff.

184

Looking northwest at the historic Potawatomi Light House on Rock Island's remote northern tip.

You will reach an old water tower and an open field offering broad lake views just before the Havamal Trail Junction at mile 3.7. Bear left (south) at the intersection, following the trail around the island's southeast corner, passing a dark cedar grove as the path swings west.

Bear left (southwest) at mile 4.5 as the Blueberry Trail cuts inland. The trail parallels the sandy shoreline here, leading into the campground area. At about mile 4.9 the trail makes a right (northeast) onto the straight grassy road known as Michigan Avenue. That route leads directly to the dock, and the end of the hike, at mile 5.2.

54 Newport State Park

Highlights:	A quiet state park featuring 11 miles of Lake Michigan shoreline and a beautiful forest.
Location:	Northeast Wisconsin, 5 miles east of Ellison Bay.
Type of hike:	A double lollipop.
Total distance:	12.2 miles.
Difficulty:	Difficult.
Best months:	April–October.
Maps:	Newport State Park trail map, USGS Spider Island (inc.) and Washington Island Southwest (inc.) quads.
Permits and fees:	State park vehicle sticker required.
Finding the trailhead:	From Ellison Bay, drive north and east 2.5 miles on Wisconsin 42 and turn right (south) on Newport Drive. After 2.6 miles turn right (south) onto the park entrance road. Drive .9 mile and stop at the entrance gate to get a trail map. Continue another .8 mile on the park road to parking lot #3, at the end of the road.
Special considerations:	The difficult rating reflects the hike's length. Newport's level ground and well-maintained trails make for fast walking. There are dispersed campsites throughout the park. Be considerate of the campers' privacy when near the campsites.
Camping:	Newport State Park has sixteen walk-in campsites.
For more information:	Newport State Park, see Appendix B.

Key points:

0.0	Parking lot #3 trailhead.
0.1	Beach, Europe Bay Trail.
1.3	Europe Bay Trail splits.
2.0	Europe Bay Trail rejoins.
2.1	Europe Bay Road.
3.4	Europe Bay Trail turns inland.
3.7	Hotz Trail Junction.
5.1	Europe Bay Road.
7.1	Beach.
7.2	Newport Trail. Parking Lot #3 Trailhead.
7.5	Sand Cove Trail Junction.
8.5	Newport Trail Junction.
9.6	Ridge Tail Junction.
10.0	Rowley's Bay Trail Junction (South).
10.7	Rowley's Bay Trail Junction (North).
11.9	Newport Trail Junction.
12.2	Parking Lot #3 Trailhead.

The hike: When it comes to finding a long walk along the state's Lake Michigan shore, this route is in the running for top honors. Newport State Park gets a thumbs up for its size, with its 11 miles of shoreline and 20 miles of

Newport State Park

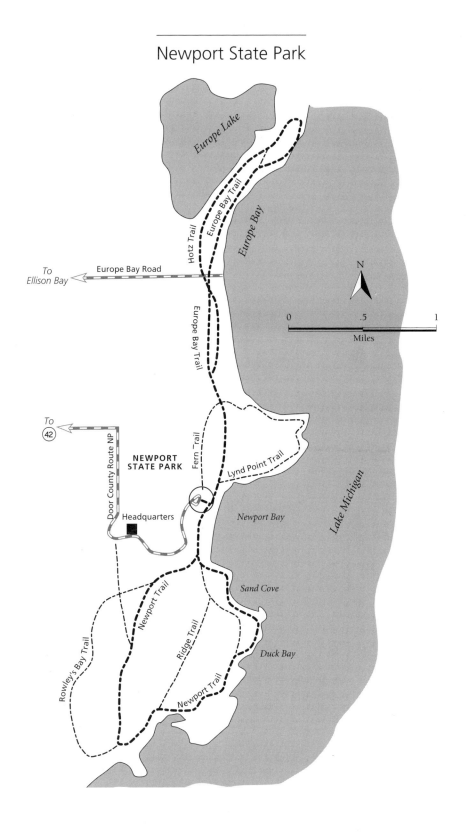

trail. Best of all, this place has ambiance. The shoreline is a quiet one and the forest is a notable beauty. Development at the park is minimal and likely to stay that way; the area has semi-wilderness status. This hike's route takes you first to Newport's north end, back past the trailhead, and then to the park's southern part.

Start the hike by walking due east 200 yards from the trailhead toward the lake. In the last low dunes before the beach, a sign indicates where the Europe Bay Trail heads north. Turn left (north) and follow that broad route north into the woods. At mile 1.3 take the right (north) choice as the trail splits into a narrow loop.

Bear right (north) at mile 2.0 as the trail's two branches rejoin. Cross Europe Bay Road at mile 2.1 and walk north. The trail skirts the edge of the woods just off the beach for a short distance then runs slightly inland. It then returns to the shoreline for a scenic .5-mile-long stretch, a fitting ending for its northward leg. A bench with prime lake views and small rock ledges decorate the shoreline stretch.

Just after a small rock chasm, the Europe Bay Trail turns west (inland) and then south. Bear right (southwest) on the Hotz Trail at mile 3.7. The Hotz Trail travels south, ascending and descending small ridges along the eastern shore of Europe Lake.

At mile 5.1 the Hotz Trail passes beneath a charming stone archway, part of a constructed gate from a previous landowner, next to Europe Bay Road. Turn left (east) there at mile 5.1 and walk 50 yards east on the road to meet the Europe Bay Trail. Turn right (south) on the Europe Bay Trail to return to the trailhead to begin the second half of the hike. Just south of Europe Bay Road, bear right (south), taking the westward option of the trail loop on your return trip.

From the trailhead at mile 7.2 of the hike, walk south on the broad Newport Trail. Bear left (south) as the Newport Trail splits at mile 7.5. Fifteen feet south of that first split you come to another intersection. Turn left (east) there at the sign that reads SAND COVE, DUCK BAY. Follow that trail as it winds around rocky points and small coves to an intersection with the Newport Trail at mile 8.5. Turn left (south) on the Newport Trail, walking first near the lake then inland as the trail cuts across a small peninsula.

Bear left (south) at an intersection with the Ridge Trail at mile 9.6. Continue walking south and turn right (north) at mile 10.0 at an intersection with the Rowley's Bay Trail. The Rowley's Bay Trail and Newport Trail share a common path as they leave that intersection and roll north through a beautiful maple forest. Bear right (north) as the two trails split at mile 10.7 and follow the Newport Trail northeast to a junction at mile 11.9. Bear left (north), retracing your steps of the first part of the southern leg of the hike, back to the trailhead at mile 12.2.

Options: The north and south segments of the recommended hike are fine outings on their own. The northern hike would be 7 miles long and the southern route 5 miles in length.

Beautiful forest and shoreline scenes alternate along the Europe Bay Trail.

55 Ridges

Highlights:	A nature sanctuary notable for its unusual habitats.
Location:	Northeast Wisconsin, 1 mile north of Bailey's Harbor.
Type of hike:	Loop day hike.
Total distance:	2.1 miles.
Difficulty:	Easy.
Best months:	April–October.
Maps:	Trail Guide ($2) from The Ridges Sanctuary, Inc. (see Appendix B), USGS Bailey's Harbor East (inc.) quad.
Permits and fees:	A $2 trail fee for adults is in effect here.
Finding the trailhead:	From Bailey's Harbor, drive .5 mile north on Wisconsin 57 and turn right (northeast) on Door County Route Q. After .1 mile turn right (southeast) into the Ridges Sanctuary entrance. Park there.
Special considerations:	This is a private nature sanctuary protecting rare habitat and plants. Treat it well. Stop at the nature center, register, and read the rules.
Camping:	There are 469 drive-in sites at Peninsula State Park, 7 miles northwest.
For more information:	The Ridges Sanctuary, see Appendix B.

Key points:
- 0.0   Nature center trailhead.
- 0.4   Bailey's Harbor beach.
- 0.5   Turn right (east) on Sandy Trail.
- 0.6   Turn left (north) on connector trail.
- 0.8   Turn right (east) on Winter Wren Trail.
- 0.8   Turn right (southeast) on Labrador Trail.
- 1.5   Spur trail to observation platform.
- 1.6   Spur trail to Solitude Swale.
- 2.1   Nature center trailhead.

The hike: Lake Michigan's influence seems to be everywhere at the Ridges. The lines of the landscape itself, the "Ridges," are crescent-shaped linear sand dunes, arranged in chronological order. Thirty in number, they also took an average of thirty years each to form. Between the dunes is a series of swales, narrow wetlands paralleling the sand ridges. This is all part of a habitat so notable that it became Wisconsin's first state natural area in 1967. Thirteen rare plant species are present. More than twenty-five native orchids bloom here, a primary motivation in the original preservation drive.

Lake Michigan still holds the key to the Ridges ecosystem. The Ridges boreal forest has an effective moat in Bailey's Harbor. The chilly waters protect the flora, remnants from a cooler era, from hot southern breezes.

Begin by walking west from the parking lot to the trailhead nature center. From the nature center, walk southeast a short distance and turn right (southwest) on the Spruce Trail. Follow that trail southwest, past a notable 120-year-old spruce tree with a double trunk.

Ridges

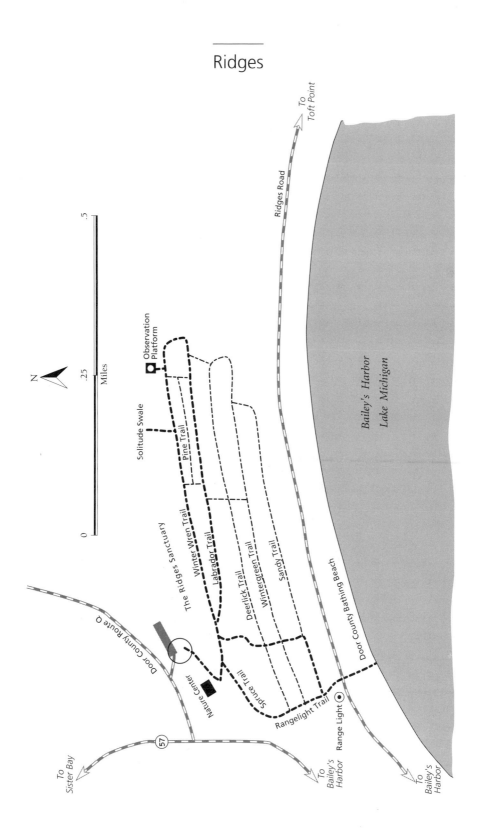

N

0   .25   .5
Miles

To Toft Point

Ridges Road

Bailey's Harbor
Lake Michigan

Solitude Swale

Observation Platform

Pine Trail

The Ridges Sanctuary

Winter Wren Trail

Labrador Trail

Deerlick Trail

Wintergreen Trail

Sandy Trail

Door County Bathing Beach

Door County Route Q

Nature Center

Spruce Trail

Rangelight Trail

Range Light

57

To Sister Bay

To Bailey's Harbor

To Bailey's Harbor

A long swale stretches east from the observation platform.

In less than .25 mile the trail turns south, becoming the Rangelight Trail. Ahead of you at the end of a long straight section is one of two of the original Rangelights that sailors used to safely navigate the rocky waters into the harbor.

Walk south across Ridges Road to the beach, and you are standing on the youngest ridge. When you are ready to continue, hike back to the north, pass the Rangelight, and turn right (east) on the Sandy Trail at mile 0.5 of the hike.

Hike east on the Sandy Trail along one of the ridges and past notable white pines. Turn left (north) at mile 0.6 onto a connector trail, crossing swales on boardwalks and going straight (north) at intersections with the Wintergreen and Deerlick Trails.

Turn right (east) at the intersection with the Winter Wren Trail at mile 0.8 and turn right again (southeast) shortly after that on the Labrador Trail. Follow that path as it meanders east .5 mile along one of the sand dune ridges. It finally turns north, crosses a boardwalk, and swings west to become the Winter Wren Trail.

At mile 1.5 turn right (north) on a short spur to an observation platform extending into one of the linear wetlands. A long, open swale extends east in a gentle arc that extends .5 mile from the observation platform. It is a rare visual corridor in the Ridges' boreal forest.

Return to the main trail and continue west to another spur at mile 1.6. Turn right (north) and walk over the boardwalk to Solitude Swale, an aptly named destination that is the farthest north part of the trail system. A bird blind there invites you to linger quietly.

From the Solitude Swale spur trail, walk west on the Winter Wren Trail to return to the nature center trailhead at mile 2.1.

56 Moonlight Bay

Highlights:	A magnificent shoreline ramble that begins in a noted boreal forest.
Location:	Northeast Wisconsin, 2 miles east of Bailey's Harbor.
Type of hike:	Loop day hike.
Total distance:	5.4 miles.
Difficulty:	Moderate.
Best months:	May–October.
Maps:	USGS Bailey's Harbor quad.
Finding the trailhead:	From Bailey's Harbor, drive north then east on Ridges Road. After 1.5 miles (where Ridges Road starts to turn south) turn left (northeast) on a shaded dirt and gravel lane. Go .2 mile to a gate and sign for the Toft Point Natural Area. Pullouts here will accommodate about six vehicles.
Camping:	Peninsula State Park has 469 drive-in sites, 7 miles northwest of the trailhead.
Special considerations:	The shoreline, off-trail segment of this hike could be hazardous under adverse conditions (storm surges, high water, or shore ice). If water levels are high, rounding the two bays described as dry might require some bushwhacking. Toft Point is a state natural area. Treat it well.
For more information:	College of Environmental Studies, UW–Green Bay, 2420 Nicolet Drive, Green Bay, WI 54301; (920) 465–2371.

Key points:

0.0   Gate, Toft Point Natural Area sign.
0.8   Old Toft resort buildings.
1.9   Tip of small, north-facing peninsula.
2.9   Southeast point of shoreline.
3.8   Southern tip of Toft Point peninsula.
4.2   Join Lighthouse Point Drive, walk north.
5.4   Return to gate

The hike: Few moderate loop hikes in this book can match this walk for its combination of intimate forest and Lake Michigan views. Most of this walk takes place within the Toft Point State Natural Area, a 700-acre preserve notable for its remnant boreal forest of balsam fir and white spruce as well as its shoreline.

Walk past the gate (northeast) on a smooth, shaded dirt road. After .5 mile you will see an opening to the north as a broad sedge meadow appears and extends to the edge of Moonlight Bay. Shortly after that the first buildings of the old Toft resort come into sight amid an overgrown meadow area. Past the last of the cabins the road reenters the woods and stops at the rocky eastern shore of the peninsula. As you step through the trees to the water's edge

Moonlight Bay

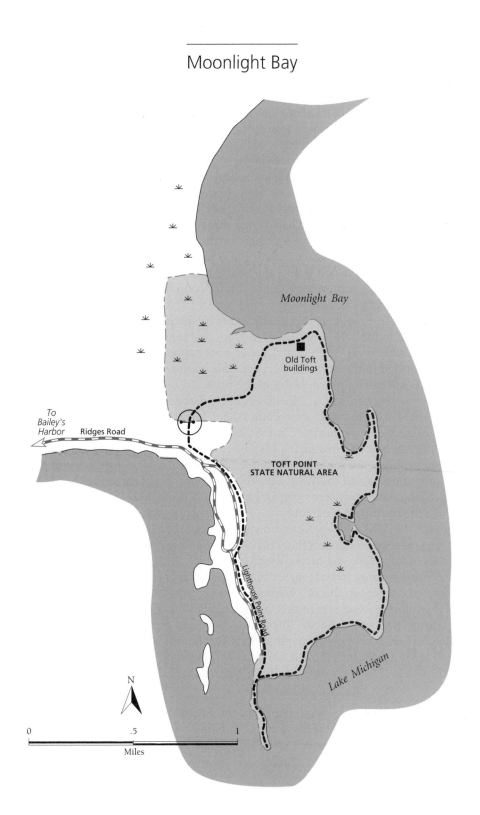

Moonlight Bay

Old Toft buildings

To Bailey's Harbor   Ridges Road

TOFT POINT STATE NATURAL AREA

Lighthouse Point Road

Lake Michigan

N

0   .5   1

Miles

you will see the beginning of the shoreline route you will follow for the next 3 miles.

The open lake is a striking sight after traversing the forest. Certainly the woods are charming in their own quiet sense, and a short distance inland mossy rocks mark an ancient shoreline. But here, next to the blue water of Lake Michigan, your senses leap from the foreground to the horizon amid wind, waves, and wildflowers.

If there is one outstanding characteristic of this hike, it is this: the juxtaposition of the micro and the macro. The relationship between forest and lake begins that theme, and the intricate shoreline continues it with style. Broad lake views are constantly in sight, while the convoluted texture of the coast leaves you constantly wondering what is around the next bend.

Two possible routes offer a choice for the next segment. A path just inside the shoreline trees leads south for .5 mile. You can follow that trail or stay on the rocky bench that is the shore. Many of the individual rocks on the shoreline are flat, and the footing varies from remarkably smooth to occasionally tedious.

Either way, .5 mile farther south you meet a north-facing bay, just as the path ends. I found the bay a dried-out flat, half sand and half dry mud, easy and pleasant travel. With higher water, you may have to bushwhack a little to get around to the north-facing peninsula on the east of the bay, your next goal. Its northern tip is mile 1.9 of the walk.

As you proceed south, Moonlight Bay broadens into the open water of the lake. Far to the northeast Cana Island Lighthouse, looking like a faint white candle on the horizon, comes into view.

Another bay, this one facing east, has a bottom as dry as the last but with considerably more rocks to assure passage. Your route continues south and at mile 2.9 turns to the west with the shoreline. The lake is rowdier here, reflecting your position on the end of the Toft Peninsula.

To the southwest a narrow spit of rocks, shrubs, and trees sticks .25 mile out into the lake and is well worth visiting. Since you left the forest you have been traversing a domain that changes hands often, sometimes land, sometimes water. Now you arrive literally at land's end, a culmination of your shoreline journey. When you sit on the tip of this peninsula, little more than a gravel bar, water almost surrounds you.

Just northeast of where this subpeninsula joins the mainland is a small parking lot east of a house. Turn north here and pick up Lighthouse Point Road where it changes from paved to gravel (at mile 4.2). Walk 1 mile north and make a right turn (northeast) into the shady lane you parked on; the gate is less than .25 mile farther. Halfway along this road walk, Lighthouse Point Road becomes Ridges Road.

Options: The 2-mile round trip from the gate to the old Toft buildings and the scenic shoreline beyond is an outstanding, easy out-and-back walk. Accessing any of the southern shoreline of Toft Point from Lighthouse Point Road is also an excellent outing.

Toft Point's eastern shore, a magnificent shoreline route.

57 Point Beach

Highlights:	A charming forest and miles of Lake Michigan beach.
Location:	Eastern Wisconsin, 10 miles northeast of Manitowoc.
Type of hike:	A lollipop day hike.
Total distance:	8.7 miles.
Difficulty:	Moderate.
Best months:	April–October.
Maps:	Point Beach State Forest trail map, USGS Two Rivers (inc.) quad.
Permits and fees:	State park vehicle sticker required.
Camping:	There are 127 drive-in sites just north of the trailhead.
Finding the trailhead:	From Two Rivers, take Manitowoc County Route O north. At mile 5.1 turn right (east) into Point Beach State Forest. Park at mile 5.4, just past the entrance station. Toilets and water are nearby.
For more information:	Point Beach State Forest, see Appendix B.

Key points:
- 0.0   Entrance station.
- 0.8   Begin Ridges Trail.
- 2.8   Molash Creek crossing.
- 4.8   Silver Creek (turn around).
- 6.8   Molash Creek crossing.
- 8.7   Entrance station.

The hike: Nowhere else on Wisconsin's Lake Michigan shoreline is there anything quite like Point Beach State Forest. Here 6 scenic miles of undeveloped sand beach border a quiet forest accented with string bogs. A well-marked system of hiking trails offers routes of different lengths through the shade of the woods while the wide open spaces of the shore beckon beachcombers. The beach segment of the hike may be mercilessly hot in the middle of a summer day. Conversely, it makes a splendid evening or moonlight walk.

From the entrance station walk west 140 yards on the entrance road. At that point turn left (south) on a broad trail (the "red" trail) marked ONE WAY, DO NOT ENTER for ski traffic purposes. Continue south .7 mile and go right (west) 50 feet on an unpaved road. Turn left (south) on the broad Ridges Trail. The "Ridge" is actually a long, low dune, a remnant of an ancient shoreline of Lake Michigan. This is typical of the topography here, linear sand ridges alternating with string bogs.

Just before you come to a paved road at mile 1.7 a cutoff trail goes left (east) over a boardwalk. Cross the road and proceed south on the Ridges Trail (also marked as the "yellow" ski loop at this area). At mile 2.4, at a spot marked by a trail map, the now-mossy yellow trail swings east as a narrow path continues south. Molash Creek, broad and marshy, appears to your south as the

Point Beach

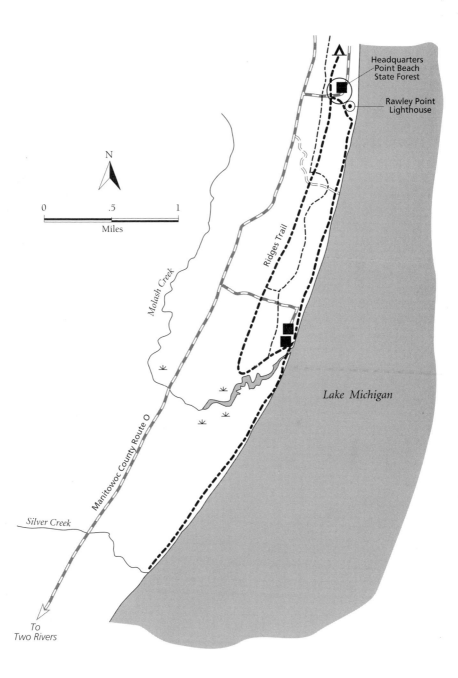

Headquarters
Point Beach
State Forest

Rawley Point
Lighthouse

N

0   .5   1
Miles

Molash Creek

Ridges Trail

Lake Michigan

Manitowoc County Route O

Silver Creek

To
Two Rivers

pathway swings to a more northeasterly direction. At mile 2.7 the woods begin to open as the trail enters the transition zone between forest and the open beach of the lake shore. Leave the maintained trail on any of several narrow footpaths that take you east 100 yards to Lake Michigan's sandy shore. Stay on the path to avoid damaging the fragile dune environment, home of rare plants. This is a good spot to contemplate the ebb and flow of Point Beach's topography. Both the forest you recently left and the beach you stand on owe their defining characteristics to the cumulative effects of the wind, waves, and sand of Lake Michigan.

At this point you are either already at the mouth of Molash Creek (mile 2.8) or slightly north of it. Turn south and cross the stream. At the lake's shoreline the creek is usually only a few feet wide and easily negotiated by a jump or a short easy wade. A few minutes' walk south of Molash Creek offers views of a breakwater in Two Rivers and Manitowoc's tallest buildings on the far off horizon. Continue walking south on the beach for 2 miles.

A low spot in the dunes is often the only sign that you are at the mouth of Silver Creek (mile 4.8) because the creek's water often disappears in the sand 100 feet short of the lake. Silver Creek is a logical spot to end your southward beach walk and turn north. Retrace your steps to Molash Creek (mile 6.8), again negotiate passage, and walk the beach north. Several buildings, part of an indoor group camp, appear at the edge of the trees.

Rawley Point Lighthouse marks the end of your walk. This 113-foot-tall steel tower sports one of the largest and brightest lights in the Great Lakes, visible up to 19 miles away. Leave the beach and follow a path just south of the lighthouse to the entrance gate.

Along Point Beach's Lake Michigan shoreline at the mouth of Molash Creek.

Options: You could eliminate the southern beach out-and-back segment and the hike would become a 4.7-mile loop. If it was too hot to walk the beach, you could stick to the ski trails for a shaded 4.5-mile loop. The cutoff trails at mile 0.8 and mile 1.7 of the recommended hike offer additional opportunities to adjust the hike's length.

58 Emmons Creek

Highlights:	A delightful trout stream and oak forests.
Location:	East central Wisconsin, 5 miles west of Waupaca.
Type of hike:	Lollipop day hike.
Total distance:	6.8 miles.
Difficulty:	Moderate.
Best months:	April–October.
Maps:	Ice Age Trail Foundation segment map #43, Hartman Creek State Park trail map, USGS Blaine (inc.) and King (inc.) quads.
Permits and fees:	State park vehicle sticker required.
Finding the trailhead:	From Waupaca, drive 5 miles west on Wisconsin 54 and turn left (south) on Hartman Creek Road. Drive 2 miles south to the Hartman Creek State Park entrance station. Obtain a trail map there and continue south another .5 mile to Windfeldt Lane. Turn right (west) and drive .5 mile to where the Ice Age Trail crosses the road. Park in the far southwest corner of the campground just to the northeast of this trail crossing.
Camping:	Hartman Creek State Park has 101 drive-in sites adjacent to the trailhead.
For more information:	Ice Age Trail Park and Trail Foundation, Hartman Creek State Park, see Appendix B.

Key points:
- 0.0 Windfeldt Lane.
- 0.5 High Point.
- 1.8 Emmons Creek Road.
- 2.4 Stratton Lake Road.
- 2.5 Far Away Valley Loop North Junction.
- 2.7 Emmons Creek Foot Bridge.
- 3.1 Far Away Valley Loop South Junction.
- 3.8 3rd Avenue/Emmons Creek Bridge.
- 4.3 Far Away Valley Loop North Junction.
- 6.8 Windfeldt Lane.

The hike: Hartman Creek State Park, with its quiet lakes, is a popular spot for weekend and vacation camping. This hike takes you away from the well-known areas of the park into its quiet southwest corner and on

Emmons Creek

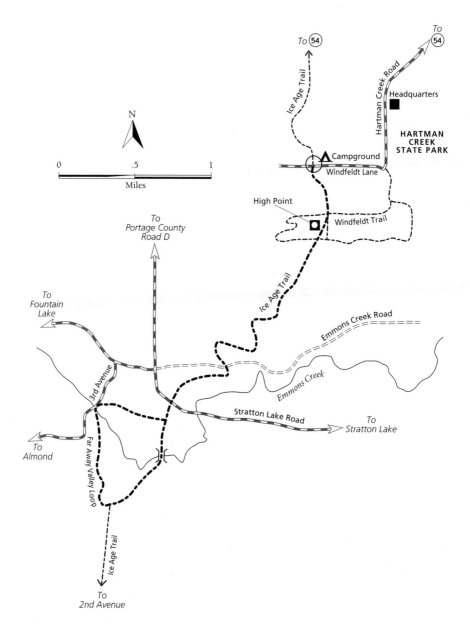

to the Emmons Creek Fishery and Wildlife Area. It's a pleasant walk through an oak forest sprinkled with an occasional pine plantation or meadow-like old field to the star of the show, Emmons Creek. That clear-running stream brightened my day. A bench, dedicated to Aldo Leopold, aids contemplation.

Begin the hike by walking south from Windfeldt Lane on the Ice Age Trail. It is a wide trail and marked with yellow paint blazes as it winds through an open oak forest dotted with pines. Almost immediately two left turns, first south, then east, bring the trail onto an overgrown field. The field gives way to a patch of woods, and another field follows.

Two intersections in this open stretch feature maps. Go straight (south) at the first one and right (west) at the second one, leading to a low knoll featuring a bench that could seat twenty hikers. This spot, shown on park maps as High Point, offers views of the surrounding fields and meadows. Hawks circle above, scanning for their next meal.

Resume walking southwest on the well-marked Ice Age Trail, now in woods. A short distance farther, go straight (south) at an intersection with a ski and bike trail. This junction, complete with map, is the last of the cluster of trails just south of Windfeldt Lane.

The trail, now a 2-foot-wide path, winds south through open oak forest, passing a sign that announces the Emmons Creek Fish and Wildlife Area near a short stretch of pine plantation. A grove of older white pines sits on the top of a short, sharp rise. At mile 1.8 the trail crosses Emmons Creek Road and shortly after that swings west on top of a ridge. The trail, a grassy old road here, runs through pine plantations before descending southward to Stratton Lake Road at mile 2.4.

Walk south across the road and through the open meadows and fields beyond. Watch for harriers here. Harriers, unlike other members of the hawk family, do not circle and scan from on high. They cruise close to the ground, taking their prey by surprise.

The trail reaches the Far Away Valley Loop North Junction at mile 2.5. Bear left (south) here, continuing on the main Ice Age Trail to the bridge over Emmons Creek at mile 2.7. A bench here makes an appealing break spot.

Emmons is a beautiful, clear stream, 10 feet wide and running between grassy hummocks and marsh marigolds blooming in April. Trout, rising for insects, dimple the surface. A boardwalk takes the trail southwest, slightly away from the creek.

The stream is again close to the trail .25 mile farther on and 100 feet down a slope to the northwest. It's well worth dodging a few bushes to make your way down to the creek and soak in the scene. Seeps and springs are abundant at the bottom of the slope, so be careful to step on the solid grass hummock areas.

When you are ready, continue walking southwest on the Ice Age Trail, reaching the Far Away Valley Loop South Junction at mile 3.1. Turn right (west), following the green blazes of that trail as the Ice Age Trail (yellow blazes) goes south. The Far Away Valley Trail meanders northwest, through scrub oaks and occasional lichen.

Emmons Creek, along the Far Away Valley Loop Trail.

The creek appears again on your right (east) and a moment later you reach 3rd Avenue and a bridge over Emmons Creek at mile 3.8. Turn right (northeast), crossing the bridge, and a moment later turn right (east) on a marked path. Walk east, passing through a pine plantation and then the open fields leading to the Far Away Valley Loop North Junction at mile 4.3. At that intersection you join the main Ice Age Trail (yellow blazes) by turning left (north) to retrace your steps back to Windfeldt Lane.

59 Devil's Lake East Bluff

Highlights:	Sweeping views of Devil's Lake, notable rock formations, and hardwood forest.
Location:	Southern Wisconsin, 3 miles south of Baraboo.
Type of hike:	Loop day hike.
Total distance:	4.4 miles.
Difficulty:	Difficult.
Best months:	April–October.
Maps:	Devil's Lake State Park trail map, USGS Baraboo (inc.) quad.
Permits and fees:	State park vehicle sticker required.
Finding the trailhead:	From Sauk City, drive north 11.3 miles on U.S. Highway 12 and turn right (east) on Ski Hi Road. At mile 12.6 turn left (north) on South Shore Road, then make a right turn (east) on Park Road at mile 13.8. At mile 14.0 turn right (southeast) into the park. An entrance station at mile 14.8 offers a chance to gather trail maps. Continue east past railroad tracks and at mile 15.0 turn right (southeast) on a park road that leads to parking at mile 15.2, with the trailhead directly to the east.
Special considerations:	Trails traverse rock sections that become very slick when wet. This hike is not a good choice for acrophobics.
Camping:	Devil's Lake State Park has 535 drive-in campsites.
For more information:	Devil's Lake State Park, see Appendix B.

Key points:
0.0 East Bluff Trailhead.
1.1 Balanced Rock Trail.
1.5 Grottos Trail.
2.2 CCC Trail.
3.0 Devil's Doorway Spur.
3.3 East Bluff Woods Trail.
4.6 East Bluff Trailhead.

The hike: Spring-fed Devil's Lake occupies a scenic gap in the South Range of the Baraboo Hills. With three 500-foot bluffs rising from its shores and notable rock formations on the bluff tops, it has attracted visitors for centuries. This route samples the best that Devil's Lake has to offer while ascending and descending the spectacular East Bluff twice. These attractive trails are not a secret, and on a fine weekend day you should expect to see many other visitors.

Begin your hike by walking east from the trailhead on the broad dirt road that is the beginning of the East Bluff Trail. The trail immediately swings to the southeast and a split occurs. The dirt road continues southeast as the East Bluff Woods (yellow) Trail. Take the right (south) choice and climb the

Devil's Lake East Bluff

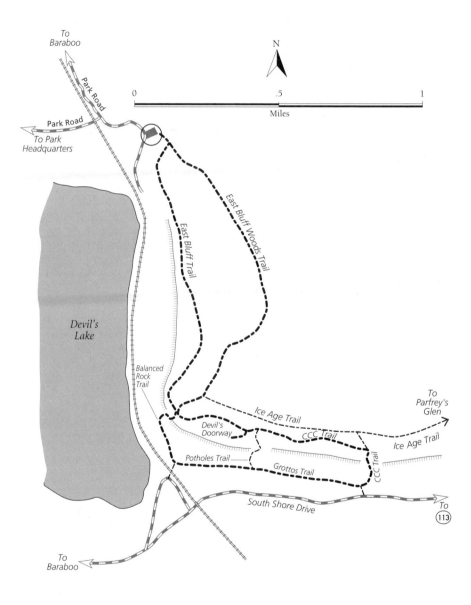

To
Baraboo

N

Park Road

Park Road

To Park
Headquarters

0   .5   1

Miles

East Bluff Woods Trail

East Bluff Trail

Devil's
Lake

Balanced
Rock
Trail

Ice Age Trail

To
Parfrey's
Glen

Devil's
Doorway

CCC Trail

Ice Age Trail

Potholes Trail

Grottos Trail

CCC Trail

South Shore Drive

To
113

To
Baraboo

constructed stone steps and asphalt of the East Bluffs (orange) Trail as it ascends through a beautiful hardwood forest.

For the next mile the trail winds between the forest and the rock outcrops that mark the edge of the escarpment while climbing to the top of the East Bluff. Along the way, numerous viewpoints offer broad views of the lake below and the West Bluff on its far shore.

At mile 1.1 the East Bluff Trail intersects the Balanced Rock Trail. Turn right (west) and begin a memorable, steep descent over talus and cemented rock steps. Halfway down, the route passes the trail's namesake boulder.

Shortly after the Balanced Rock Trail finally leaves its chaotic rock route for the security of dirt and the valley floor, it intersects the Grottos Trail at mile 1.5. Turn left (east) and take this broad path through an oak forest as it parallels the rock debris at the base of the bluff's slope.

Turn left (north) on the CCC Trail at mile 2.2 as it steeply ascends the bluff on rock steps. Near the top it snakes through several cliff bands before swinging left to follow the top of the escarpment west. At mile 3.0 a short trail to the left (south) leads to one of the most famous rock formations, the Devil's Doorway. The 100-yard spur leads down stone steps and across a broad rock ledge to the best vantage point for viewing this natural stone arch.

Return to the main path and walk west to the intersection with the Balanced Rocks Trail at mile 3.3. Turn right (north) on a broad jeep road, a route for emergency vehicles. Shortly after swing left (north), ignoring the jeep road that goes straight, and follow the yellow markings of the East Bluff Woods Trail.

The rock formation known as Devil's Doorway, high above Devil's Lake.

At first the trail traverses the oak woodlands that characterize the top of the bluff. As the trail descends to the north, a damper climate, maple begins to dominate the forest. At mile 4.6 the trail returns us to the trailhead, just a stone's throw past the fork where the East Bluff (yellow) Trail joins your route.

60 Devil's Lake to Parfrey's Glen

Highlights: A through-hike connecting sweeping bluff-top views at Devil's Lake with the intimate charms of Parfrey's Glen.

Location: Southern Wisconsin, 3 miles south of Baraboo.

Type of hike: Point-to-point shuttle hike.

Total distance: 9.9 miles.

Difficulty: Difficult.

Best months: April–October.

Maps: Ice Age Trail segment map # 29, USGS Baraboo (inc.) quad.

Permits and fees: State park vehicle sticker required.

Finding the trailhead: From Sauk City, drive north 11.3 miles on U.S. Highway 12 and turn right (east) on Ski Hi Road. At mile 12.6 turn left (north) on South Shore Road, then make a right turn (east) on Park Road at mile 13.8. At mile 14.0 turn right (southeast) into the park. An entrance station at mile 14.8 offers a chance to gather park trail maps. Continue east past railroad tracks and at mile 15.0 turn right (southeast) on a park road that leads to parking at mile 15.2 with the trailhead directly to the east.

Special considerations: Trails traverse rock sections that become very slick when wet. This hike is not a good choice for acrophobics.

Camping: Devil's Lake State Park has 535 drive-in campsites.

For more information: Ice Age Park And Trail Foundation, see Appendix B.

Key points:
- 0.0 East Bluff Trailhead.
- 1.1 Balanced Rock Trail.
- 1.5 Grottos Trail.
- 2.2 CCC Trail.
- 2.5 Ice Age Trail connector.
- 2.6 Ice Age Trail.
- 2.7 Steinke Basin Trail.
- 4.4 Ice Age Loop Junction.
- 4.5 Wisconsin 113.
- 6.4 Solum Lane.
- 8.5 Parfrey's Glen Trailhead.

Devil's Lake to Parfrey's Glen

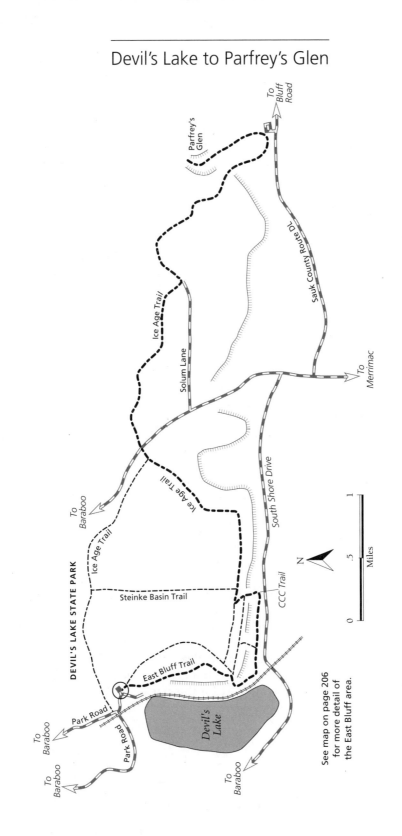

Parfrey's Glen

To Bluff Road

Sauk County Route DL

Ice Age Trail

Solum Lane

To Merrimac

To Baraboo

Ice Age Trail

South Shore Drive

N

.5

1

Miles

0

Ice Age Trail

DEVIL'S LAKE STATE PARK

Steinke Basin Trail

CCC Trail

East Bluff Trail

Park Road

To Baraboo

Park Road

To Baraboo

To Baraboo

Devil's Lake

To Baraboo

See map on page 206 for more detail of the East Bluff area.

9.2 End of Parfrey's Trail.

9.9 Parfrey's Glen Trailhead.

The hike: Two of the most scenic hikes in south central Wisconsin, the East Bluff of Devil's Lake and Parfrey's Glen, anchor each end of this route. Along the way, it skirts cliff tops and traverses a hardwood forest at the east end of Devil's Lake State Park. Rolling east, it ascends through old fields and small wood lots to Sauk County's highest point and long views stretching to Blue Mounds, 30 miles to the southwest. Finally, it drops to the valley floor to sample the intimate charms of Parfrey's Glen.

For the first 2.5 miles, this hike's route is the same as the Devil's Lake East Bluff Hike. (See Hike 59 for a description of that segment.) At mile 2.2 of the hike the route begins a steep ascent of the East Bluff on the CCC Trail. As the trail reaches the lip of the bluff it turns sharply west. Just after that turn, at mile 2.5, turn right (northwest) on a narrow path that connects with the Ice Age Trail 90 yards later. Turn right (east) there at mile 2.6, on the broad, graveled Ice Age Trail. Go straight (east) 200 yards later at mile 2.7 where the Steinke Basin Trail goes north.

The Ice Age Trail continues east, rising 100 feet onto a high spot on the bluff and running close to the top of the escarpment. Garage-size chunks of granite litter the top of the slope and quiet hikers can spot turkey vulture flocks roosting in the rock fields. The South Bluff, rising .5 mile away across the valley, screens views in that direction, but to the southeast long vistas open up to Lake Wisconsin and beyond.

Swing north, still walking in a fine hardwood forest, to an intersection at mile 4.4. Turn right (east) on the Ice Age Trail and shortly after cross Wisconsin 113 at mile 4.5.

East of Wisconsin 113 the trail's route takes on a more pastoral flavor, running through small sections of woods and meadow-like old fields. About 1.25 mile east of Wisconsin 113 follow the crest of a broad ridge before turning south in a meadow bordered by scrubby woods. Long views open up to the southwest, across the Wisconsin River Valley, to Blue Mounds and beyond. Hawks work the open spaces, riding the bluff top breezes.

At mile 6.4, the trail passes the eastern end of Solum Lane and swings northeast, beginning a gentle ascent. The radio towers ahead of you mark Sauk Point, the highest spot in Sauk County, a reminder to turn around from time to time and check for views. A meadow offers a view to the south before the trail turns east and begins to descend.

Follow the trail southeast, in and out of woods, as it steadily drops. For the last .75 mile the path goes through a pleasant stretch of older maple forest before arriving at the Parfrey's Glen Trailhead at mile 8.5. Turn left (north) and follow the description in Hike 61 for this portion of the hike.

61 Parfrey's Glen

Highlights: A charming sandstone glen, gurgling brook, and small waterfall.
Location: Southern Wisconsin, 3 miles north of Merrimac.
Type of hike: Out-and-back day hike.
Total distance: 1.4 miles.
Difficulty: Easy.
Best months: April–October.
Maps: USGS Baraboo (inc.) quad.
Permits and fees: A state park vehicle sticker is required.
Finding the trailhead: From Merrimac, drive north 2.5 miles on Bluff Road and turn left (west) on Sauk County Route DL. At mile 2.7 turn right (north) into the Parfrey's Glen DNR parking lot.
Special considerations: Parfrey's Glen is a state scientific area that requires visitors to remain on the maintained trail.
Camping: Devil's Lake State Park, 5 miles west, has 500 drive-in sites.
For more information: Devil's Lake State Park, see Appendix B.

Key points:
0.0   Parfrey's Glen Trailhead.
0.7   End of trail.
1.4   Parfrey's Glen Trailhead.

The hike: Parfrey's Glen, a picturesque, .25 mile long sandstone gorge, cuts through the Baraboo Hills' south slope 5 miles east of Devil's Lake. Robert Parfrey, the site's namesake, operated a grain mill near the mouth of the narrow canyon in the 1870s.

Today the glen has state scientific area status to protect its rare plants. The glen is a moist, shaded environment, harboring plants such as white pine, yellow birch, and mountain maple that are more typical of northern Wisconsin.

From the trailhead walk north on a gently ascending lane, first in an old field and then in thickening woods. The road becomes a 4-foot-wide path made of stones and crosses the first of several bridges over Parfrey's Glen Creek.

Here the drainage is still a broad ravine, but where the trail ascends seventeen stone steps the canyon begins in earnest. Forty-foot-high walls, sheltering shaded nooks, soon grow to nearly 100 feet in height.

The path continues, using small bridges and boardwalks, to a point where a pile of fallen rocks lies on the canyon floor. Just on the other side is the end of the trail, a walled viewpoint. From this spot you can actually see out of the upper end of the gorge, as well as a small, 6-foot high waterfall some 30 yards in front of you.

Parfrey's Glen

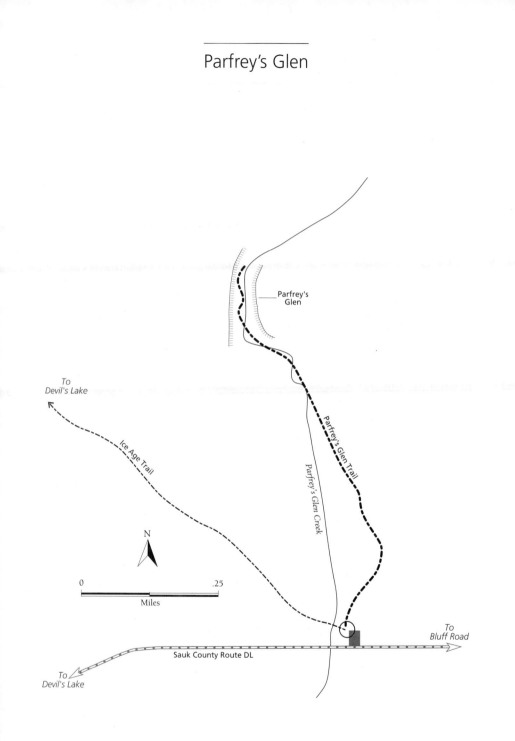

Parfrey's Glen Gorge, boardwalk at bottom.

62 North Kettle Moraine

Highlights:	A shaded walk along the top of a moraine.
Location:	Southeastern Wisconsin, 4 miles northeast of Dundee.
Type of hike:	Lollipop day hike or backpack.
Total distance:	10.3 miles.
Difficulty:	Difficult.
Best months:	April–October.
Maps:	Ice Age Park and Trail Foundation Parnell segment map #10, Kettle Moraine State Forest Trail Map, USGS Cascade quad.
Permits and fees:	State park vehicle sticker required.
Finding the trailhead:	From Dundee, drive 3 miles east on Fond Du Lac County Route F, which becomes Sheboygan County Route F, and turn left (north) on Pine Road. Drive 1.2 miles north and turn left (west) on Sheboygan County Route V. Drive .3 mile west. Park on the wide shoulder on the south side of the road as it descends into an open area.
Camping:	Shelter #4 with permit from Kettle Moraine State Forest. Long Lake, 3 miles west of the trailhead, has 200 drive-in sites.
For more information:	Ice Age Park and Trail Foundation, Kettle Moraine State Forest Northern Unit, see Appendix B.

Key points:

0.0	Sheyboygan County Route V.
0.9	Spur path to Parnell Esker.
1.3	Scenic Drive.
3.1	Sheboygan County Route U.
3.4	Parnell Trail Junction (South).
3.7	Parnell Trail Junction (North). Shelter #4.
6.3	Parnell Tower.
6.9	Parnell Trail Junction (South).
10.3	County Route V.

The hike: Of all the 60-some miles of Ice Age Trail in the Kettle Moraine State Forest, this is the trail segment with the longest continuous stretch of woods. The woodland ambiance along this hike is a pleasure for the eye, but there is a practical angle here as well. This shady, up-and-down the moraine, 10-mile route is one of my favorites for a sunny summer day.

Begin by following the broad Ice Age Trail north from Sheboygan County Route V as it follows the crest of the moraine. A broad marsh begins to the west while the first of a series of small wetlands appears in a bowl to the east. About .5 mile north the trail skirts an open field for .25 mile, reenters the woods, and ascends the moraine in a short, steep climb. On a fine spring day the kettle wetlands along this stretch will be noisy with the chorus of

North Kettle Moraine

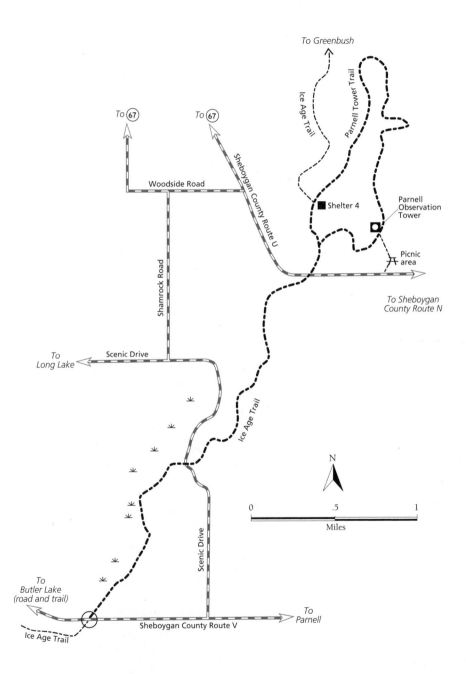

To Greenbush

Ice Age Trail

Parnell Tower Trail

To 67

To 67

Woodside Road

Sheboygan County Route U

Shamrock Road

Shelter 4

Parnell Observation Tower

Picnic area

To Sheboygan County Route N

To Long Lake

Scenic Drive

Ice Age Trail

N

0   .5   1
Miles

Scenic Drive

To Butler Lake (road and trail)

Ice Age Trail

Sheboygan County Route V

To Parnell

spring peepers, frogs rejoicing in the warm weather. During the summer, watch for tiny frogs, the size of your smallest fingernail, along the trail.

The Ice Age Trail continues northeast, with minor wetlands on either side, and crosses Scenic Drive at mile 1.3. Follow the trail north as it dips and rolls through a pleasant hardwood forest. At about mile 2.8 the path passes through a notably pleasant glade featuring a grassy forest floor beneath widely spaced trees, before crossing Sheboygan County Route U at mile 3.1.

North of County Route U the trail ascends to a junction with the Parnell Tower Trail at mile 3.4. Bear left (northwest) following both the blue blazes of the Ice Age Trail and the yellow blazes of the Parnell Tower Trail for the next .25 mile. The combined path descends an eroded slope to the west before swinging north to a junction at mile 3.7, where the two trails split. Trail shelter #4 is nearby to the east. Bear right (northeast) at that split, following the yellow blazes of the Parnell Tower Trail north.

After a little more than a mile, the path, a loop route, begins a swing east and then south. Keep walking south as the trail, at times a rock garden, ascends the higher part of the moraine and arrives at the Parnell Observation Tower at mile 6.3. The view from the top, taking in large parts of Southeastern Wisconsin on a clear day, is well worth the climb. A water pump and toilets are southeast of the tower.

When you are ready, locate the continuation of the trail, just south of the tower. The path runs southwest slightly and then turns west, rejoining the Ice Age Trail at mile 6.9. This is the same intersection you saw at mile 3.4 of the hike. Turn left (south) and retrace your steps on the Ice Age Trail to return to County Route V.

Trillium blooming along the Ice Age Trail.

63 Lake La Grange

Highlights:	A quiet footpath leads from a historic log cabin through a mature hardwood forest to a peaceful lake and marsh rich in wildlife.
Location:	Southeast Wisconsin, 6 miles east of Whitewater.
Type of hike:	Out-and-back day hike.
Total distance:	9 miles.
Difficulty:	Moderate.
Best months:	April–October.
Maps:	Ice Age Trail Foundation segment map #17, USGS Whitewater (inc.) and Little Prairie (inc.) quads.
Permits and fees:	State park vehicle sticker required.
Finding the trailhead:	From Palmyra, drive 3.8 miles south on Jefferson County Route H, which becomes Walworth County Route H. Turn right (west) on Bluff Road and at mile 4.9 turn left (south) on Duffin Road. Park on the wide grassy shoulder at the Oleson Cabin (mile 5.7).
Camping:	Shelter #3 with permit from Kettle Moraine State Forest. Whitewater Lake, 4 miles southwest of trailhead, has sixty-two drive-in sites.
For more information:	Kettle Moraine State Forest Southern Unit, Ice Age Trail Foundation, see Appendix B.

Key points:

0.0   Oleson Cabin.
0.2   Junction with Ice Age Trail.
0.8   Spur trail to shelter #3.
1.0   Duffin Road.
1.7   Log bench, top of ascent.
4.5   Bench at Lake La Grange, sandy shoreline, spur trail to Big Spring Drive.

The hike: When you step out of your car at the Oleson Cabin the quiet ambiance of this hike begins. You won't find any of the crowds here that are at some southern Kettle Moraine trailheads.

A restored two-story log cabin is 100 yards east of the road. Ole Oleson, a Norwegian immigrant, built this home for his family out of Tamarack logs hauled from the nearby Scuppernong Marsh in 1846.

Follow the path east to a signed intersection with the Ice Age Trail. Both trail maintenance and markings are good on this segment of the Ice Age Trail. Turn south and follow that path through brushy meadows and pine plantations to the spur trail (at mile 0.8) for the #3 shelter (100 yards off Ice Age Trail). Shortly after that you cross Duffin Road, round a spring fed wetland, and enter the beautiful hardwood forest you will spend the next hour crossing.

You will receive a quick lesson in the tumbled topography of the Kettle Moraine region as the trail ascends almost 200 feet. At .7 mile from the road, the trail passes some large mossy tree trunks lying on the ground and then

Lake La Grange

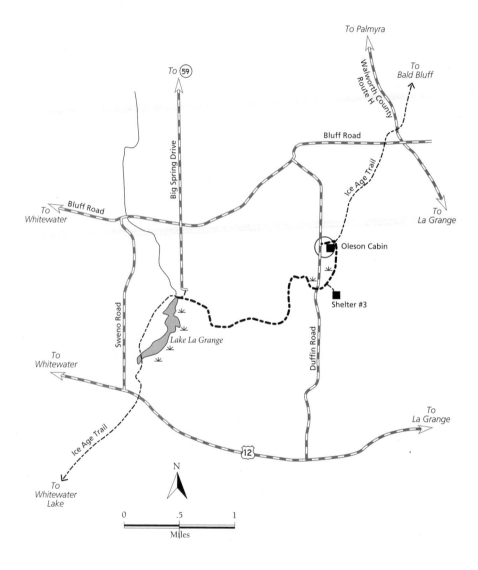

a large log arranged as a bench, capable of seating a dozen. This marks the end of the climb, and it will be another 1.5 miles before you begin the slow descent to Lake La Grange.

Three miles after entering the woods at Duffin Road the trail emerges into the extensive fields and meadows that border Lake La Grange. The open space is exhilarating after your sojourn in the woods and adds a harmonious balance to the day's outing. Hawks work the tall grass. A small rise offers views of the sparkling lake and the hills beyond.

A little farther on you will notice a bench to the north of the trail, overlooking the lake. This area makes a fine destination for your hike. The shoreline beyond the bench is sandy and pleasant. Fifty yards west a short spur trail leads north 100 yards to the end of Big Spring Drive (see Options). Retrace your steps on the Ice Age Trail to return to the Oleson Cabin Trailhead.

Options: You could walk this hike in the opposite direction, starting from the Lake La Grange area. This alternative might be attractive to backpackers wishing to stay at shelter #3 (permit required). One way to do this is to start from the south end of Big Spring Drive (limited parking). Another choice is to start from U.S. Highway 12, which adds 1.5 miles to the distance of the hike. Unfortunately, this is a noisy trailhead next to a busy highway, but as you walk north along the lake the road noise fades.

64 Beulah Bog

Highlights:	A boardwalk to the center of a primeval bog.
Location:	Southeastern Wisconsin, 3 miles north of East Troy.
Type of hike:	Out-and-back day hike.
Total distance:	1 mile.
Difficulty:	Easy.
Best months:	April–October.
Maps:	USGS East Troy quad.
Finding the trailhead:	From East Troy, drive north 1 mile on County Route G and turn left on St. Peter's Road. After .5 mile turn right (north) on Stringer's Bridge Road and drive 1.4 miles to the trailhead parking area on the right (east) side of the road.
Special considerations:	Beulah Bog is a state natural area. Treat it well. Do not attempt to step off the boardwalk, both for the plants' well-being and yours.
For more information:	DNR, Southern Kettle Moraine State Forest, see Appendix B.

Key points:
0.0   Trailhead.
0.4   Boardwalk begins.
0.5   Boardwalk ends.

Beulah Bog

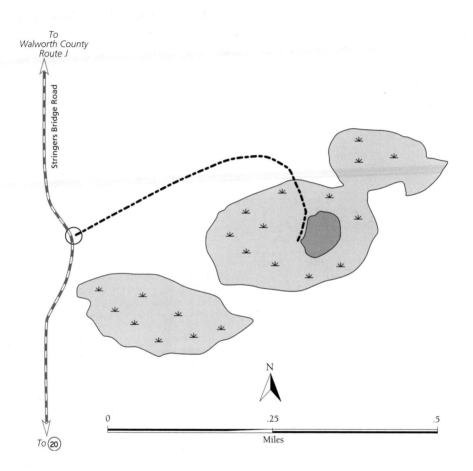

The hike: Name the least-disturbed natural habitat in this corner of the state and it would have to be bogs. Beulah Bog is a good example of these Ice Age relics; its impressive list of credits includes several rare plants and six carnivorous ones. This wetland also features floating mud flats, a bog lake, and a tamarack forest. Best of all, it has a way to get to the middle, a boardwalk. Bogs are neat, intriguing places, but they are inaccessible, too wet to walk and too thick with vegetation to canoe.

Walk east from the trailhead on an unmarked but well-worn trail. This path wanders east and northeast through overgrown old fields and scattered oak trees.

A turn to the south, descending a wooded hillside on steps, announces the path's approach to the bog's north shore. At the bottom of that small slope at mile 0.4 the boardwalk begins with a bang. Seven fifty-gallon drums, laid horizontally, provide flotation for the first segment of the boardwalk.

If you have crossed trail bridges suspended from cables, "swinging bridges," the effect is similar. This is a viable span, but one that rewards rhythm and steady nerves.

After that exciting start, the boardwalk settles down to a series of wood planks, with crossbars spreading the weight onto the oozing mass below. Continuing its 150-yard run into the bog, the boardwalk passes through a dense stand of tamaracks, with a verdant, mossy carpet below.

The boardwalk ends at the bog's lake, a picturesque spot at mile 0.5 of the hike. Retrace your steps to return to the trailhead.

The boardwalk leads to Beulah Bog's lake.

Appendix A: Glossary

Bog. A wetland of spongy, wet peat featuring sphagnum moss and tamaracks.

Bottoms. A floodplain area, usually a mixture of forest and wetland.

Dike. An elevated earthen causeway, passing through a wetland or along a river.

Dolomite. A rock similar to limestone and consisting largely of calcium magnesium carbonate.

Esker. A ridge of fine gravel and sand carried by a glacial stream.

Goat Prairie. A steep, bluff-top prairie located on dry, south-facing slopes.

Kame. A round knoll of gravel or sand deposited by vertical streams of glacial melt water.

Kettle. A rounded depression formed by a block of glacial ice melting.

Marsh. A shallow wetland, largely filled with reeds, cattails, and water lilies.

Moraine. Gravel and debris left by glaciers, in either linear or mound-like forms.

Portage. A trail used for transporting boats from one body of water to another or around obstacles.

Slough. A wetland that is part of the flood plain, or a backwater of a river.

Swale. Marsh-like low ground.

Woods road. A dirt road in the woods that is past being used by wheeled vehicles. Can be in various stages of revegetation.

Appendix B: Useful Addresses for More Information

Alma Office
Department of Natural Resources
P.O. Box 88, Courthouse
Alma, WI 54610
(608) 685-6222

Amnicon Falls State Park
(715) 398-3000 (May–Oct.)
Pattison State Park (during off season)
(715) 399-8073
6924 S. State Road 35
Superior, WI 54880

Apostle Islands National Lakeshore
Route 1, Box 4
Bayfield, WI 54814
(715) 779-3397
www.nps.gov/apis

Bayfield County Forestry Department
117 E. 5th St.
Washburn, WI 54891
(715) 373-6114

Black River Falls Office
Department of Natural Resources
910 Highway 54 East
Black River Falls, WI 54615
(715) 284-1400

Brule River State Forest
6250 S. Ranger Road
P.O. Box 125
Brule, WI 54820
(715) 372-4866

Chequamegon-Nicolet National Forest
Eagle River Ranger Station
P.O. Box 1809
4364 Wall Street
Eagle River, WI 54521
(715) 479-2827

Chequamegon-Nicolet National Forest
Glidden Ranger Station
P.O. Box 126
Glidden, WI 54527
(715) 264-2511

Chequamegon-Nicolet National Forest
Laona Ranger Station
Route 1, Box 11B
State Highway 8
Laona, WI 54541
(715) 674-4481

Chequamegon-Nicolet National Forest
Medford Ranger Station
850 North 8th, Highway 13
Medford, WI 54451
(715) 748-4875

College of Environmental Studies
UW-Green Bay
2420 Nicolet Drive
Green Bay, WI 54301
(920) 465-2371

Chippewa Moraine Interpretive Center
Ice Age National Scientific Reserve
13394 Colorado Highway M
New Auburn, WI 54757
(715) 967-2800

Copper Falls State Park
RRT 1, Box 17AA
Mellen, WI 54546
(715) 274-5123

Devil's Lake State Park
S5975 Park Road
Baraboo, WI 53913
(608) 356-8301

Door County Parks Department
P.O. Box 670
Sturgeon Bay, WI 54235
(920) 743-3636

Florence Natural Resources Center
Route 1, Box 83
Florence, WI 54121
(715) 528-5377

Friendship Office
Department of Natural Resources
Highway 13, Box 100
Friendship, WI 53934
(608) 339-3385

George W. Mead State Wildlife Area
S 2148 County S
Milladore, WI 54454
(715) 457-6771

Governor Dodge State Park
4175 State Road 23
Dodgeville, WI 53533
(608) 935-2315

Governor Knowles State Forest
P.O. Box 367
Grantsburg, WI 54840
(715) 463-2898

Hartman Creek State Park
N2480 Hartman Creek Road
Waupaca, WI 54981-9727
(715) 258-2372

Ice Age Park and Trail Foundation
207 East Buffalo Street, Suite 515
Milwaukee, WI 53202-5712
(800) 227-0046 or (414) 278-8518
iat@iceagetrail.org
www.iceagetrail.org

Interstate State Park
Highway 35, Box 703
St. Croix Falls, WI 54024
(715) 483-3747

Iron County Recreation
c/o Extension Office–Courthouse
Hurley, WI 54534
(715) 561-2695

Kettle Moraine State Forest–Northern
  Unit
N1765 Highway G
Campbellsport, WI 53010
(414) 626-2116

Kettle Moraine State Forest–Southern
  Unit
S91 W39091 Highway 59
Eagle, WI 53110
(262) 594-6200

La Crosse Office
Department of Natural Resources
3550 Mormon Coulee Road, Room 104
La Crosse, WI 54601
(608) 785-9000

Lower Wisconsin State Riverway
C/o Tower Hill State Park
5808 County Highway C
Spring Green, WI 53588
(608) 588-2591

Manitowoc Office
Department of Natural Resources
1314 Highway 310
Manitowoc, WI 54220
(920) 683-4926

Marinette County Extension Office
1926 Hall Avenue
Marinette, WI 54143
(715) 732-7510

Newport State Park
475 County Road NP
Ellison Bay, WI 54210-9801
(920) 854-2500

North Country Trail Association
Wisconsin State Coordinator
Cable Natural History Museum
P.O. Box 416
Cable, WI 54821-0416
(715) 798-3890
nctrail@cablemuseum.org
www.northcountrytrail.org

Northern Highland–American Legion
  State Forest
8770 Highway J
Woodruff, WI 54568
(715) 453-1263

Pattison State Park
6294 S. State Road 35
Superior, WI 54880
(715) 399-8073

Peninsula State Park
P.O. Box 218
Fish Creek, WI 54212
(920) 868-3258

Perrot State Park
P. O. Box 407
Trempealeau, WI 54661
(608) 534-6409

Point Beach State Forest
9400 County Highway O
Two Rivers, WI 54241
(920) 794-7480

Price County Tourism Department
Price County Courthouse
Phillips, WI 54555
(800) 269-4505

The Ridges Sanctuary, Inc.
P.O. Box 152
8270 Highway 57
Baileys Harbor, WI 54202-0152
(920) 839-2802

Rock Island State Park
RR1, Box 118A
Washington Island, WI 54246
(920) 847-2235
(920) 854-2500 (winter)

Sandhill State Wildlife Area
P.O. Box 156
Babcock, WI 54413-0156
(715) 884-2437

St. Croix National Scenic Riverway
Marshland Visitor Center
Route 1, Box 134
Pine City, MN 55063
(320) 629-2148

Sylvania Wilderness
Ottawa National Forest
Watersmeet Ranger Station
Watersmeet, MI 49969
(906) 358-4551

Tower Hill State Park
5808 County Highway C
Spring Green, WI 53588
(608) 588-2591

Trempealeau National Wildlife Refuge
Rte. 1, Box 1602
Trempealeau, WI 54661
(608) 539-2311

Viroqua Office
Department of Natural Resources
220 Airport Road
Viroqua, WI 54665
(608) 637-3938

Wilson Nursery Office
Department of Natural Resources
5350 Highway 133 E, Box 305
Boscobel, WI 53805
(608) 375-4123

Wyalusing State Park
13081 State Park Lane
Bagley, WI 53801
(608) 996-2261

Appendix C: Good Reading

Seasonal Guide to the Natural Year for Minnesota, Michigan, Wisconsin. By John Bates. Fulcrum Publishing, Golden, Colorado, 1997.

Wisconsin Wildlife Viewing Guide. By Mary Judd. Falcon Press, Guilford, Connecticut, 1995.

Wisconsin's Outdoor Treasures. By Tim Bewer. Prairie Oak Press, 1997.

About the Author

Eric Hansen's first recorded hike was an ascent of New York's Bear Mountain at the age of four. His parents encouraged him to roam the woods with curiosity and confidence, the beginning of a lifelong love of exploration and route finding in the outdoors. Topographic maps were the wallpaper of his childhood bedroom.

He has hiked and backpacked extensively and now divides his time between the mountains and canyons of the West and the woods and waters of the Midwest. Eric's background includes successful climbs of most of the high peaks in Montana's Glacier National Park and over a dozen rim-river-rim treks in the Grand Canyon. After twenty years of exploring Wisconsin's natural areas, he hiked 800 miles to research this guidebook.

He is a frequent contributor and gear reviewer for *Backpacker Magazine*. His local outdoor writing credits include *Milwaukee Magazine, The Milwaukee Journal-Sentinel,* and *Shepherd Express,* as well as *Silent Sports Magazine.*

American Hiking Society (AHS)
is the only national nonprofit organization dedicated to establishing, protecting, and maintaining America's foot trails—the same trails that are detailed in this book and around the country.

As a trail user, your support of AHS is important to ensure trails are forever protected and continually maintained.

Join American Hiking Society today and you will learn about trails to hike, their history, their importance, and how you can help protect them. American Hiking Society is:

A strong voice. With increasing threats to our treasured open space and wilderness, American Hiking Society exists to actively represent hikers' interests to safeguard these areas. To protect the hiking experience, AHS affects federal legislation, shapes public lands policy, collaborates with grassroots trail organizations, and partners with federal land managers. As a member of AHS, feel assured that while you are hiking, AHS is going *the extra mile* for you.

A helping hand. With more than 200,000 miles of trails in America, AHS steps in with needed maintenance for trail managers and hiking clubs. Through our Volunteer Vacations program, we provide more than 24,000 hours of trail work annually to help preserve some of the most scenic places in America. As an AHS Member, you can take advantage of this opportunity to give back to the trails that you use and love.

A critical resource. Each year, crucial trail funding continually falls behind trail maintenance demands. Your favorite trail will **not** be next, thanks to American Hiking Society! Our National Trails Fund annually awards financial grants to local and regional hiking clubs for land acquisition, volunteer recruitment, and trail maintenance. As you support AHS, you share in the satisfaction of helping grassroots trails clubs nationwide.

Join TODAY!

American Hiking Society

1422 Fenwick Lane · Silver Spring, MD 20910 · (301) 565-6704
www.AmericanHiking.org · info@AmericanHiking.org